EQUAL TIME

Books by Marcia Lasswell and Norman M. Lobsenz

No-Fault Marriage
Styles of Loving

Books by Marcia Lasswell

Love, Marriage, Family   (with Thomas E. Lasswell)
Marriage and the Family   (with Thomas E. Lasswell)

Books by Norman M. Lobsenz

How to Stay Married   (with Clark W. Blackburn)
Nobody's Perfect   (with Hendrie Weisinger)
Writing As a Career
Is Anybody Happy?
   A Study of the American Search for Pleasure
Farewell to Fear   (with Thelma Keitlen)
Emergency!
The Complete Guide to Successful Retirement

EQUAL TIME

The New Way of Living, Loving, and Working Together

MARCIA LASSWELL &

NORMAN M. LOBSENZ

1983

DOUBLEDAY & COMPANY, INC.

GARDEN CITY, NEW YORK

Library of Congress Cataloging in Publication Data

Lasswell, Marcia E.
    Equal time.

    1. Marriage. 2. Sex role. 3. Interpersonal
relations. I. Lobsenz, Norman M., 1919– .
II. Title.
HQ734.L3358 1983   306.8'72
ISBN 0-385-17473-X
Library of Congress Catalog Card Number 82–45254

CONTENTS

EQUAL TIME

THE NEW CHALLENGE: GROWING TOGETHER

One day each year the men and the women of the Greek village of Monoklissia observe an ancient custom. For twenty-four hours they trade places. The men remain on their farms or in their houses to cook the meals, take care of the children, milk the cows, and do the other routine household chores. Their wives, meanwhile, gather at the taverna in the village square to gossip, play cards, and drink the potent *retsina* wine of the region. Any man found on the streets of Monoklissia during that time period risks the traditional punishment: a thorough soaking in the town fountain.

In our times, in our towns, men and women are also "trading places"—not just for twenty-four hours but for the years ahead. Freed from the strictures of generations of cultural conformity, both sexes are increasingly choosing life-styles that suit their needs and their skills rather than the dictates of society. Women in large numbers are taking their places in occupations once monopolized by men. In turn, many men are beginning to share equally with women in homemaking and child care, and some are even choosing to stay at home and be house-husbands. Women are learning that it is not unfeminine to be assertive, and men are learning that it is not unmasculine to be dependent. Both women and men are taking advantage of the full range of options they can now choose from in the emotional and intimate areas of their lives. They are deciding to marry later, or not at all; to live with a lover, who may be of either sex; to have children or to be a non-parent.

Unlike the Monoklissians, those who resist or challenge these changes in the social structure, or who do not take them seriously, or who do not grasp the significance of their sweeping effects, risk no mere dunking. Their destiny is considerably more serious. For their human relationships will flourish or suffer depending on how well they understand and deal with the new definitions of masculinity and femininity; and on how effectively they apply these new definitions to such matters as intimacy, commitment, trust, fidelity, and conflict in the context of being husband or wife, mother or father, coworker, friend, or lover.

"Ladies' Day" in Monoklissia is an annual charade that probably represents a dim, anemic vestige of some lusty pre-Christian ritual that honored the Mother Goddess. But the changing and merging of sex roles in American life during the past decade is no empty ritual. The resulting shock waves have been felt by every woman and man, regardless of her or his chosen life-style. Most of the changes, of course, have occurred in the roles of women. But when women change their definitions of femininity and the kinds of behavior that are appropriate to the female sex role, men will also change. Every couple constitutes a single emotional "system." And since there are no signs that women and men are any less emotionally involved with each other than they ever have been, changes that affect one sex must necessarily lead to changes in the other.

Such a major social transition (especially one so basic) carries enormous potential for both good and ill. On the one hand, the prospect of anything new or different tends to promote anxiety. Old ways, like old clothes, are familiar and therefore reassuring, even though they may be unfashionable, uncomfortable, or no longer functional. So we postpone coming to grips with change; and when we do, we do so, for the most part, reluctantly. Firm convictions and deeply imbued ways of behaving are slow to change, if at all, despite our best intentions and most sincere efforts.

On the other hand, change has the advantage of exposing us— or forcing us to expose ourselves—to ideas and feelings, to skills and achievements, and to ways of relating that hold the promise of greater emotional fulfillment. In short, change offers a man and a woman the opportunity to help each other grow and, perhaps more important, to enjoy each other's growth. Many people, still hemmed in by outdated or prescribed roles, are dimly trying, and failing, in both areas.

If the quality of a relationship is linked to how well partners agree on their roles, then many women and men are headed for trouble. One recent survey showed that out of more than thirty different complaints that spouses registered when filing for divorce, conflict over sex roles ranked second among husbands and eighth among wives.

It is hardly surprising, then, that we believe the overriding task for women and men today, and in the years immediately ahead, is to learn how to rebuild their partnerships so as to *benefit* from the sex-role changes that have taken place. This means couples must take a whole new look at each other, deal with a host of unexpected feelings and reactions, find fresh paths to mutual joy.

That is why we are not so much concerned in this book with describing the changes in roles and relationships as with exploring how you can minimize or avert the stresses these changes have created, and how you can enhance the growth of intimacy within the framework of change. Some women and men have already begun to do that. "I believe that a quiet movement has been going on among American men for some years," writes Betty Friedan in *The Second Stage*. "If I am right, the new questions men are asking about their own lives will converge with women's new questions—and provide a new power and energy for solutions that only seem impossible . . ."

When we talk about helping women and men to get along better with each other in these changing times, we are not talking about going "back" to some of the old ways or some of the old "rules." That is impossible. Thanks to expanded options and resources, today's woman functions from a new kind of power base. But though she is freer to get more pleasure out of her relationships with men, that very freedom also creates a different set of anxieties and needs. Today's man, too, operates from a different power base than when he carried (or was supposed to carry) the whole burden of economic responsibility. In losing some of his control he has gained the right to express his feelings and to drop the image of "masculine mystique." But, again, that right involves him in new problems and responsibilities.

Think of it this way. Can you imagine going back to your childhood home? Chances are it has a new roof, it's been painted a different color, the plumbing has been improved, perhaps a new room has been added. It's still the old home, yet if you tried to live in it as an adult, it would very likely feel strange to you, perhaps at first unworkable. But eventually you would adjust to the changes, develop a new perspective, and learn to be comfortable in the house. So it is with the eternal relationships—love, marriage, family. The fundamental framework—like one's childhood home—remains even though there have been changes in the way it has been put together. To make it work satisfactorily for you and your partner, each of you needs to approach it with a new perspective. The aim of this book is to help you develop that perspective.

For generations women and men have measured themselves against "ideal" characteristics appropriate for each sex. There have always been certain traits considered desirable for women and certain others approved for men. As far as we can tell, there probably always will be. It is not, therefore, that we have emerged into a "roleless" society but, instead, that our definitions of feminine behavior and masculine behavior are changing in important ways.

Masculine and feminine traits traditionally lay at opposite ends of a continuum, so that some of the approved characteristics for women were specifically *not* approved for men and masculine traits were taboo for women. In this way, masculinity and femininity were defined as opposites. If aggressiveness was considered masculine (and it usually has been), a woman who exhibited aggression was judged to be unfeminine; since feminine traits usually included submissiveness and modesty, these characteristics were considered undesirable in a man. Men who showed traits considered peculiarly feminine were labeled "sissies." Women who were competitive or dominant—both stereotypical male traits—often were said to be "castrating" or to have "unresolved gender problems."

These "bipolar" stereotypes became so entrenched in our society that each generation carefully taught the next generation that there were "good" and "bad" ways for boys and girls to behave. Accepted patterns of femininity and masculinity were translated into family responsibilities and work roles with equal care. Boys grew into men who were taught it was their role to represent the family in the community and the world of work. Girls grew up expecting to nurture the family by tending to its physical and emotional needs. Men managed their families' economic interests by controlling access to the outside world; women controlled men's access to affection, sex, and nurturance (unless men found these resources outside the home). The implication of these "opposite" roles was that if men were powerful in the family's interface with the world, then women could not be. Similarly, if women were dominant in controlling the family's emotional resources, then men could not be. Perhaps the most significant aspect of changing sex roles is how these stereotypes have been challenged. As large numbers of women have entered the labor market, for example, it has become more acceptable for assertiveness to be included in definitions of femininity. As men are more and more involving themselves with child care, nurturance has come to be seen as an acceptable masculine trait and function.

As ideas have changed of what women should be and do, and what men should be and do, we've learned that the sexes have not been cast by evolution in totally separate molds. Research is breaking important new ground in showing us how the sexes differ and how they are alike. There are the obvious differences in physiological equipment. But while anatomy is *not* destiny, there are important biological differences that cannot be denied—mainly in the form of the sex hormones and their effects, and in the actions of the chemical transmitters that spark neural impulses in the brain. Current research highlights other sex differences that may be biological, or may be learned, but are nonetheless very real. We know, for instance, that women and men respond differently to sounds, visual stimuli, tactile sensations, and problem-solving challenges. (But "different" does not mean one sex's reactions are necessarily "better" or "worse" than the other's.)

The research of Stanford University psychologists indicates that while the sexes are equal in general intelligence, they seem to process information differently. By the age of ten or eleven girls excel in verbal ability, and boys suffer more from such language problems as stuttering and reading disabilities. Conversely, by adolescence, boys seem to excel in mechanical skills, mathematics, and the kind of spatial reasoning essential to map-reading and other scientific endeavors. (But by adolescence, girls—and educators—have already been "taught" that boys are better in these fields, and thus this "difference" becomes a self-fulfilling prophecy.)

Moreover, studies of brain structure and development suggest that many—if not most—of these cognitive differences may be due in part to the fact that girls mature physically earlier than boys. For example, the right side of the brain is the center of spatial reasoning, among other factors, and the left is the center of language skills. In early maturers the two sides have less time to specialize. Since both halves of the female brain share these and other tasks, women may be able to integrate more information and process it faster. (Some experts feel this may account for what has been called woman's "intuition.")

Unfortunately, such biological differences have been used to distort the fact that literally from infancy we are culturally conditioned to prescribed sex roles. Harvard University biologist Richard Lewontin speaks for many researchers when he says that the determining influence in the development of a person's sexual orientation is that people "are called 'boys' and 'girls' from the day they are born." In a classic experiment, subjects were asked to describe the behavior of a group of newborns. When the infants were dressed in blue diapers (the conventional color for boy babies), the observers said that they were "very active." When the same infants were presented in pink diapers, the subjects commented on their "gentle" behavior. And when the babies were put into yellow diapers the observers, according to Lewontin, "got upset. . . . They started to peek inside the diapers to see their sex."

In sum, then, the sciences are telling us that while there are physiological differences between the sexes, they are far fewer than we once thought; that the differences ought to be relatively unimportant in setting the pattern of our social and sexual roles; and that the similarities between women and men are greater than the common wisdom ever believed or admitted. The fact is that there are sex-linked chromosomes in *every* cell of our bodies, and their physical effects are widespread and profound. At the same time, how we judge the rightness or wrongness, propriety or impropriety, of male and female behaviors is the result of social learning. To force the issue of whether heredity or environment, biology or culture, is more important in determining sex roles is like forcing the issue of which blade of a scissors cuts the cloth more effectively.

The real issue for women and men in day-to-day living is not what makes particular people behave in particular ways, but how constructively we respond to that behavior: to give our partner a sense of human dignity, a chance for joy, and the freedom and energy to achieve his or her goals in life. The task is not merely to substitute new rules in relationships for the old rules; the task is to get rid of rules and open new horizons.

The new information about how a woman and a man differ from yet resemble each other has, paradoxically, left most people both wiser and more confused. Let's look for a moment at just one issue basic in the debate over sex-role function that we referred to earlier: whether women are born to be nurturers and men born to be protectors and providers, or whether these roles are learned rather than innate and therefore capable of modification and change.

Both positions have been argued passionately if not always eloquently. Those who speak for innate differences base their case on the fact that each gender has its specific reproductive function, and for hundreds of thousands of years has specialized in doing what each does best. Others cite the role of prenatal hormones, which some scientists believe predispose males to be more aggressive than females. Combined with the knowledge that on the average men are physically larger and stronger than women, the conclusion has been drawn that males are indeed "programmed" to protect and provide. By the same token, women, since they give birth to and nurse children, are assigned the role of nurturer.

But these and other gender differences have been called irrelevant by those who say that such stereotyped sex roles are chiefly the result of child-rearing practices, the educational system, the media, and other sources of socialization. Reproductive differences, they claim, are of secondary importance; that women bear and nurse children is not the crucial factor. Instead, it is the fact that women have always been culturally charged with the responsibility of child care that spells the major difference between the roles of women and men in our society.

A major obstacle to resolving these opposing views is that it is

nearly impossible to determine just when sex-role learning begins.
Studies show that from the earliest days of life girls are responded
to more quickly when they cry than boys are. Mothers increase
the amount of attention they give to a fussy baby girl and are
more likely to interpret her crying as fear. They reduce the
amount of attention they give to boy babies because they perceive
their cries as a show of anger. Does this maternal behavior subtly
program girls to learn to be more nurturant and boys to be more
aggressive?

Infants cannot label such differential treatment as "the way
girls should be treated" and "the way boys should be treated."
But by the time children can walk and talk, they know quite
clearly what sex they are, and by the age of three they have
learned many of the "proper" masculine and feminine ways to behave. Yet we still cannot say with any certainty whether these behaviors are the result of biological predisposition, of direct in-
struction, of subtle social learning, of a child's amazing ability to
imitate the behavior of parents and other adults important to
them, or (most likely) from a combination of all of these. It is a
chicken-and-egg puzzle. Do boys prefer to play with cars and guns
because they are by nature aggressive, or do parents give them
such toys because the parents think boys *should* be aggressive, or
because cars and guns have come to be considered the *right* toys
for boys? Do girls play with dolls because they are innately nurturant, or because they are early on encouraged to play with dolls
and assume the nurturant role?

Most women and men today seem to have decided that it will
be a long time, if ever, before these questions are finally answered.
What is more important, they say, is to find new ways of relating
to each other—ways that will free them from those aspects of
traditional sex roles that limit personal growth and interpersonal
intimacy, and at the same time let them keep hold of those aspects that provide important emotional rewards. Pressured (or
eager) to change in some areas of their lives, and wanting to
remain unchanged in others, women and men are fumbling for
workable solutions to the unexpected and unfamiliar conflicts this
dilemma is causing. For example:

• As women increasingly move into once male-dominated fields
of work, and men are increasingly involved in domestic respon-

sibilities, what feelings are aroused and what power balances are upset? What happens between a couple when she earns more than he does? When she gets a promotion and has a higher career status than he does? When he must move because she has been offered a better job? When their work separates them geographically? When her new bargaining power in their partnership entitles her to a stronger role in decision making?

• Trust has always been a key ingredient in a couple relationship. In the past it focused on a woman's trust in her man, since he had more independence and mobility in the world outside the home. Today the emphasis is on *mutual* trust, and how a couple can build and keep it in the face of woman's growing freedom.

• Friendship between the sexes is raising questions that disturb many women and men. Are non-sexual, non-romantic friendships possible? Can they stay platonic? What functions do they serve? What problems do they cause? How can they be protected?

• Having children, not too long ago an almost automatic choice for most couples, is now a complex decision to make. Is the price of being a parent (including the loss of a working woman's income and the possible handicap to her academic or professional progress) too high? Should couples wait to have children? How long? Do they want children at all? Does one partner want a child, but not the other? Do children strengthen a marriage or do they add to its stresses?

These are but a few of the key areas where sex-role changes are making it necessary for women and men to learn new ways of being together and growing together. There are no facile answers to the problems involved in balancing the best of the past with the best of the present and future. On the one hand, sex stereotypes—deeply rooted in religion, education, economics, and countless generations of family history and ritual—are slow to die. A man today still usually identifies himself in terms of the world outside his home: his work, his school, the organizations he belongs to, his practical accomplishments. A woman still tends to identify herself (even now, twenty years after the women's movement raised her consciousness) as a daughter, a wife, a mother. Moreover, the changes that have been evoked have aroused more rage and created more conflict than anyone anticipated.

In counseling we see women and men who are uncertain about

what to make of the new options and directions in their lives, and others who resent the consequences of this new freedom. We also see couples struggling to bridge the gap that still exists between the ideology of equality, and the need to make it work on a practical basis in day-to-day relationships. Advances by women (they've reaped more benefits from sex-role changes so far than men have), plus slowly growing acceptance of the new human environment by men, have lessened the climate of hostility. In the decade between 1970 and 1980, for instance, the number of women and men who favor the new sex-role patterns has substantially increased. According to a Roper poll, more than half of the women and men questioned in 1970 said they did not support efforts to strengthen the status of women; in 1980 fewer than one quarter opposed the idea.

Yet the truce that exists is an uneasy one. Neither sex, having traded conventional certainties for unorthodox options, quite knows how to deal with the other. Thus, the critical issue for today and for the years ahead is sharply defined: How can women and men successfully come to grips with the changes that are taking place in their roles and relationships and still retain the positive qualities—trust, intimacy, emotional security, mutual respect —that make it possible for them to live together, love together, work together, grow together? In the pages that follow we shall show, out of our own experience and that of the women and men we have counseled, how that challenge can be met.

1 — INTIMATE CARING, INTIMATE SHARING

If, as George Bernard Shaw once said, "marriage combines the maximum of temptation with the maximum of opportunity," we can also say that any intimate relationship combines the maximum opportunity for caring with the maximum risk of revealing one's deepest self. For there can be no true intimacy without self-disclosure; in a very real sense one is the "flip side" of the other. Yet to many women and men the prospect of self-disclosure, of making themselves emotionally vulnerable, is scary. Do you tend to avoid intimacy rather than risk being disappointed, hurt, perhaps rejected? Or are you willing to take that chance in order to gain the rewards of intimate caring and sharing? The dilemma is a classic one. Each of us must learn to resolve it if we are to have a rewarding adult emotional relationship.

We must also learn to define what intimacy means to us. Nowadays it has become a catch-all description for closeness of many kinds, from "steady dating" to live-together arrangements to marriage, and in some cases beyond marriage to "extended networks" where groups of partners share intimacy. Intimacy is considered essential to a good male-female relationship, important in a friendship, necessary for a child's development. But the higher the value we place on intimacy, the less we are able to say exactly what we mean by it. To clear up some of the confusion, family-life authority Dr. David Olson, of the University of Minnesota, points out that there is a significant difference between an intimate *experience* and an intimate *relationship*.

According to Olson, an intimate experience is a sense of sharing with another person that can exist in any of seven areas. He cites emotional intimacy (a closeness of feelings); social intimacy (having friends in common); intellectual intimacy (sharing ideas); recreational intimacy (enjoying the same hobbies or sports); spiritual intimacy (having a similar view of religious faith or the meaning of life); aesthetic intimacy (sharing the same concepts of beauty); and, lastly, sexual intimacy. "It is quite possible," says Olson, "to have intimate experiences with a number of persons without developing an intimate relationship with any of them. True intimacy is a process that develops when two persons share many such experiences over a long period of time." Moreover, true intimacy is never completed or fully accomplished: "It is foolish to assume you have 'achieved' intimacy or that you no longer have to work at maintaining it."

In the past, partners set, or had set for them, boundaries to intimacy that were socially defined. Today, changes in accepted sex roles give women more freedom to explore intimacy—to have cross-sex friendships, to control their own sexual lives—and give men more freedom to express their emotions, to open themselves up to greater self-disclosure. This growing emancipation from role-playing has allowed both sexes to penetrate the boundaries that formerly circumscribed their relationships. As a result, each sex is better able to experience itself through the other. Neither can easily take refuge behind the comfortable shield of mystery or the "safety" of the wall that once separated the "male" world from the "female" world.

But while lifting this barrier has had many positive effects, it has, paradoxically, also aroused much anxiety. Breaking down the boundaries between women and men increases the prospects for intimacy. At the same time, it increases the concerns about vulnerability. The situation has been described in terms of the parable of the two porcupines: Their delicate task was to learn how close they could be together without hurting each other with their prickly quills. It is not surprising, then, that ways of assimilating and practicing the new definitions of intimacy, and ways of coping with new kinds of vulnerability, do not come quickly.

The old patterns, of primitive origin and thus entrenched in the unconscious, have a way of surfacing unexpectedly, of sneaking up on us without warning. Moreover, we spent years learning them. Many of the barriers to adult closeness are a legacy from childhood experiences. As young children we are necessarily dependent—certain adults, usually parents, have to be there in order for us to survive. As a result, we begin life knowing that intimacy makes us extraordinarily vulnerable; the idea of being abandoned, physically or emotionally, is terrifying.

For most children the time comes, usually in young adulthood, when they separate themselves from parents and establish autonomy. This adolescent struggle to redefine one's boundaries is marked by alternate periods of "distancing" from one's home base and returning there for emotional and physical refueling. Only when we succeed in feeling fully secure in our autonomous adult identity are we ready and able to form intimate links with others. But few, if any, of us feel secure all the time. When we are faced with difficult situations that challenge our self-sufficiency, the long-buried childhood feelings resurface and we retreat into the seeming safety of familiar behavior. Thus it is that when women and men begin to feel vulnerable in their new roles and patterns of relating, they fall into the traditional "dance between the sexes." Intimacy needs propel us one step forward; fears of loss and dependency drag us two steps backward.

This unfortunate foxtrot is at the root of most relationship problems with which therapists are asked to deal. In one version, one partner presses for more intimacy while the other runs from it. The partner who shies away from closeness has been dubbed the "dance-away lover"—better at forming relationships than sustaining them. When one partner seeks a deeper level of intimacy, the fear of being vulnerable leads to intricate avoidance maneuvers—everything from workaholism to extramarital affairs can serve as ways to elude a partner who insists on more closeness.

In another variation, *both* partners fear the vulnerability that intimacy brings. Their solution often is to keep some emotional distance from each other; this allows them to feel relatively safe, defended against what they see as an unwelcome intrusion into their personal territories. Couples who form this kind of relationship usually complain about a vague sense of loneliness, of having drifted farther apart than they intended. They cannot conceive that intimacy is possible without being overwhelmed by fears of losing control if they should let down their guard. At the same time, their need to love and be loved continues. The result: a great deal of emotional frustration.

An unusual case that came to our attention illustrates how certain kinds of occupations can intensify this need to be constantly on guard against letting anyone get too close emotionally. The woman who arrived for a counseling appointment told her story briskly, but with an undercurrent of sadness. She was more concerned about her husband than herself. "He's a state trooper, a fine man, good to his family," she said. "But I feel, sometimes, as if we talk together through a closed door. He always seems to hold back a part of himself." Ultimately the problem was traced to the pressures of the husband's job which dictated that he be wary and maintain emotional control at all costs.

"Men whose work involves danger often have trouble with intimacy," the therapist told the woman, "because their very lives may depend on never allowing themselves to lose control, never permitting themselves to be open in their dealings with others. Your husband may be unable to separate the way he *has* to feel when he is on the job from the way he would *like* to feel when he is with you." Since his wife was not a threat nor an enemy, it was not necessary for the man to behave emotionally at home the same way he did on the job. "It will help if you talk to your husband about your feelings," said the counselor, "and if you can encourage him to do the same. Self-disclosure is one way for people to overcome the fear of vulnerability."

Sometimes both partners in a relationship have the forward-backward struggle going on *within* themselves. They alternate between wanting to be close and wanting to pull away. What complicates their "dance" further is that they rarely synchronize their individual movements. One partner attempts to move close only to meet withdrawal from the other; when he or she, in self-protection, then takes a backward step, the other moves forward. They manage never to connect. It is not surprising that with such bad timing these couples have a lot of sexual complaints, too. (Of course, even couples who handle intimacy comfortably have, as we shall see, periods when they each want to be closer and periods when they each desire more separateness. But they do not exhibit the "yo-yo" effect typical of those who bounce almost rhythmically from one extreme to the other.)

All of these patterns share a common factor. They interfere

with, or perhaps stem from, one partner's inability to make an emotional commitment to the other. The struggle to protect the "self" paralyzes any movement toward commitment. One or both partners resist what is perceived as a path of no return because their fears require that they always have an escape route.

Committed friends, lovers, or spouses share a dedication to the growth of their relationship. Each partner learns just how close he or she can be to the other without risking the loss of individuality and freedom. Their boundaries are clearly defined, their linkage clearly differentiated from any other relationship they may have. They have a shared set of meanings unique to themselves. They give a high priority to time for each other. They do not believe commitment is a trap.

To some, commitment seems suffocating. "I always need to have one foot out the door," a man said recently. "I have an affair now and then to prove I can walk away from my wife any time I choose to." Extramarital affairs are, indeed, a common sign of the flight from commitment. Having an outside "focus" for a while helps to neutralize the tension created by the pressure for commitment. But, then, affairs ultimately create their own tensions. One set of anxieties is merely replaced by another.

Commitment, private time and space, sexual fidelity, the balance between separateness and togetherness, the conflict between self-disclosure and self-protection—all are integral aspects of intimate caring and sharing. This section explores how today's men and women are learning to deal with them, and to get more pleasure out of being together.

Living Together: Old Wine in a New Bottle

Those who, often to their surprise, must grapple with *all* of these challenges to intimacy are the couples who choose to live together without marrying. (After experimenting with a number of esoteric terms for live-togethers—CUs for "consensual unions" or UNMALIAS for "unmarried liaisons"—sociologists have settled on the rather grim-sounding but accurately descriptive word, "cohabitors.") Since it first blossomed on college campuses in the early 1970s, cohabitation has become an increasingly accepted way of life. Census Bureau statistics indicate that more than one million couples now identify themselves as what the Bureau calls

"POSSLQs"—Persons of the Opposite Sex Sharing Living Quarters. Though cohabitation is currently most prevalent among persons under forty-five years old, it occurs in all age groups. Many cohabiting couples are women and men in their middle years who choose to remain unwed; or, having been through a divorce, are in no hurry to remarry. A substantial percentage of cohabitors are over the age of fifty-five—senior citizens who seek companionship and intimacy without having legally to merge their financial assets or risk losing any retirement benefits that might be affected by marriage. Indeed, the social acceptance of cohabitation is dramatized by the fact that the number of live-together couples increased by 250 percent between the beginning and the end of the decade of the 1970s. For couples where both were twenty-five or younger, the increase was 800 percent, making cohabitation virtually an integral part of normal courtship. Even so, less than 3 percent of the population of the United States are cohabitors.

This rapidly growing popularity of living together can be attributed mainly to the thrust of the role changes. Cohabitors are more accepting of the new sex roles: Men are more emotionally supportive than non-cohabiting males, and women in these relationships more assertive. Moreover, the liberalization of sexual codes has transformed our attitudes toward intimate relationships. For instance, the virtual disappearance of the double standard, so that premarital sex is now condoned for women as well as for men; for instance, the growing acceptance of the idea that being in love (or even persuading oneself that one is in love) justifies sex without marriage. But though freer sexual attitudes have helped to make this shift in intimate life-styles feasible, sexual availability is not the only reason cohabitation has proliferated. Others—directly or indirectly traceable to changing ideas about sex roles—include:

• Idealism about intimate relationships. "What a man and woman feel for each other is more important than any ceremony they go through," said one person. Couples say they value emotional commitment more than legal commitment. A man commented that "being there every day because I want to rather than because I have to represents a greater commitment than marriage does." Couples say they can share their lives "more honestly" by living together: "What we feel in our hearts is more meaningful than any ceremonial vows. If we are secure in our love, why do we need a license to express it?"

• Cynicism about marriage. Many women and men point to a divorce rate that has risen 65 percent over the last ten years. They ask, "Why bother to marry when the chances are you'll just have to go through more legal red tape to get divorced?" More significantly, they have been disillusioned by the sterility or the breakup of their parents' marriages.

• Rationalism about the demands of togetherness. Some couples see cohabitation as a way of combining emotional closeness with the kind of emotional freedom they fear would be lost in wedlock. "We don't want to be hung up on possessiveness and jealousy," one couple said. "We want to give each other some degree of individuality, of emotional privacy. Love should be a gift, not an obligation."

However, the very reasons that women and men offer for living together leave them unprepared to deal with the delicate and complex dilemmas of intimacy that cohabitation frequently creates. (Indeed, two of every three live-together couples break up within two years.) Paradoxically, their problems arise largely from the conflicts that cohabitation is theoretically supposed to avert. There is no question that couples who see living together as a chance to combine emotional closeness with emotional freedom work hard to achieve that goal. Linked by love and mutual concern, they are able to give each other areas of both spiritual and physical privacy. For some, however, there is a major conflict between theory and practice, especially when it comes to sex. Many such couples we have talked with who say they believe in the idea of individual sexual freedom are to all intents and purposes monogamous. "The theory is that we're both free to sleep with other people," one woman said. "But he'd be jealous as hell if I did, and vice versa."

Another woman—thirty years old and previously married and divorced—who has been living with her partner for more than a year, said she does feel free to date other men, but doesn't want to because the possibility of sex with them makes her uneasy. And a man of thirty-one, an attorney, said he and his partner had ruled out sexual freedom, but not because they felt jealous or possessive. "We're working hard at living together," he declared, "and if either of us gets involved with someone else, we'll deprive our relationship of emotional energy."

Obviously there is an irony implicit in such qualms about "faithfulness" when changing sex codes place less emphasis on fidelity as the bedrock of intimacy. Yet jealousy (as we shall see in a later section) is not so easily rooted out of our natures. Nor can we easily shed the cultural dictates of the past even though in our new roles we may not want to be burdened by them.

A few individuals who have sexual relations with people other than their live-together partner are surprised to find they feel *guilty* about it. "I didn't think you could feel guilty about something you had permission to do," one woman observes. "When you know intellectually it's okay, that you've both agreed to it," a man says, "it's even more upsetting to discover that lump of guilt."

Another development that surprises a good many cohabiting couples is that as time passes it becomes more and more difficult for them to avoid falling into conventional marital roles and patterns. Take household chores, for instance. No matter how firmly living-together couples set out to share them, to avoid traditional sex roles, there is a tendency for the woman to inherit most of them. Even if she also holds a job, it may not be long before she is doing the cooking, cleaning, and laundry, while he performs the traditional American male task—taking out the garbage. When living-together couples socialize, their friendships tend to be couple-oriented—the same two-by-two social life married persons have. (However, there's also far more tolerance for each partner's separate friends, and for friendships that cross sexual lines, than exists in marriages.)

Part of the reason, perhaps, that some cohabiting couples are drawn into traditional patterns is that they tend to assume—albeit with varying degrees of reluctance—the camouflages of marriage in order to avoid legal and social problems or family pressures. Gradually this pretense becomes the shape of their reality.

Experts who have analyzed cohabitation arrangements identify four major patterns for such relationships:

1 – The "Linus blanket" (named for the character in Charles Schulz' *Peanuts* comic strip): Sometimes couples decide to live

together because they are insecure and dependent. Many young persons who have recently left their families but who are not yet ready to live alone drift (or rush) into cohabitation in order to have someone to lean on. Usually these relationships end when one or both partners grow strong enough to move on. If one remains dependent while the other grows more secure, the one who no longer needs a "security blanket" may feel used or trapped. The insecure one is left with more anxieties and less self-esteem than he or she had to begin with.

2 – Emancipation: Some younger women and men seem to use cohabitation as a way of struggling to free themselves from family controls, or of claiming adult status. Persons in this category usually have a history of several short-term live-together relationships.

3 – Convenience: In this pattern, one or both partners are trying to meet selfish personal needs at the other's expense—clearly the converse of intimate caring. In some instances the woman is trading sex for financial or emotional security (usually a false security). Such exploitative relationships do not endure for long unless the partners are, for the time being, fulfilling more important needs. One such couple (call them Fred and Nancy) had lived together for nearly two years. During that time Fred, a bearded advertising copywriter, became increasingly demanding, and Nancy, a slender dark-haired teacher, finally rebelled. They entered counseling. (Significantly, cohabiting couples account for as much as 25 percent of the case load of marital therapists.)

> *Nancy:* I always envied youngsters who grew up in loving families. Mine was cold and unaffectionate. My father was a domineering man, and my mother always gave in to him. I guess my idea of a wife was someone who mostly did the laundry, cooked, and took orders. I was determined that I wasn't going to become that kind of a woman.

> *Marcia Lasswell:* And what kind of a childhood did you have, Fred?

> *Fred:* Well, I was an only child, and my folks usually gave me anything I wanted. If we're talking about control, I'd say I was the most powerful one in my family.

ML: So perhaps you unconsciously thought that if
you married, you would have to give up, or lose, some of
that control?

Fred: That's possible.

The dynamics of this cohabiting couple were obvious. When
Fred felt anxious he made demands on Nancy in order to reassert
his control. When that happened, Nancy fought back in an effort
to maintain her independence. For them, living together was essentially a convenient way of dealing with their hidden fears
about a more permanent kind of intimacy.

4 – Testing: This last cohabitation pattern is essentially a trial
marriage in which couples hope to find out if their relationship
can *survive* the vicissitudes of living together. They sincerely try
to learn more about themselves, about each other, and about
their reactions to intimacy. Should these couples finally decide to
wed, they are likely to have worked through many of their problems. As a result, their marriages tend to be more successful than
the average. But even couples who decide *not* to wed after having
lived together usually say it was a worthwhile experience.

On balance, the factors that make marriages work are so complex it seems doubtful that cohabitation would ever be the deciding factor. Perhaps the greatest benefit cohabitation affords the
success of marriages in general is that it keeps some persons from
marrying each other at an early age, having children, and later
divorcing. As one study concluded: "The best divorce you get is
the one you get before you get married."

There is as yet no definite answer to whether the chances for
success in marriage are enhanced for partners who live together
before they wed. In a recent study, two psychologists at the University of California, Los Angeles, interviewed couples applying
for marriage licenses in that city, and contacted them again four
years later. The psychologists found that those who had lived together first were just as likely to have gotten divorced as those
who had not lived together.

Ultimately, the future of a live-together couple seems to depend on the degree of commitment each brings to the relationship. We'll be talking in more detail about commitment
somewhat farther along in this section, but we want to touch on

it here because the basic conflict in cohabitation often has to do with what "commitment" means to each partner in the relationship. Not long ago a woman came to us with this concern:

> My nineteen-year-old daughter and the young man she has been dating for the past year are planning to move in together. She says it will help them to decide whether or not to marry by testing their commitment to each other. Is this a realistic view?

The answer, as so often in these cases, is, "It depends." One of the things it depends on is whether this young couple are being honest with themselves or deluding themselves. Quite frequently younger women and men use cohabitation as an unconscious way of *avoiding* commitment. They invariably say the "daily freedom to stay or go" that is implicit in a living-together situation makes them more committed to each other. But these couples often have to work harder at their relationship precisely because of this freedom. If the door is always open, couples do not have to try to resolve differences; one or both can always leave. And eventually that "daily freedom" can undermine commitment by creating an atmosphere of doubt and anxiety. Getting close to someone isn't as frightening as staying close.

The answer depends, too, on how the two persons involved define commitment. Women tend to define it in a different way from men. Men (especially young men) usually feel that commitment takes the form of an increased willingness to share and enjoy sex. But a woman's commitment is more likely to be to the permanence of the relationship. (Interestingly, cohabiting women see themselves at a greater disadvantage in their relationships than women who are steady-dating but not cohabiting; some experts feel it may be easier for non-cohabiting couples to have an equalitarian relationship.) In any event, no relationship can long survive unless the partners continue to give concrete signs of their commitment to it. As long as each person displays evidence of increasingly greater commitment as time passes, intimacy deepens. But the Catch-22 for most couples who live together is that the ultimate commitment—and the ultimate intimacy—is, of course, marriage.

The Risk of Caring Enough

My husband swears that he loves me, but when I ask him for words or signs of affection, I might as well be talking to a stone wall. When I feel depressed enough about this to register a serious complaint, his response is to bring home a present for me, or to give me money to buy something for myself. But this is not what I want. Why can't he just tell me how he feels?

I have a strange problem. The woman I live with says she loves me and is happy with me—*but* she occasionally urges me to go out with other women, and even suggests that I go to bed with them. I don't know what to make of this.

The person who is unafraid of intimacy is always puzzled by a partner who backs away from it. "In such men," says psychotherapist Rollo May, "we see the fear . . . that too much responsibility will be heaped on them by the woman, the fear of enchainment to a woman's emotions and a woman's needs. Obviously, women have the same fears of men: fear that they'll be enveloped by the man, lose their autonomy, be . . . subordinated to a 'woman's role.'"

But what is there, actually, to be afraid of? We struggle all our lives with the hope that we can be "one" with another person—and at the same time with the fear that we may become submerged in that oneness. Carl Whitaker, a renowned family therapist, refers to it as "the delusion of fusion." For many years Whitaker kept in his office a six-legged coffee table that he had built himself. A series of hinges underneath the top allowed the table to be separated into two halves, each of which could stand separately on its three legs. The table, of course, was supposed to provide symbolic proof that true closeness in a relationship did not depend on a total permanent fusion but rather on some kind of rhythm between being together and being apart. And that a woman and man who each relished the opportunity to be separate from time to time would ultimately find a greater intimacy when they were together.

Unfortunately, many women and men are unable to enjoy the experience of aloneness. (This must be distinguished from loneliness. As we shall see, not until you know how to function as an individual are you able to be alone *without* feeling lonely.) Some of us have simply never had the chance to develop this sense of autonomy. Those who marry young (and despite the number of people who delay getting married nowadays, the average age for a first marriage in the United States is still in the early twenties) move directly from dependence upon parents to dependence upon a partner, without having time to learn to depend on themselves. Within an intimate relationship such persons may begin to feel trapped.

"I've never had a chance to make any choices for myself," one woman said. "I lived at home until I was nineteen, got married, and moved straight from my father's house to my husband's." For such a person the only way to survive seems to be to resist intimacy out of the fear of being swallowed up. Without a solid sense of one's own identity, what the world calls intimacy comes to seem like "engulfment." Anyone who feels that togetherness implies surrender is not likely to be capable of giving or accepting intimacy. He or she may feel there is no boundary between the self and the partner.

"All my life I've been dominated by women," one man said. "First my mother and, after she died, then my older sister. In college I dated a girl I liked but didn't love, yet she almost convinced me to marry her. That's why I break off any relationship that seems to be growing too intimate. I'm afraid I'll never be able to escape, to be myself again." At the other extreme, however, lurks the fear of abandonment, left over from childhood. To escape it we yearn to be "all in all" to another person. That requires letting down one's guard completely, sharing all ideas and feelings with the other person. But when we do this it leaves us extraordinarily vulnerable. The person who has not learned the value of separateness finds that this vulnerability can set off great anxiety. And if one partner in a relationship allows this fear of abandonment to become too important, he or she may make such excessive demands on the other for closeness that the pressure may actually drive them apart.

At first glance the fear of abandonment might seem to be the diametric opposite of the fear of engulfment. The fact is that both stem from the same source: a lack of self-esteem that results in anxiety about self-disclosure, and an exaggerated vulnerability to rejection. In the first case one dreads intimacy—even though wanting to be close—due to the fear of being deserted; in the second, one resists intimacy out of the terror of being swallowed up. True intimacy exists only when both partners *want* it to exist, not because either person *forces* it on the other, *needs* it from the other, or *demands* it from the other.

When women and men could play out their traditional sex roles, questions of intimacy and vulnerability could be avoided or disguised. In today's world it is not so easy to do this, and sorting out one's true feelings is often confusing. For example, not long ago we received this letter:

> I'm forty-five, an attorney, recently divorced. I meet many attractive girls—but I seem to appeal to those who immediately get serious and talk about marriage. Are there no truly liberated females who don't want to rush into wedlock?

This was our reply:

> Of course there are truly "liberated" women around, if by that you mean women who are happy to be on their own and can take care of themselves. But, as you have discovered, there are also many women who still fantasize about finding a Prince Charming who will take care of them. You *may* be giving off the message that you view a woman as someone to be taken care *of*. Without reading too much into your choice of words, it may be worth asking yourself why you refer to women, presumably in your own age range, as "girls." Most of the self-sufficient females we know prefer to be called "women" and would steer a wide path around any man who calls them "girls."
>
> Do you suppose you may be setting yourself up for what you get? We suggest that you think carefully about the kind of person who attracts *you*, as well as whom you are attracting. You may be surprised to discover that

you really prefer "girls" to more self-sufficient women. Perhaps you are not sure you can handle an independent woman. Perhaps you unconsciously would rather be with a dependent female who will make you feel needed. While you decry their wish to be close, you may feel uncomfortable with a person who is both able and satisfied to be alone.

Can You Be Sure Love Will Last?

I'm twenty-four and my friend is thirty. We've been together nearly two years, and over the past few months Rob has pressed me time and again to marry him. But we've been happy the way things are, we don't want children yet, and I can't see why he wants to change anything. We're starting to argue about it more, and I'm afraid we may break up.

Rob is evidently one of those people who equate marriage with commitment. For them, it often does signify the ultimate commitment one can make. It can also be a way of trying to lock in the other person. But the basic question here may be not so much why this young man wants to be married, but why this young woman is so resistant to the prospect.

To what extent have the changing rules and roles of relationships affected women's and men's willingness to pledge their time, energy, and loyalty to each other for the sake of mutual goals? Do women and men define commitment differently? Studies indicate that they may. It seems that men define it as being involved in a relationship that is enjoyable, provides good companionship and sexual fulfillment, and respects each partner's right to make decisions of his or her own. Men also tend to believe that today's new women define commitment in the same way. But they do not. Most women still see commitment primarily in terms of sexual exclusiveness and dedication to the permanence of the relationship. As one researcher put it: "Women, more than men, are holding to the traditional sex role ideology."

Experts have identified several psychological and sociological components of commitment (though the average person thinks of it as a single characteristic). They are:

- dedicating oneself to continuing the relationship;
- rejecting competing relationships;
- limiting one's activities to the accepted kinds of social behavior for a "committed couple";
- sharing personal feelings of attachment.

In a time when emotional ties seem so often to be at the mercy of sudden or capricious change, it is not surprising that most of us seek such reasonable assurances of stability in our intimate relationships. But the problem is that hardly anyone knows quite what commitment means anymore, or what specific qualities of heart and mind go to make it up.

For earlier generations, commitment was implied in the marriage vow: to love, honor, cherish and obey, in sickness and in health, "till death us do part." Since divorce was rare then and life expectancy shorter, the form, if not always the spirit, of that promise was usually observed. One might eventually come neither to love, honor, cherish, nor obey one's spouse, but one generally stayed with him or her, and, therefore, with the marriage.

Today commitment is more a matter of choice than obligation. Moreover, it means different things to different people. At a convention of family therapists, we asked a number of them what they thought it meant. "Commitment is an interesting concept," one said, "but I'm not sure I know what it signifies nowadays." Another felt that current attitudes toward personal freedom and sexual fidelity make the promise of a permanent commitment unrealistic.

Indeed, most of the therapists we spoke with found they could more clearly define what commitment is *not*. "It is not a promise of unconditional love," one person said. "Only a mother can say —and mean—'I will always love you, no matter what you do.'" Another observed that commitment is not something for which we can contract in advance. "There is no guarantee that a relationship will continue to work," she remarked. "Men and women can be expected to live up to a contract for their behavior, but not necessarily for their thoughts and feelings."

Yet, though they can't precisely define commitment, virtually every therapist agrees that it is vital to a successful relationship. Without at least a *sense* of commitment between partners, the way is open to the demons of jealousy, mistrust, loneliness, and alienation.

Here is a particularly apt and touching example of the destructive effects of a cavalier approach to commitment. The excerpt is from a letter written to us by a middle-aged woman whose partner—she describes him as "a very sexy man"—has a job that takes him out of town for weeks at a time:

> It is very important to me for someone to be completely true. He and I seem to mean two different things by that term. He feels if he tells me all, he is being true and faithful. So while he is on the road, if he goes out with someone else he feels everything is O.K. if he tells me about it. But it upsets me! I am a one-man woman. He tells me what we have is so special that he doesn't feel anyone could come between us. I'm getting tired of hearing that, but he doesn't seem to understand. I have told him how I feel about all this. But it seems like it is water off a duck's back to him.

Much of the difficulty people have in dealing with commitment is that they tend to think of it as something monolithic—a single, massive building block, self-contained, in the structure of a relationship. The fact of the matter, however, is that commitment can exist in a variety of shapes and forms. For example, the marriage ceremony creates a legal (and in some cases a religious) commitment even though the couple may hate each other by the time the honeymoon is over. Conversely, one can be emotionally or intellectually committed to a partner without being married. Some wives and husbands are committed to marriage itself as a state of being even when there is little or no commitment to the spouse; these are the people who remain in a relationship "despite everything" because, for a variety of reasons, it is important to them to be married.

Even sexual commitment can be a relative matter. X may feel a moral or religious duty to remain faithful to Y, no matter how emotionally empty their relationship. But that traditional concept of fidelity no longer holds for those couples who do not necessarily consider sexual loyalty an integral part of their commitment. Indeed, in an "open" relationship part of the couple's mutual commitment may be to give each other sexual freedom.

In his book, *Freedom and Destiny*, Rollo May tells of a woman who announced, in her first meeting with a therapist, that though she had no desire to have sex with anyone other than her lover, *he* felt something was wrong if she did not *want* to sleep with other men. May then asks this question in light of such current attitudes toward sexual commitment: "Is not an essential part of being free the freedom to have sexual intercourse with whomever one wants, whenever one is so inclined?" Or, we might add, the freedom *not* to have sexual intercourse whenever one is so inclined?

Given this flexible nature of commitment, we can establish three basic standards by which to measure it. One is *duration*—how long a person is willing to give unreserved love and support to another. Many people think of duration as the most important sign of commitment: "They've been together twenty-five years—they must be absolutely devoted." But, as we know, the time span of a relationship does not necessarily have anything to do with its quality. For example, consider this excerpt from the case history of a recent counseling client:

Husband: My wife and I have been reasonably happily married for thirteen years. I feel completely committed to her and to our marriage, yet two or three times a year I spend the night with women I meet when I am away from home on business. The involvement is purely physical, and I never see these women again. I don't feel guilty about my behavior, but I sometimes wonder if it is possible for me to do this without having it affect my commitment to my wife. Am I just kidding myself?

ML: I would say, yes, to some extent you probably *are* kidding yourself. If you were not at all concerned, it would be easier to believe those casual infidelities did not affect you. But the fact that you raise the question indicates that you probably do feel some guilt.

Let me ask you a question. When you say you are "completely committed" to your wife, what are you talking about?

Husband: Well, I don't have any plans to leave her. What else do you have in mind?

ML: Does commitment mean that you are devoted to her except for sexual loyalty? Does it mean that you think that a person can have one kind of commitment at home and another on the road? And, what does commitment mean to your wife?

Husband: I guess I had never really thought about how I define commitment. And I have never asked my wife how she feels.

ML: You might want to have a frank talk with your wife about how each of you views the responsibilities of your relationship. After you hear what she has to say, you may be better able to decide whether your infidelities do or do not violate your joint definition of your life together. You might, for example, find that your wife's ideas about casual sex are similar to yours. In that case you will need to decide whether you feel comfortable allowing your wife the same kind of sexual freedom you assume for yourself.

A second dimension of commitment is *intensity*—the strength of feeling and depth of concern that a woman and man are prepared to invest in each other. Just as enduring relationships may be emotionally shallow, brief encounters may be emotionally intense. Those for whom intensity is important may make more than one personal commitment during a lifetime, but in each case it is the emotional investment in the partner that counts.

A third dimension is the *priority* one gives to the relationship. We know couples who would be shocked if you questioned their commitment to each other. But we see in them a husband who is a virtual stranger to his wife and family because he works long hours and travels constantly on business. Or a woman who gives far more love and attention to her children, parents, or job than to her spouse. The priority that partners give to their *mutual* involvement is one way in which they show the extent of their commitment.

Unmarried partners face the same conflicts. A young man recently observed that it was hard for him to spend time with his fiancée because it took too much time away from his work. "If you have a career going," he said, "you can't afford to spend much time on anything else." Some young women feel the same way. They do not want to get "tied down" until they have established themselves economically. Many of them are more committed to careers than to men; as a result, their main bonds of intimacy are likely to be formed with colleagues and coworkers. "That shouldn't be so surprising," one woman said. "After all, they are the people with whom I share interests and objectives."

What all three dimensions of commitment—duration, intensity, and priority—have in common, of course, is the implication of responsibility. One authority, Dr. James Ramey, put it this way: "Commitment occurs when two people value the bond between them more than anything else—and when they are willing to assume the responsibility to maintain it."

What does this entail? For one thing, the willingness to work out problems and conflicts. For another, the willingness to change in significant ways for the sake of the mutual bond. And for a third, real concern for what is good for each other.

A word about women and men who can neither give nor accept commitment: Women's inability to give or accept is more familiar, and the reasons span the entire spectrum of our natures, and of our social environment. Role changes have produced a generation of women—strong, independent, assertive—whom some men see as rivals rather than as friends or lovers. Moreover, changing attitudes toward sex and work are making many women and men view emotional commitment (of any but the most transitory kind) as a trap, a giving up of open-ended opportunities for financial independence and sexual adventure.

Psychologically, commitment implies being responsible for and to another person. Some people simply do not have the maturity to handle that kind of assignment. So they play at being emotionally elusive; or they become perfectionists, searching endlessly for the impossible-to-find person who can meet all their often conflicting ideals (i.e., the sexually knowledgeable virgin, the dominating but tender man); or they cultivate an air of detachment, of being "cool," that permits them not to care much about anything or anybody.

This fear of commitment also occasionally manifests itself in sexual disturbances. One therapist reported the case of a man who, though able to have an erection, often could not reach orgasm. A physical examination uncovered no medical reason for this; therapy sessions, however, revealed the man's deep-seated fear of commitment to intimacy. With a casual partner he had no sexual hang-up; but when he was with a woman he cared for, anxieties about getting too emotionally "involved" took over. Unconsciously he withheld his orgasm as a way of denying his feelings.

The person who cannot *accept* commitment commonly has trouble believing that he or she is worthy of it: once again, the specter of low self-esteem. A bewildered man asked us recently how he could convince his wife that he truly loved her and was not planning to leave her. The answer may seem simplistic, but in most cases it is the only way to deal with this situation. We told him what was most likely to work was regular reassurance, in words and actions, that she is the person he cares most about: "When you have a tender thought or warm feeling for her, do not let it pass without telling her. Praise her accomplishments and skills, ask for her advice and opinions. By letting her know, over and over, how much you care for her and appreciate her, you may help to build her self-esteem to the point where she can eventually be able to accept what you say."

Some studies indicate that it takes as long as three years after marriage for a couple to develop a sense of bonding, to see themselves as *we* instead of two I's. (That may have a good deal to do with the fact that the divorce rate is highest in those first three years of marriage.) Unquestionably, something happens during that time to carry most couples past this crucial period. What happens, we submit, is the gradual strengthening of the bond of their mutual commitment.

Many people believe that until at some specific point they consciously *make* a commitment, none exists. This belief is emotionally self-defeating; like the illusive quest for happiness, such a state can be found only when striving for it ceases. Couples sometimes find, to their astonishment, that an emotional evolution has taken place between them in spite of their caution or resistance. Indeed, it is possible that all commitment is essentially involuntary, that it grows whether we seek it or not. Therefore, in the long run it may not be particularly important to try to define commitment or to go searching for it. Instead, simply accept that it happens.

Forsaking All Others . . . ?

Sexual fidelity has always been considered the *sine qua non* of intimate caring. One was faithful if for no other reason than to preserve the emotional security of an intimate partnership. Or one's own moral image was felt to be at stake: "I wouldn't sleep with another man even if Jeremy couldn't possibly know," a woman told one researcher. "Whatever I did, I would be doing it to myself as well as to us."

Such an attitude seems almost quaint in a time when, statistics show, the incidence of infidelity is rising, especially among younger middle-class women and men. Surveys differ in actual numbers, but it is generally agreed that more than half of all married men, and nearly half of all married women, have been unfaithful at least once. Reasons for the increase are not hard to come by: a more mobile and urban society; the existence of effective birth-control methods; the widespread use of sexual symbols and lures in the media; the increasing number of women who work in once-traditionally male occupations, maximizing women's opportunities for sexual encounters; the emphasis on personal gratification. The new sexual image of the women's liberation movement also has its influence. With a determination to control her own life and body, today's woman often believes she should not be "owned" or dominated by her partner in any way, including sexually. Fidelity, such a woman believes, should be a matter for choice.

But a funny thing has happened on the way to the bedroom. Along with statistics showing sexual unfaithfulness rampant, other sets of statistics—less publicized but equally reputable—report that an overwhelming majority of women and men *disapprove* of infidelity. In a nationwide study by family specialist David L. Weis, two men out of three said that extramarital sex was "always wrong." A survey conducted for a national magazine produced figures showing that 86 percent of those questioned believed infidelity was "always" or "almost always" wrong.

Does this mean there are two contradictory standards operating, one for what we do and another for what we think we *ought* to do? If so, it would not be the first time that women and men did not conform to their ideals. It is more likely, however, that this discrepancy has a more down-to-earth explanation.

For one thing, statistics about infidelity may not present as accurate a picture as researchers would like to think. For example, the interpretation of the numbers themselves may be suspect. A person who is unfaithful only once (perhaps for reasons that have little or nothing to do with his or her love for a spouse or partner) is lumped along with those for whom the behavior is chronic. And in addition, that one-time transgressor—and even someone who was once a chronic offender—may now have a completely different view of the meaning and importance of fidelity. Conversely, a person who stands foursquare for faithfulness today may change his or her opinion tomorrow—when marital conflict, or a sudden infatuation, or perhaps a partner's sexual disinterest creates a new set of emotional circumstances.

So how one acts or feels or thinks about fidelity at any particular time may not accurately indicate how one will feel or act about it next month or next year—and may not reflect how one felt about it in the past. "Never in my wildest dreams did I imagine I would ever do anything like that," one woman said as she told about a casual sexual encounter she had with a man in her office. "It went against all my principles—and yet it happened."

A second reason for the discrepancy in the statistics is that some people may disapprove of unfaithfulness as a *general* standard of behavior but see their own actions as an exception to the rule. "You didn't ask how I felt about the question as it affects *me* personally," one man said. "Of course I think infidelity is wrong. But in my case there was a good reason for it. My girl friend and I were having some hard times, and she refused to sleep with me. I was hurt and angry, so I found someone who would."

It is also possible that the disparity between the statistics on unfaithful *behavior* and those on *attitudes* toward unfaithfulness are a measure of the respondents' needs to conform—to *say* what they think is socially acceptable, while *doing* whatever they choose to. The disparity, in any event, reflects the basic ambivalence of our feelings about sexual fidelity. Dr. Laura Singer, a former president of the American Association for Marital and Family Therapy, once declared that, "If we are honest with ourselves, we realize that almost everyone, at one time or another, has sexual desires for other than his or her partner." Indeed, in one study of middle-aged couples, half of the sexually faithful husbands admitted (in confidence to the researcher, of course!) that they would "like to have" a chance for an illicit sexual experience. Three out of four of these men, and nearly half the women, agreed that most happy couples sometimes wish they could have sex with someone other than their partners.

These conflicting findings raise several critical questions for couples forming intimate relationships in today's flexible sexual climate: Do modern sexual attitudes and the search for self-fulfillment make the whole concept of fidelity an anachronism? Can true intimacy exist without sexual fidelity? What does "fidelity" really mean to this new generation? When an adult couple engage in behaviors that they jointly perceive as sexual, what does it mean to them or about them? What does it mean when two people have slept in the same bed overnight? What does it mean if an adult married to someone else is invited to have sexual intercourse?

These questions have almost as many answers as there are people to answer them because there are almost as many sexual scripts as there are people. For one person, in one situation, intercourse means permanent bonding. For another it means rebellion; for a third, conquest; for still another, defilement. Sexual intercourse may be an affirmation of gender, of adulthood, of relationship status. It may mean reaching for immortality through producing children; it may mean fun and games; it may mean security and contentment; it may mean "restoring one's soul."

But whatever one's script may be, we submit that changing times and changing roles make it necessary to expand the script—to take "fidelity" or "infidelity" out of its narrow sexual connotation and place it where it more properly belongs—in the context of the total partnership between women and men. With so many social factors increasing the opportunity for sexual temptation and providing a climate of tolerance for yielding to it, we believe that it is time for a redefinition of fidelity. Rather than limit the meaning of the word specifically to sexual loyalty (and the meaning of infidelity to a specific act or acts of sexual intercourse), we see it as something more positive and encompassing. That something is a primary commitment to a partner based on the desire for exclusive intimacy *of all kinds*. Such a commitment may or may not have sexual exclusivity as its most important ingredient.

For example, one husband told us he felt more unfaithful when he confided his emotional troubles to a woman friend than he would have if he had gone to bed with her. "I should have had the courage and honesty to discuss them with my wife," he said. "Talking about my marital problems with another woman was really a breach of the trust between me and my wife." In another instance, a young woman who planned to spend a weekend with a man told her live-in lover she had to go out of town on a business trip. She changed her mind at the last minute but said, later, that she felt unfaithful anyway, "because I really meant to do it." The pattern works in reverse as well. Another wife left her husband not because she discovered he was having an affair, but because of who the other woman was and how the affair was conducted. "She was a neighbor and a friend, and everyone knew what was going on before I did. I probably could forgive my husband if it was just a matter of sex, but I can't forgive him for betraying me emotionally in such a cruel and humiliating way."

As more and more women and men come to believe that infidelity in a relationship involves something far more crucial than an isolated sexual act, it would benefit couples to explore the topic frankly with each other. Just what is each partner's definition and expectation of fidelity? What emotional values does each one consider most important? Questions like these need to be discussed together; it is far too easy (and too dangerous) to assume that both persons share the same attitudes.

In Ingmar Bergman's prize-winning film, *Scenes from a Marriage*, Liv Ullmann as the wife confronted with her husband's sexual unfaithfulness, says, "Fidelity is not a vow we make; it must be something we choose to do." But why do women and men choose to do it? There are any number of reasons for remaining faithful—many of them negative. In some respects they parallel the six levels in the development of the capacity to make moral decisions identified some years ago by psychologist Lawrence Kohlberg. At the lowest levels, he said in effect, we do "the right thing" in order to avoid pain or to achieve a balance between frustrations and rewards. Later on we conform to social pressure and the conventional morality of the times. In other words, our moral choices are largely a reaction to "outside" authority. It is not until we internalize moral values, said the psychologist, that we make certain choices for their own sake.

At the lowest level, for instance, are the "pain-avoiding" feelings: the fear of being caught, the inability to deal with deception and guilt. "I honestly believe that if Ellen didn't know about it, it would not make any difference to her," said an engineer. "But is it worth what could happen if she found out? The one who would be hurt is me—because I'd have to live with the knowledge that I had betrayed my promise." The deceptions that often must accompany sexual cheating are distasteful, particularly to women. "It's a messy and tawdry business," one said, "making up cover stories, being careful never to make a slip." Other women and men refrain from infidelities out of concern for social pressures and respect for religious mandates.

Fidelity that exists for these reasons alone is neither true faithfulness to a relationship, nor can it be counted on to last. Not until we reach Kohlberg's highest level, the wish to stay faithful because of an internalized set of principles, do we find a reason that stems from personal commitment.

Andrew Greeley in *Sexual Intimacy* takes fidelity beyond the sexual act. "Fidelity," he writes, "requires that you commit yourself never to wait for the other to take the initiative to heal a separation, and never to reject the other's initiative." To turn to one another when lonely, discouraged, frustrated, says Greeley, is itself an act of faithfulness, since it means we are willing to share intimate feelings of weakness and vulnerability.

We suggest that the new definition of fidelity is making it possible for couples to do just that. Love exists, said psychiatrist Harry Stack Sullivan, "when the satisfaction or security of another person becomes as significant as one's own." And when a woman and man feel that way toward each other, fidelity exists as well. For to be other than faithful, in the newest and best sense, would impair the emotional intimacy and security of them both.

How Close Is Too Close?

He's a stockbroker, on the phone most of the day with clients and under constant pressure to make split-second decisions involving many thousands of dollars. The woman he lives with is a computer programmer. For most of her day she works alone, the quiet broken only by the click and clatter of machines. "I'm tired and tense when I get home," the stockbroker says. "I'm not good company till I have a chance to be by myself for a while. But Ann is bursting to talk, wants my attention right away. If I say I'd like some time alone, to unwind, she feels hurt."

Jill has a somewhat different problem. "I like Howard a lot," she says, "but when he comes over to my apartment he drives me crazy following me from room to room. If I go into the bedroom to dress, he stands in the doorway and watches. The other night I pushed him aside and shut the door. To my amazement, he opened it and walked in. 'You don't have to be alone,' he said. 'You can be with me.'"

And then there's Penny, who was in love with a novelist. "But he kept asking what I was thinking, why I said what I did, how I felt about other people. When I objected, he said it was a writer's habit to *probe*. I told him to probe some other woman's mind, and said good-bye!"

Like each of these couples, most of us at one time or another have trouble squaring away our desire for closeness with our need for some privacy. In an intimate relationship that dilemma can become a prime cause for conflict. American society is unique in its emphasis on the premise that couples linked by love or marriage should function in all things virtually in tandem. In most other societies partners are freer to have separate identities, individual friends, personal interests. But in this society when a woman or man wants time or space to be alone, outsiders tend to speculate that the relationship is in trouble:

> My husband and I sleep in separate bedrooms [a friend told us recently]. He likes to read until quite late, and I have to get up early to be on campus in time to teach my eight o'clock class. When my sister, who was visiting us for a few days, saw our sleeping arrangements,

she took me aside and, in what she thought was a tactful
way, asked if we needed any help with our "sexual problems"!

Different sleeping patterns arise because many couples, like this
one, have "scheduling" problems or because one partner is a
"morning person" and one a "night person." One partner may
snore loudly, or want to keep the windows open or the heat up
high, or want to watch the late-late movie on television, while the
other needs absolute silence in order to fall asleep. True, sleeping
apart *may* be a sign of sexual incompatibility or estrangement—
but the fact is that where one sleeps has little to do with one's
sexual interests or activity. Couples who have separate bedrooms
or separate beds are usually just as active sexually as those who
share a double bed. Indeed, many such couples say that being *invited* into each other's bed adds a touch of romance and sexual
excitement. Even in these days of increased personal independence for both sexes, many women and men obviously are still
ensnared by the idea that in a good relationship both persons
should share the same interests, hold the same values, and never
—well, hardly ever—be apart. "The notion that the same thing
will make two people happy at the same moment is a pleasant enough fantasy," says Ellen Goodman, whose syndicated col-
umn often muses on questions of separateness and togetherness.
"But the reality," she goes on to say, "is often mutual sacrifice
rather than mutual satisfaction."

One definition of adulthood describes it as that stage of life
when one has a sense of self-sufficiency. This includes the ability
to be one's own person, to function on one's own, and to enjoy
the experience of autonomy. Marital therapists believe that this
sense of identity is a vital ingredient in whether or not an individual will be successful in his or her intimate relationships. Psychologist Laura Singer writes: "In the early stages of marriage, couples inevitably discover certain things that can be very distressing.
I often hear the dismayed reactions of people the first time they
realize that they and their partners are separate individuals. Being
dissimilar creates anxiety, and it usually stems from the unconscious sense that if we love each other, we should be the same.

And if we're different, then something's wrong. Maybe we don't love each other."

Until the sense of identity and the feeling of being able to depend on oneself develops, it is difficult to achieve a truly intimate adult partnership. Until one has this sense of being able to be a separate person, the fears of abandonment or engulfment that we discussed earlier will remain as barriers to intimacy. One cannot be truly close to another person unless one can also be alone. (Incidentally, some women and men who remarry after a divorce seem better equipped for true closeness, perhaps because they have learned the hard way how to grow as separate individuals. A happily remarried couple we know believe that the main reason they are so well-mated is that the experience of being divorced forced them to develop their emotional resources and to depend on themselves. "Now, if one of us retreats from the other for a while, we understand," they told us. "Being able to enjoy our separateness makes it possible for us to appreciate our closeness.")

Even for the most loving couple constant companionship eventually cloys; being one half of a twosome begins to wear thin. Yet as time passes it grows increasingly difficult to say, "I need some time to myself . . . I need a place to be alone." Some people can stand the pressures of togetherness better than others. Psychologists don't know why A needs more privacy than B. They think it can be traced to childhood influences. But they cannot agree on whether the desire for aloneness is the sign of a neurotic "loner" or the hallmark of a well-adjusted person. A desire for aloneness (a more inclusive term for privacy of both time and space) is often misinterpreted as a sign of secretiveness, selfishness, or withdrawal. But there is a basic human need to have some part of yourself that is not shared, even with someone you love.

Today's woman has a special problem with this concept. Women have been taught for generations that they have a duty to be available constantly to meet the needs of lover, husband, family. The lesson has been so well-ingrained that even in this equalitarian time many women still find it difficult to assert the right to private time and space. A marriage counselor reports, "I see more and more women who say they feel like running away from home. They aren't unhappily married; they don't want to break up a relationship; they just want breathing space for a few days." Working women are especially likely to have little opportunity for privacy. "At least a housewife has *some* time for herself when her husband and kids are gone during the day," says a woman who works as a truck dispatcher. "But I'm surrounded by people all day long. I can't get away even though I often need to."

The need for personal space varies. But each of us has some sense of what social psychologists call "territoriality," our own invisible envelope of space we strive to maintain. Invasion of that area is likely to cause anxiety or anger. (In one test, researchers sat at a library table at varying distances from women readers. The researcher was ignored if she sat several chairs away. If she sat in the adjoining chair, however, the woman would avert her head or turn her back, shift the chair farther away, or use books as a "barrier" to protect the boundaries of her space.) "This invisible bubble may expand or shrink as the occasion requires," write Paul M. Insel and Henry C. Lindgren, experts on the psychology of crowding. But, they add, territorial behavior involves a specific place that we identify as ours alone. "The fact that we can lay claim to territories such as a home, an office, a desk, a bed, a chair, or whatever," they say, "makes it possible for us to withdraw at times from having to cope with others." For some couples, territoriality may even be keyed to an automobile:

> Bill and Diane, live-together law students, share a tiny apartment. The enforced closeness was making both of them irritable. Finally Diane asked Bill if he would mind taking the bus to school some of the time and letting her drive alone in their car. "That time on the freeway is precious," she says. "I feel suspended in space. Someone asked Bill and me to join a car pool, but I said no, thanks. I don't want anyone in that car with me!"

Significantly, married people seem more "territorial" than unmarried ones. According to Dr. Paul C. Rosenblatt, a University of Minnesota sociologist, that may be because it helps them compensate for the normal lack of privacy that is part of marriage. Moreover, he says, setting boundaries seems to be evidence of commitment to a long-term bond. Unmarried couples do not have this need to the same extent.

How couples deal with this conflicting need to be together and apart can create problems. If one partner wants some time alone, the other often feels resentful or rejected. In turn, the one seeking privacy may feel guilty for doing so—and then also resentful that there seems no way to have some solitude:

After twelve years of marriage Karl and Kristin are on the verge of divorce. Karl, an ardent fisherman, wants to spend every weekend at their lakeside cabin. Kristin has, all this time, gone with him uncomplainingly. But now she wants more time to enjoy her own interests—a Saturday concert, a Sunday exhibit at the art museum—in the city. Every weekend has become a struggle of wills. "You don't want to be with me anymore," Karl accuses. "That's not true," Kristin retorts. "I just want a chance to do something that interests *me*."

Luke is a young man who enjoys physical activity. He bowls, plays tennis, jogs, swims at an indoor pool. "I need the exercise after sitting at a desk all day," he says, "but my wife would like me to spend every night at home with her, watching TV or playing cards. If I say I'm going out to bowl or swim, she gets upset. How can I convince her that leaving her alone for a couple of hours two or three times a week doesn't mean I'm rejecting her?"

We told Luke, "It is more a matter of 'convincing' your wife. It is a matter of finding out why she feels as she does. For instance, she may get all the stimulation she needs from her work and look forward to quiet evenings with you. Clearly, she needs more closeness than you do. Maybe she unconsciously feels that your leaving her, even for a short while, means you don't love her enough to want to be with her.

"It may sound unrealistic to you, but it could be very real for her. You need to work on the problem together. Help her find ways to entertain herself when you are out; find more things both of you would enjoy doing together. Most of all, reassure her that you just need to exercise to let your tensions drain away so that you can enjoy being *with* her."

Privacy extends to thoughts and feelings, too. To ask, "What are you thinking about?" can sometimes be an intrusion. When it produces the usual response—"Oh, nothing"—the questioner feels rebuffed, left out. But the person who insists on sharing everything runs the risk of alienating a partner rather than drawing him or her closer. One woman said she and her man acknowledge each other's need for private thoughts by avoiding questions like "What did you do today?" or "Who did you talk to?" As she put it, "If we have information we want to share, we offer it. We consider with whom we lunched or who we telephoned to be as personal and private as our mail." Asking too many questions she says, tends to force secretive or defensive behavior.

How can you build an intimate relationship that balances separateness and togetherness? It is not an easy assignment for women and men who have learned to live more independently as a result of changing sex roles. It helps to keep in mind that the more you respect your own need for aloneness, the less threatened you will be by your partner's need for the same privilege. Here are some specific suggestions:

• Talk frankly to each other about your desire for, and concern about, privacy. Avoiding the issue only guarantees that it will flare up when you are least prepared to discuss it calmly. Quite often a conflict over privacy can develop simply because one person is honestly unaware of another's needs.

• Be specific about the kind and extent of privacy you would like to have. Just to say, like Greta Garbo, "I want to be alone" isn't very helpful. Tell your partner the kinds of times when you prefer to be alone. Perhaps it's right after you come from work; perhaps it is the quiet hours of early morning or late night, when you are best at problem solving. It may help if you and your partner can agree on special times for privacy. If, say, being alone for half an hour after work is an accepted part of a couple's routine, no one is going to feel guilty or rejected when each partner claims his or her private time.

• Don't confuse privacy with isolation or loneliness. A woman we know spends many evenings with her lover in a comfortable shared silence. She reads or studies while he listens to music on stereo headphones. "We're separate, yet together," she says.

• Try to understand and accept the dialectical nature of separation-togetherness rather than view it as an either/or situation. Separateness need not be pursued in a vacuum. Indeed, it develops as well, if not better, within a loving relationship. The reason? Privacy helps each of us discover and enhance our own uniqueness. When women and men lack that privacy they ultimately find they have little of themselves to give to each other. Whatever you give to another person remains forever a part of that person, and whatever you receive from him or her remains forever a part of you. But only when we are free to claim and to grant personal privacy are we secure enough to share ourselves with one we love. The reward for the woman and man who can give each other this privilege of aloneness is that when they are together they will share a greater intimacy.

2 — BEING FLEXIBLE

When you stop to think about it, it seems almost impossible to expect lovers or married partners to survive years of close emotional and physical proximity without some damage to the relationship—or at least substantial wear and tear—from the inevitable friction. We know that friction is a universal force. On the cosmic scale we are helpless to stop its drag. The action of oceanic tides slows the rotation of the earth an infinitesimal few milliseconds every decade. On more familiar ground we take what steps we can—adding oil to our car's engine, for instance—to reduce friction's abrasive effects on close-fitting moving parts. Yet when it comes to the most potentially abrasive and important ground of all, personal relationships, we tend merely to cross our fingers in the foolish hope that friction won't be a factor.

But of course it will. And the only lubricant that can offer any realistic protection against it is the quality of temperament we call *flexibility*.

There has perhaps never been a time when the quality of personal flexibility was as important as it is today. Flexibility makes it possible for us to keep our balance on the emotional tightrope that stretches between being able, on the one hand, to adapt to changing life situations and, on the other, to achieve stability in our relationships. That delicate balance must be maintained if love and marriage (surely the most delicate juxtaposition of "close-fitting, moving parts") are to survive and flourish.

Personal flexibility manifests itself in two areas. One involves the give-and-take between partners who are equals. When women and men moved to a carefully choreographed pattern of duties and obligations set by social custom, there was little likelihood they would step on one another's toes. Today the pattern is confused, each person moves to his or her own tune, and there is a large potential for collision. Women and men need a new and more forgiving sense of balance and direction to keep the music going, the dance flowing.

The other area of flexibility involves the capacity to adapt to change. "There is nothing permanent except change," a Greek philosopher said. And while adjusting to the rapid pace of technological change is demanding enough, the changes to which we must be most alert and responsive are those that occur in the persons we live with and love.

In this section we'll be examining key areas where flexibility can make the difference between a relationship that grinds harshly and one that functions smoothly. One such area is personal change. There is something extraordinarily reassuring about the *status quo*, even when it is not particularly satisfying. We have known women and men who would rather fight change—in themselves or in a partner—than face the unpredictable future change might bring about. This is not surprising. We all get ourselves stuck, at one time or another, in a comfortable rut: a role we play, a habit we cling to, a pattern of relating that seems to work for a while. But as a colleague, Lynn Hoffman, has remarked, inherent in all living organisms is the power "to transcend the 'stuckness' and move to a different stage." When someone you care about suddenly changes—an outgoing man becomes taciturn, a frugal woman turns spendthrift, a submissive lover becomes assertive—it is only by transcending the "stuckness" that partners can incorporate the change into their relationship so both can benefit from it (or, at worst, so the least possible friction will result).

This is true even of minor interactions in the day's routine. We're reminded of the time when friends of ours went through a minor crisis because the husband decided to jog for an hour every day before dinner. The wife, who had a part-time job and was involved in community affairs several evenings a week, found the timetable she had worked out for dinner, children's bedtimes, and so on rudely thrown off schedule. For a while the couple were at an impasse. "Being married to a runner is to be married to a man obsessed," the woman wailed. Each resisted the change in plans for weeks; eventually they did find a way to "transcend the stuckness" and accommodate his jogging to her needs. (We'll explore some of these methods in the following pages.) That result was foregone, for though no one can force his or her partner to change, it is a fact that when one person does change the other one ultimately will have to change, too.

Obviously not all change is automatically for the better; nor must change be accepted for its own sake. But we need to react to change in a realistic way. Fighting it—trying to cling to "what is" no matter how unproductive or even destructive it may be to the relationship—is a futile waste of energy.

The enormous changes in sex roles that have led women and men to make major adjustments in their expectations of each other also make personal flexibility an essential quality. As the nature of the power balance between the sexes has shifted, for example, women have increased their input into and control over the decisions that a couple make. We may not like to think that power is an issue between friends or lovers, but it clearly is. Power —most often defined by family experts as influence or authority over a partner—often rests with the woman or man who has the most resources: skills, information, income, physical attractiveness, physical strength, and similar personal assets. The person who has, or is believed to have, the most resources usually makes the most decisions. As the change in sex roles has vastly increased the resources and, consequently, the power of women, flexibility is crucial for couples who hope to avoid friction in the decision-making process.

Another prime example of the change in power concerns sex and the need for couples to learn to cooperate in setting and reaching mutually acceptable sexual decisions. Today's emphasis on freer sexual expression and assertiveness makes many women and men reluctant to compromise their intimate needs and wants. Again, flexibility is the tool with which each person can shape his or her sexual choices to fit the other's with the least friction.

Adapting to change . . . making decisions . . . Does it strike you as anticlimactic to add to these grave concerns where flexibility counts something as trivial sounding as minor irritations?

It should not, for we may need more of that quality, and more often, to deal with the small annoyances that plague every couple almost every day: leaving the gas tank on the edge of "empty"; eating in bed; not putting something back from where you took it; the nervous cough; forgetting to call to say you'll be late.

Abraham Maslow, the father of humanistic psychology, once commented that if you see anyone worrying about aphids in the rose garden, you can be sure they have no worries about food or shelter. There is clearly some truth to this view. But that is not to say that small vexations are not real, or not important, or not worthy of attention. It has been our experience that when two people are getting along well in the major aspects of their relationship, minor problems are somehow less annoying. It is simply easier to be tolerant when our primary needs are being met. When petty differences are blown up into serious confrontations, they are almost certain to be symptoms of some larger area of dissatisfaction. Thus, minor irritations, albeit inconsequential in themselves, can become emotionally corrosive if they are not managed with enough flexibility to prevent them from escalating. In other words, a partner is most irritating to us when we are feeling the most irritable. At the very time when flexibility is most important it may be least available. A good relationship is made up of innumerable such "small transactions"—one person yielding a bit here, the other giving a bit there. Successful couples learn the differences between forced compromise, self-deception, and reasonable flexibility.

When Someone You Love Suddenly Changes

In an ideal world, lovers and spouses would be able to adjust readily to change and reach out to each other in mutual support. Unfortunately (or perhaps fortunately), we do not live in an ideal world. Instead of accepting change as a potential opportunity for growth in a relationship, we all too often see it as a threat, or as a personal affront. Some of us revert to childish attitudes, put our partner in the position of a parent, and in effect ask, "Why are you doing this to me?"

Family therapists recognize two kinds of personal change. One, called "first-order" change, arises out of the natural progressions of life. It comes about by degrees and, more important, fits sensibly into the normal patterns of emotional development. People marry and have children, children grow and adults mature, relationships deepen or fade away—these changes we can accept and understand. They are likely to occur for both partners over generally the same period of time, and couples can usually deal with such transitions together—or at least have a degree of understanding about what is going on so they're able to weather the other's "natural" disruptions.

But there is another type of change that puzzles and disturbs us. An apparently contented wife and mother suddenly decides to go to college. A corporation executive quits his job to become an artist. Therapists call these "second-order" changes, and because they occur (or seem to occur) abruptly, unpredictably, and with no discernible cause, their effects are often disruptive. Here is one such example:

> *Husband:* In the past few months my wife has transformed herself. She has had her hair restyled and colored. She has gone on a diet and lost twenty-five pounds. She goes to an exercise class twice a week, and has bought a closetful of sexy clothes. I like the "new look"—though I never objected to the old one—but I can't help worrying about what can be going on here.

> *ML:* When you use the phrase "going on" it seems to me you are giving away your real concern.

> *Husband:* What do you mean by that?

> *ML:* It's the phrase people use when they are suspicious. What was your first reflex reaction to your wife's changed appearance—that she might be having an affair?

> *Husband (reluctantly):* Well, I suppose so. But isn't that a logical reaction?

> *ML:* Perhaps. But it's just as logical to suppose your wife wants to be more attractive for *you.*

Actually, any number of things may be going on. The most obvious probability is that this woman, having reached what she considers a critical mid-life stage, wants to recapture an appearance that reflects or bolsters her self-esteem. But the new look could also be a reflection of other changes taking place in her life. Is she in psychotherapy? Is she planning to look for work, or perhaps aiming for a promotion in her present job? Is she thinking of running for office in a community organization? Has she recently become friendly with younger or more fashionable women? Any of these changes can be a reason for her wanting to look and feel younger and prettier.

There could also be psychological reasons for her changed behavior. Some women "redo" themselves when the youngest child leaves home and they no longer see themselves primarily as a mother figure. Or it may be that the man's wife never realized that he liked the way she looked before and has changed her appearance because she feared he might become attracted to other women. These are the kinds of answers to "What's going on here?" that might have been produced by a more flexible approach to change. The only way this man is going to be able to satisfy his curiosity, or quell his doubts, is to ask his wife the question he asked the therapist. And (unless she *is* having an affair) the flexible response should be to pay her the attention her new appearance requests.

One of the problems women and men face in coping with a partner's change is that most people tend to assume it will be of the first order—predictable and therefore not particularly unsettling. Only recently has adequate attention been given to the fact that adults go through specific periods during life when crises can spark a host of seemingly sudden second-order changes. A significant birthday, for example, can set off an abrupt shift in behavior. One woman tells how, shortly after her husband's fortieth birthday, he discarded his conservative wardrobe for sport shirts and jeans, took up Yoga, and bought a motorcycle.

In another more vivid and evidently disconcerting instance, a man sought counseling to help him deal with his partner's sudden interest in experimenting with different sexual techniques. "We've been together eight years," he said, "and I guess our sex life has been fairly routine. But," he added quickly, "satisfying to both of us—at least I thought it was to her. I'm not averse to trying something new, but what bothers me is—where did she learn about these new techniques? Why are they suddenly so important?"

Again we see the reflexive response of suspicion when someone we love changes. In this particular case, as counseling sessions brought out, the woman's desire for sexual experimentation stemmed from feelings stirred up by conversations with friends, by books she had been reading, by her growing knowledge that today's woman has the right to be sexually more assertive. Realizing she had been missing certain sexual experiences, she wanted to try them out. And she demonstrated *her* flexibility by feeling comfortable enough to ask her partner to share these experiences with her. How could this man have responded in kind? By saying something like, "It seems as if you've totally changed your approach to lovemaking. I'm willing to try new things, but I've been wondering what happened to cause the change?" If both partners agree they find new approaches to sex mutually satisfying, the effect on their relationship can only be positive.

We say such second-order changes are "seemingly" sudden because the forces that generate them may have been unconsciously at work for a long time. One can clearly see the physical changes that take place in a partner as time passes. But the equally real changes in his or her feelings and goals, though just as gradual in development, usually cannot be detected as they evolve.

When someone experiences a second-order change, it usually means that both persons have to restructure the pattern of their relationship. When partners are adaptable, for the most part this works out satisfactorily. A man whose wife went back to her premarriage career as a fashion designer was enthusiastic about their new life-style. "It means more housework for me," he said, "but it's worth it. I can't imagine going back to living the 'old' way, when she was so much less vibrant and independent."

Unfortunately, one partner's second-order change does not usually produce such a flexible response in the other. The partner who changes is in a powerful position. In effect, by a unilateral action he or she is requiring the other person to change as well. Not surprisingly, the latter is often frustrated, resentful, angry: "I don't want this situation, I had nothing to do with it!" or, "Look at what's happening to us, and it's all your fault!"

Retirement often produces such a situation. When a person who has worked or run a business all his life (in this older genera-

tion it is still almost always the man who is the retiree) suddenly
has no place to invest his time, skill, and energy, a sudden change
in his behavior is not an uncommon occurrence:

> We have been happily married for nearly forty years [a
> woman writes]. But since my husband retired all we do
> is argue. He is constantly underfoot and gives me orders
> as to how to rearrange the kitchen shelves, the closets,
> etc. I realize he has little else to do, but he is driving me
> crazy.

Few things are more irritating to a woman of that generation
than to have a man messing up "her" kitchen. It is natural for
her to be annoyed. Her husband is in a very real sense intruding
on her "territory." But it is important that she have the flexibility
to understand the circumstances and to deal with them tactfully.
She might, for instance, suggest to her husband that his help with
specific chores would be more useful than generalized advice.
She might suggest they agree on dividing them so each would be
"in charge" of certain ones. And without wounding her husband's
feelings, this woman might suggest that he get some post-retire-
ment counseling.

How can you best deal with a partner's second-order change?
To begin with, communication is essential. No matter how puz-
zling or hurtful the change may be, there are almost always reasonable motives for it. Finding out what they are—discovering
the emotional *intent* behind the new attitude or behavior—makes
it easier to understand what is happening.

Second, the change must be acknowledged and accepted. To
deny a person the right to change, however destructive or illogical
it may seem to you, is to deny his or her integrity and individuality. Nevertheless, many women and men refuse to acknowledge
change in a partner. Some people fight it. They say things like,
"You can't do that to me!" or, "I won't allow this to happen!"
But this is like trying to sweep back the ocean with a broom.
Some people try to deny change. They say, "This isn't like you,"
or, "You're not acting like the person I know." They wait for the
change to disappear: "By next week you'll feel different." Or they
ascribe the change to a temporary aberration.

And some people distort the change in an effort to find a "reason" for it that they can understand. A man encouraged his long-time companion to go back to college and get her degree. When she did, however, his orderly and comfortable life fell apart. The woman now had neither the time nor the interest to cook elegant dinners, to entertain their friends, to go on weekend trips. But rather than face the fact that a fundamental change had occurred and that he was partially responsible for it, this man tried to distort what had happened. At first he denied it by saying in mild rebuke, "It's not like you not to be home." Eventually, he blamed the "women's movement," "She's turned into one of those feminists."

To acknowledge a second-order change does not mean one must approve it. That is especially true if the change is carried out in a deliberately non-caring way. But most people do not say, in effect, "I'm going to do what I want, and you'd better shape up and get used to it!" Rather, most changes come as somewhat of a surprise even to the one who changes.

Sometimes a partner's change can be accommodated by making changes of one's own. This does not mean "giving in"; it means developing flexibility. We recall talking with a young husband who was deeply upset because his wife—they'd only been married two years—announced she wanted to go away by herself for two or three weekends every year. "She says she needs to be alone some of the time," the man said. "Would she need to be alone if she were happy being with me?"

We told the young man that each of us has a unique need for solitude, and perhaps being off by herself was the only way his wife could satisfy her need. "Try to see the situation from her point of view," we said. "Sometimes being with another person— especially one you love—creates pressures to adjust to that person's needs. If you were with her, your wife would have to mesh her activities with yours. Alone, she can be free to cater to her own whims, follow her own rhythms." We suggested that instead of being a lonely martyr while his wife was away, the husband treat himself to a weekend on *his* own, doing exactly what and when *he* chose. By meeting change with change, both partners adapted to the situation beautifully.

Yet most of us tend to resist making such "accommodating"

changes. "Why should I have to change my way of life just because you did?" we protest. But any relationship between partners is, in the sociological sense of the word, a "system." If one element in a system changes, the other must adapt in order to maintain the system's balance, and adaptation means change. A system cannot function or even survive if one person changes while the other does not. It may seem from what we have been saying that change is largely a negative process. Nothing could be further from the truth. The fact that we *can* change offers constant hope for our future. How depressing it would be to think that the ones we love would always stay the same!

Who Decides What?

Decision making is one of the key day-to-day challenges couples face as they work out ways of living together compatibly. Yet many couples are not quite sure *how* they reach decisions, or why they sometimes have trouble coming to agreement. For instance, one young woman declared that when she and her fiancé had a choice to make, the one who "felt more strongly" about the issue was the one who made the final decision. But the man later admitted to us that he often deliberately underplayed his feelings. "If she sees I care a lot," he said, "she usually opposes my view. So if I want her to agree with me, I try to appear indifferent to the decision." Another young couple—newlyweds—said they never decided anything without talking it through until they were agreed. "But surely," we asked, "there must be a time when you can't totally agree . . . when one or the other of you has to yield a little. What happens then?" "Oh," the woman said, smiling, "if I really want to do something he doesn't want to do, I throw a little tantrum. Then we usually decide my way."

Research confirms the fact that most couples are unaware of such inconsistencies between what they *think* goes on in their decision making, and what actually goes on. But it's not surprising that this should be so. Most women and men grow up without much chance to learn how decisions are made. The discussions and the give-and-take by which our parents reach decisions, for instance, are usually carefully screened from us when we are youngsters. At work, decisions are handed down by superiors without much attempt to explain the thinking that went into them. And during courtship, women and men are so eager to please each other that thrashing out a decision is seldom necessary.

Family experts believe that the partner who makes the most decisions is the one who has the most "power," and that power resides in a person's "resources": his or her earning potential, skills, wisdom, attractiveness, sexual accessibility, education, social status, and similar personal assets. Traditionally, a woman who was financially more dependent on a man, according to this theory, was more likely to defer to his wishes than if she had her own source of income. (Sometimes, of course, it works out that a man who is more interested in a woman sexually than she is with him —or, significantly, more than he *thinks* she is—may back away from making decisions that might alienate her.)

But the upheaval in sex roles is changing the traditional power balance. As women move more confidently into the workplace they have greater financial independence. Today's woman is just as likely as her man to be well-educated, skilled, assertive, competent. She has a greater sense of self-esteem, and is not about to give in on matters she considers important out of the fear that if *this* particular relationship ends she may not be able to find another that suits her. Men, aware that their one-time dominance in the resources that contribute to decision-making power no longer exists, are seeking, along with women, new and more flexible ways to deal with the process.

The problem is that while most of us like to think we are reasonable and logical—open to discussion, willing to hear different opinions, ready to cooperate—in practice most of us do *not* make decisions on this reasonable and logical basis. Instead of setting real ground rules for effective decision making, most couples eventually work out (or stumble into) some sort of "system" that all too often is flawed and self-defeating.

Do you know how you and your partner arrive at decisions? As a test, ask yourself these questions to see if you agree on how each of these decisions was reached:

• How did you choose the last three movies you saw together?
• How did you decide where to eat the last three times you went to dinner together?

• How did you decide on your last major purchase? Where to spend your vacation?

• If you have moved to a new house or new city in the last several years, who decided that?

• Who decides when you will make love?

Did one or the other of you make the majority of these decisions? Were they made emotionally or on impulse? Were they decided only after an argument? Did it "just happen" without either of you making an actual choice? If the answers here are "Yes," you may need to make some changes in your decision-making techniques.

Moreover, the person who makes most such decisions is not necessarily the one who is in control of the decision-making process. The person who, openly or covertly, delegates which partner will make the decisions often holds more power. One of our counseling clients was sure that he usually chose the place where he and his wife go for their vacation: "I'm better at planning ahead, so I do it." But his spouse put a new light on it when she explained that, "It's true he does decide where we go, but that's because I *let* him. I'm too busy to get stuck handling all the travel details." The basic question, then, is not simply "Who decides?" but "Who *decides* who decides?"

There are patterns of decision making, and couples tend to fall into the habit of using a particular one or ones quite early in a relationship. Unfortunately, the pattern they use is not always the one most suited to their temperaments or their interaction. That's why it is important for a couple to be able to identify their pattern of decision making and, if advisable, change it.

Partners sometimes agree to give each other authority over the areas of daily life in which one or the other is more competent or better informed. Traditionally, men have made decisions about mechanical things—cars and home repairs, for example—and women about home decoration and child care. But as male and female "roles" increasingly intertwine and overlap, these stereotyped "areas of expertise" are changing. Today couples must be sufficiently flexible to decide for themselves who is better equipped to make which decisions. Moreover, it's often difficult to keep these areas separate. If a woman is going to be driving as

much as her man, she is entitled to her share of input into the
choice of car they buy. If a man is going to be sharing the care of
a baby, he should have a voice in deciding whether to use dispos-
able diapers or a diaper service.

In another pattern, one or the other partner may avoid decisions as long as possible: One merely "waits to see what happens"
and allows events themselves to force the issue. For example:

> The man I'm going with has a terrible time making
> decisions. When he finally does make one it takes him
> ages to do what he said he was going to do—and he
> often changes his mind several times along the way.
> This makes me furious, especially if I am counting on
> him to carry out a decision we made together.

One of the reasons people hesitate to make decisions is that
they really *don't* want to carry them out. We know a woman
whose husband kept pressuring her to quit her job so she could
travel with him. Reluctantly, she agreed. But though she "made"
the decision to leave, she kept finding excuses to avoid telling her
boss. A year later she was still working. Some people who cannot
make up their minds are obsessed about the possibility of being
wrong. They are so fearful of criticism or failure that they literally
get stuck at the choice point or resist committing themselves to
action.

Still another reason for procrastination lies in a pessimistic belief that it doesn't matter *what* one decides, since something un-
foreseen will sabotage the choice anyway. This "why bother?" attitude is often reinforced by poor decision-making skills. When
one repeatedly makes choices that do not work out well, one is
likely to blame somebody else rather than the process that led to
dissatisfaction in the first place.

All of these reasons for postponing decisions are also possible
reasons for delaying action on them. But when a person who
makes decisions reasonably well balks at implementing them, the
problem usually can be traced to either uncertainty or a lack of
enthusiasm for the choice that was made. One solution is to
rethink the decision and locate the source of the resistance to it.
If the decision is a Hobson's choice—between options that are

equally objectionable—self-discipline about following through is the only answer.

For those who seem unable to make decisions, the question is whether they put off *all* decisions or only certain ones. If you are often indecisive about issues that involve your partner, you may have some angry feelings toward that person which you are handling in this way without realizing it.

It is one thing to *choose* not to take any action in certain circumstances; sometimes waiting for further developments, or doing nothing at all, is a wise move. Defaulting on a decision, however, often means living from crisis to crisis. This system may save stress when minor matters are involved, but the danger is that one may become locked into it even when important questions come up. Essentially, this pattern reflects a *fear* of making choices. Such people may actually let outsiders make their decisions for them—friends, relatives, church or school authorities, alleged "experts" in specific fields. (We once had a couple in therapy who literally let their seven-year-old son make their decisions. He was the one who usually chose what they would eat, what they would watch on television, where they would go on vacation!)

Another pattern that yields poor results occurs when one partner acts as "parent" and makes all or most of the decisions except for those he or she delegates to the other person. Often the controlling partner does not value the other's ideas or feelings, and speaks of him or her almost as one would of a child. "My wife decides things on emotion, or what she calls intuition," an attorney remarked condescendingly. "She just isn't capable of reasoning things through." And the wife of a successful physician says, "If I left financial decisions to my husband we'd be up to our ears in debt. He never thinks about planning for the future."

But sometimes the decision-making partner has a need to impose his or her will regardless of the other person's competency. In some instances, this is accomplished under the guise of superior knowledge or authority that stems from being, say, a teacher, a cleric, a psychotherapist. In other cases, it reflects the fact that he or she holds the power in the relationship. Here's a prime example of the "need to control":

Wife: My husband travels a greal deal on business. I make whatever decisions need to be made while he is away. But when he comes home he immediately "takes over," often changing my decisions. The result is confusion—and a lot of resentment on my part.

ML: "Taking over" sounds as though you believe he is asserting his right to make decisions out of a desire to show you who's in charge.

Wife: What other reason could he have?

ML: It's possible he feels guilty about being away so much and about making you carry what he thinks should be his responsibility. However, it doesn't seem that is a good enough reason for causing confusion or for countermanding decisions you have made. It might be useful to point out that when he is away he has, in effect, delegated decisions to you, and that it is neither fair nor efficient to interfere with your judgments.

If you are right in thinking there is a power struggle over decisions, it might help to talk with your husband —before he leaves on his next trip—about things that may require decisions while he is gone, and get his opinion. But tell him firmly that you do not approve of his retroactive interference. If he trusts you to start something, he must trust you to finish it.

Paradoxically, decision-making power does not always rest with the person who seems to have it. Some women and men surrender their right to make decisions because they honestly feel incapable of making wise ones. Some yield out of apathy or a desire to avoid conflict, like the security analyst who makes crucial financial decisions all day at work and "when I get home I'm in no mood to make more decisions about where we'll go or whom we will see . . . I just leave that up to my boyfriend." Other women and men use manipulative techniques to control the decision-making process. For instance, Janet wants to accept a better-paying job even though it means she will have to work two or three evenings a week. Ted would not think of imposing his opinion on her. Instead, he says, "It's your career, you have the right to make your own choice. But of course you know how unhappy I'd be coming home to an empty house at night."

Must every decision that a couple makes be a joint one? Here's an interesting case history that was resolved with a technique that can be useful:

> My husband and I [a woman writes] respect each other's independence, but try to agree on decisions. Yet, more and more we find ourselves arguing when decisions must be made. Is there anything we can do to stop this?

Not long ago a colleague, family sociologist David Olson, observed that even in these days of personal independence and flexible sex roles many women and men are still stuck with the idea that in a good relationship partners should make all decisions jointly. He suggested that couples learn to think in terms of "I" as well as "we." Thus, our letter-writer and her husband might want to categorize issues into "I-decisions" and "we-decisions." The former would concern matters affecting each of them *individually* and would be up to each to resolve independently; the latter would be matters affecting them as a couple in which both would have a say. I-decisions might concern personal appearance, personal values, self-development goals. We-decisions might concern family finances, life-style, mutual friends, all matters pertaining to children. Remember that these areas themselves are flexible. What one couple agree is suitable for I-decisions may be something another couple would consider a we-decision.

For couples who wish to restructure the way they make decisions, here are some guidelines:

• Define the issue, gather relevant information and discuss the facts.

• Take each other's wishes, priorities, and values into consideration. Decisions made on the basis of facts alone without paying attention to feelings are those you are most likely to regret.

• Explore the available alternatives and select one. Sometimes this is a clear-cut choice. Occasionally the decision will have to be one that neither of you would have chosen if left to your own devices, but rather is a compromise you both can live with.

• Set down in detail the steps necessary to implement your decision. This will help make sure you are not working at cross-purposes. It also prevents shilly-shallying about putting a decision into action. Many couples make good decisions but fail to follow through.

At another time, when you are not actually making any decisions, you might want to take a look at the patterns by which you and your partner seem to operate. As a basis for discussion, answer the questions we posed at the outset of this section. Then:

• Sort out which decision areas each of you feels qualify as "major" or "minor" ones. Since there is no formula to determine this, couples often disagree. Some couples feel that "major" decisions need to be made so infrequently in the ordinary course of events that the partner who makes the bulk of the day-to-day "minor" decisions really is the controlling one. Make sure that each of you understands what sort of issues are important to the other.

• Don't get locked into one set pattern of decision making, but develop a variety of techniques to be used depending on the situation. At certain times, it may be just as well to "wait and see" what happens; at other times, one partner's clear expertise in a particular matter may mean it's best for him or her to decide.

• Be aware that as life-cycle changes affect you, you will need to remain flexible and find new ways to settle issues. A woman who takes a full-time job may find she no longer has the interest or the time to make all the household decisions; but since she is now contributing to the family income, she may want a larger voice in financial matters.

Sexual Decisions

We live in a period of sexual paradox. On the one hand, new psychological knowledge and new emotional attitudes are making it possible for women and men to understand their sexual responses better and to enjoy them more fully and freely. Yet therapists today see an increasing number of couples who complain that their intimate sexual times together are disappointing—clouded by resentment, hurt feelings, guilt. And much of the problem stems from conflicts over sexual decisions: How often should we make love? When should we make love? Who should make the first move? Should I go along with my partner's desire even if I feel no desire of my own at the moment? We hear these questions time and again:

• "I prefer to have sex at bedtime, just before going to sleep. She'd rather make love in the morning before she goes to work. I don't have time in the morning; she says she's too tired at night. What do we do about this?"

• "I would like to make love more often than my husband wants to. Our discussions turn into arguments. Am I supposed to resign myself to this situation, or can it be changed?"

• "My wife feels quite free to reject my sexual advances without giving me any reason for doing so. This hurts my feelings and makes me angry. But she says that if she has to give me a reason, it's the same as giving up control over her body or her sexual life."

Each of these situations calls for certain decisions to be made. And since sex is so entwined with unconscious emotional responses that neither facts nor reason carry much weight, it is all the more crucial for couples to understand how they arrive at decisions about it. In all of the above instances the problem is not so much one of dealing with individual preferences as it is of dealing with each partner's desire to hold on to the position he or she has staked out in the sexual arena. In each case a not-too-difficult compromise would seem to offer the best solution.

Take the couple who can't agree on when to make love. Certainly they could agree to alternate between morning and evening, or to save their main lovemaking sessions for a weekend. The woman who wants more loving than she gets is not in a hopeless situation. Indeed, as women become more self-confident sexually many have had—and resolved—this conflict. Instead of talking about it in a general way (which is what usually starts arguments) she should focus on specifics. For example, she could begin by asking her husband how often he would like to have sex if the decision were left entirely to him. Then, after telling him what frequency she desires, the couple could reach a compromise if each were willing to make a mutual adjustment.

And what about the woman who feels that being made to explain why she doesn't want to make love trespasses on her sexual independence? Actually, the shoe is on the other foot. Since the man in this instance seems always to be the initiator, and the woman is the one who says "yes" or "no," in effect she is in sexual command. The resentment this man feels when his wife refuses his advances may be due as much to repressed anger at her control of the situation as to his sense of rejection. We suggest he encourage his wife to propose lovemaking from time to time. Since the man would then be free to say "yes" or "no," neither could feel the other was always in control, or trying to exert control. Both partners need to realize, however, that every person has the right to say, "I don't feel like making love right now." If this is said in a loving way (and not every time) the other person should have no reason to feel rejected.

But because many people *do* feel personally rejected when sex is refused, the unwilling partner tends to make up reasons that can be accepted as legitimate even if they are not true. Deliberately or unconsciously, he or she converts "I don't want to" into "I can't" to avoid getting involved in potentially difficult explanations. So we get the bedtime litany of "I'm exhausted," or "I've got a headache," or "I have to get up too early." It would be preferable to be able to say, for example, "I love you but I'm not in the mood tonight," accompanied by a hug and kiss. But even a simple "no" is sometimes wiser than having to defend the validity of an excuse.

The trouble couples have in matching moods and schedules so they will be equally aroused at a mutually suitable moment is not surprising. Pressures of work, family, home, and community obligations often make it seem impossible to find the time, energy, or peace of mind that allow for proper lovemaking. Just as so many of us find we are having our meals on the run, we may fall into the habit of having sex on the run. Yet if we constantly postpone sex for that elusive "perfect" time, we would not have it very often.

Some couples try to circumvent the problem by making what are, in effect, advance reservations. They set aside a day, an evening, a weekend—some period of time when they will be sure of privacy and freedom from outside demands. Theoretically, this is a good idea, but in practice it all too often is booby-trapped by excessive expectations. Having arranged for undisturbed and enthusiastic lovemaking, couples tend to expect this time together to provide a peak sexual experience—to be romantic, passionate, intensely satisfying.

Let us call this goal a "Level One" response of emotional and sexual intimacy. When it occurs, it is a magical sensation. Some couples remember (or imagine) that this was how sex was in their early months together. For others it is an ideal yet to be achieved—but still an ideal. Anything less seems disappointing. But how realistic is it to expect that two people can reach this ideal whenever they set out to? Even when circumstances are at their best, should you both expect to respond sexually with the same degree of enthusiasm and arousal? The odds against this are so great that Level One sex occurs far less frequently than we hope—and expect.

If a couple is locked into the idea that nothing but a Level One response is worthwhile, they are depriving themselves of a considerable range of other interesting and rewarding sexual activity. For example, what about those times when one partner is quite aroused and the other is only mildly interested? Or when the circumstances are not entirely perfect for lovemaking, and it doesn't look as if the "right" moment or situation is likely to occur soon?

It is still possible under these conditions to have a satisfying sexual experience at what we call a "Level Two" response. This might be labeled the "Well, okay, why not?" category. That is certainly not the attitude we might wish for in a partner, but neither is it a refusal. Yet in many instances, when one person reacts with a Level Two the other is automatically turned off! "If you can't be as emotionally or physically involved as I am, forget it!" But if Level Two opportunities are always passed over because of the less than enthusiastic beginning, many rewarding sexual moments may be missed. If both partners can accept a Level Two response for what it is, sex can be mutually warm and gratifying. Indeed, such experiences often turn out better than anyone anticipates. In the course of lovemaking, what was at first a mild stirring of interest frequently grows into more passionate excitement. The time proves to be not so inappropriate after all.

There is another variety of sexual encounter—the "Level Three" response, which many couples foolishly and wrongfully deny themselves. It begins as a potential refusal to make love by a partner who is, at the moment, *not at all* sexually interested. But sensing and responding to the need or desire of the other person, the reluctant partner offers to go along with the idea. The unspoken (or sometimes spoken) reaction is, "I don't feel much like it, but I will if you really want to."

Actually, he or she is offering a special gift of love. But the offer is often rejected—turned down not out of consideration but in anger, "Don't do me any favors!" Part of the failure to recognize the gift for what it is may be due to the way in which it is offered. Put forward with an implication of hostility, resignation, or self-sacrifice, it can make sex seem like a duty or a chore—or, worse, like an act of charity. But for couples who can learn to convey these feelings tactfully and to give and accept this sort of loving gesture from time to time, Level Three sex provides another opportunity for unexpected intimacy.

All in all, if we wait for the perfect time to make love or always expect the perfect experience, we place unnecessarily destructive conditions on sexual pleasure. It is important to recognize that there is a flexible range of sexual-response decisions. Each of them can, in its own special way, contribute to a fulfilling relationship.

The Toothpaste-cap Syndrome, and Other "Minor" Irritants

• "Can you tell me why the man I live with always locks the bathroom door even if he's only shaving or brushing his teeth? He's not all that modest in other things, and it's a nuisance when we both have to get ready for work at the same time. It's a small thing, but it's driving me crazy."

• "Isobel is *always* late. I've learned to live with it, to stop expecting her to be on time, but it still annoys me."

• "Am I old-fashioned, or isn't it still bad manners to fix your face in public? My girl's lovely, but she constantly fusses with her makeup when we're out together."

It's the little things in life that count, we're told—but, unhappily, those little things often turn out to be annoyances rather than pleasures. Thus, many of the stresses couples experience result not from major differences but from comparatively minor irritations. They are so familiar as to be clichés: *He* never puts the cap back on the toothpaste; *she* leaves panty hose draped over the shower; *he* drops ashes on the rug; *she* is forever talking on the telephone. Counselors probably hear as many complaints about such trivial faults and flaws as they do about more serious and often underlying problems.

Sometimes a minor irritant is simply that—a minor irritant. (Even Freud, when accused of turning every image and dream into a sexual symbol, jestingly admitted that "sometimes a cigar is just a cigar.") And good man-woman relationships are no more immune to such irritations than are troubled ones. Living intimately with another person inevitably produces small annoyances. What often makes them even more abrasive is that we feel ashamed of being irritated by them. Why, we wonder guiltily, do we let the "little things" get under our skin when all the big, "important" things are going so well?

But counselors do not brush off these minor irritations as inconsequential. Indeed, they spend a considerable amount of time and effort helping people to cope with them. For though each annoying habit or act may seem picayune in itself, the guilt or embarrassment we feel at being annoyed by it—or the resentment we sense if we repress that annoyance—can become corrosive over time. It is another example of the emotional attrition that friction can produce in a relationship.

Because petty annoyances *are* so petty, they are difficult to deal with. Ignore them? Try it and see how far you get, or how long you can continue to do so. Complain about them? Doing that often makes the complainer seem petty. Force the issue? It's usually not a big enough issue to *be* forced. Mindlessly humming off-key, forgetting to clean the bathtub—these are the stuff that bad TV situation comedies are made of. But when endlessly repeated, such behavior can eventually come to be seen, at best, as evidence of a partner's thoughtlessness or uncooperativeness. At worst, one may come to feel the other person simply does not care enough—love enough—to mend his or her ways. But whether you choose to put the best or the worst construction on minor irritants, to deal with them effectively requires a range of flexible responses. Otherwise the cumulative impact of these exasperating trifles can escalate them into a major problem.

How can I make my fiancé dress properly when we go out? He likes to wear what he calls "casual" clothes— but I call them old, wrinkled, and out of style. He could

look so nice if he wanted to. How can I make him care
more about his appearance? It can certainly be disconcerting when I'm all dressed up and he is not.

Before the woman who brought these questions to us sets out
to try to remake her fiancé's sartorial image, she needs to have a
clearer idea of *why* the man dresses as he does. "Some people,"
we told her, "women as well as men, though that's less usual, use
clothing to show their hostility toward others or to express rebel-
liousness against authority and conformity. The question is, is this
defiance of conventionality an expression of great personal security or does it mask insecurity? If it is the latter, it might help if
you can give your fiancé the support and encouraging feedback
he needs to feel more comfortable about himself and the way he
looks, so that he does not have to use clothing as a way of 'pro-
testing too much.' If he dressed casually out of enormous ego
strength, so that it really does not matter to him what others
think of his appearance, you might ask him to care more about
your feelings. Is being comfortable—or even rebellious—more important to him than making you feel at ease?"

There may be a number of other reasons why the man clings to
his irritating habit. He may lack the amount of self-esteem necessary to feel that he *deserves* to be dressed well. Perhaps he grew
up in a poor family where the budget didn't stretch to include
"good" clothing. Or he may be one of those men who simply
don't know how to dress properly for certain occasions. Clearly,
his companion's response must be flexible enough to take into account these different motivations. Basically, she needs to know if
her man wears jeans to a dinner party out of some emotional
hang-up, pure inner strength, or simple miscalculation. Once she
knows the why of the matter she can enlist his cooperation into
developing a "dress code" they can both live with.

Such minor irritants grow more significant when, as sometimes
happens, they are symptoms of major conflicts that a couple may
not be consciously aware of or have been refusing to bring out
into the open. A woman complains that her partner watches ball
games on television all weekend; but what she *really* may be saying, or feeling, is that he pays no attention to her. Here is an excellent example of a "minor irritation" that cloaked a major conflict:

Why is it [a counseling client asked] that my husband
is never ready on time when we have to go somewhere?
Sometimes I think he does it just to spite me because he
knows I hate to be late.

On the simplest level, it could be that time has a different meaning, a different importance, for each of these spouses. The woman
may have been taught, as a child, that promptness is a cardinal
virtue; her husband may have been raised in a family where other
values took priority over punctuality. If something like this were
the case, we would suggest that the couple try to work out a system of differentiating between occasions when they really should
be on time—for the theater or a business appointment—and occasions where promptness isn't crucial—a large party, a casual
visit with friends. And if both agree that punctuality is more important than competing values, the woman can't be accused of
nagging when she calmly reminds her husband of the hour.

But, we have pointed out to some couples with such a problem,
consistent lateness may indicate more rancorous motives at work.
Being late when one's companion wants to be prompt often is a
passive-aggressive way of exerting control over the other person; of
silently saying, "You are not going to tell me what to do or when
to do it." Conversely, a woman's insistence on punctuality in situations where it is *not* vital may indicate *her* unconscious attempt
to control her husband. "Are the two of you using time as a
weapon in a struggle for dominance?" we might ask. "That's
something we need to find out in future counseling sessions. If so,
then what you both choose now to view as a minor irritant is a serious symptom of a major problem."

In another instance a man accused the woman he was living
with of shirking her responsibilities at home. She, in turn,
charged him with refusing to do his share. What seemed at first a
trivial difference of opinion proved to have more significant roots.
The woman had recently entered law school and was trying
to combine her domestic responsibilities with an exhausting
classroom-and-study schedule. She felt her companion owed it to
her to carry more of the household load so she could give more
time to her studies. But he—a college dropout with a routine,
dead-end job—was threatened by her ambitions and her progress.

The only way he knew to protect his vulnerability was to retreat into a shell of uncooperativeness.

How can a couple tell when a minor irritation threatens to turn into a larger problem or when it is symptomatic of deeper conflict? One way is to work directly on the situation to see if it can be solved. A man grew annoyed with his wife because she fell asleep every night around ten o'clock, "just when I begin to relax, just when I want to talk with her." He felt she was deliberately avoiding him, saying with body language that she did not want any sense of intimacy. As it turned out, the woman's early-evening sleepiness was simply the way her biological clock was set. "Day" people who live with "night" people often run into this problem. But there are ways of dealing with unsynchronized biorhythms. We offered several suggestions: Perhaps the couple could arrange to share intimate time earlier in the evening, over a glass of wine before dinner; on the other hand, perhaps they could get up earlier and talk over a leisurely breakfast; perhaps the woman, if she's a housewife, could plan to take an afternoon nap that would leave her more alert and receptive later in the evening.

The fact is that when "a cigar is just a cigar," minor irritants can be smoothed away with a modicum of these ingredients of flexibility: common sense, consideration, caring. And if one eventually finds that deeper issues are involved, any small accommodations a couple may have been able to make can serve as building blocks on which to base solutions to the larger difficulties.

3—TALKING TO EACH OTHER

There are countless recipes for a good relationship. One of our favorites comes from Rebecca West's novel, *The Thinking Reed*: "There was a definite process by which one made people into friends, and it involved talking to them and listening to them for hours at a time." It would be hard to find a better formula—not only for making people into friends, but for making friends into lovers, lovers into partners, and for sustaining those relationships.

How well a woman and man get along with each other depends on how well they communicate; and how well they communicate depends on how well they get along. The first principle is widely accepted. There seems no question that as two people attach personal meaning to each other's words and gestures, these gradually symbolize their closeness. The second principle is perhaps less firmly established. But it makes common sense, for when two people feel content about their relationship they are likely to be more receptive to each other's messages.

Then too, warm feelings give rise to a tolerance for imperfection, a margin for error that allows each person to give the other the benefit of a doubt, to increase trust, to reduce suspicion, to take less seriously words spoken in anger. Such women and men often communicate without words. They have learned to understand the significance of a touch, a glance, a tone of voice, a smile, a shrug, a silence. They develop a set of signals unique to themselves. Nowhere do we see this operate more clearly than in sexual communication.

But to use words and signals in these ways, we must be able to control them—to understand what we are saying, how we are saying it, and perhaps most important, why we are saying it. In an era of changing roles, particularly, women and men need constantly to be aware of whether they give and receive intimate information with the same degree of clarity and openness that characterizes other aspects of their new ways of dealing with one another.

"When I married," a middle-aged woman told us recently, "we *assumed* we'd have children, we *assumed* I'd be a homemaker. But our son can't assume what his partner will do with her life, and our daughter can't take it for granted that the man she married will want children. Today you need to talk out those choices and listen them out; otherwise you will have to deal with a choice you didn't expect." The question of having time to talk is also a relatively new problem. "I work, she works, we both go to evening classes on different nights, weekends are filled with chores, church, socializing," a young husband said. "We don't ever seem to have time to talk."

Communication is often defined as a sharing, a linking, an opening up of one person to another. But there can be no sharing, linking or opening up without the kind of communication that creates an atmosphere both intimate and secure. A biblical prophet aptly summed up the essential value of creative communication: "Speak, that I may know thee."

How to Say What You Really Mean, and Vice Versa

Clear communication is the main avenue by which women and men arrive at harmonious living, and through which they learn to work effectively together. It is the kind of talk that involves the interchange of ideas and feelings. Yet this kind of talk, evidently, does not take place nearly as much as it should. Research indicates, almost unbelievably, that the average couple spend less than an hour a week in such conversation. Even in a better-than-average relationship, the amount of time a woman and man spend in constructive, revealing, or intimate talk together is seldom more than that.

But there is one significant difference that distinguishes communication between couples in successful relationships from that of couples who are less satisfied or actually in conflict. It isn't so

much what a couple talk about, nor even how much they talk together (although both factors are always important); rather, what
seems to matter most is how *clearly* they communicate with each
other: How careful they are to avoid "buzz words" that substitute
clichés for reasoned discussion . . . How skilled they are at probing beyond and beneath stereotyped "mental sets" about chauvin-
ism and feminism, about male and female roles . . . How insightful enough they are to realize when they use words (or silences)
to hide rather than to reveal feelings of resentment, hostility, dis-
trust.

Here's a rather typical instance of clouded communication
drawn from a case history in our counseling files. The couple had
lived together for nearly a year and were planning to marry soon:

> *Ellen:* It bothers me that Greg won't let me help him
> when he is worried about things. I can tell when he's
> upset over problems in his work, but he won't share
> them with me.

> *ML:* Is that true, Greg?

> *Greg:* Pretty much. I do keep some things to myself.
> But I don't see why I need to burden Ellen with some-
> thing she can't do anything about.

> *ML (to Ellen):* Do you talk to Greg about it when
> *you* have job problems?

> *Ellen:* I'd like to, but I feel that I can't, under the cir-
> cumstances. I mean, if he doesn't want to share with
> me, I expect he doesn't want me to burden him.

And Greg, it turned out, *was* using the pose of being the strong
silent male not so much to spare Ellen, but so he wouldn't have
to listen to her troubles. "By keeping your problems to yourself,"
the counselor suggested to Greg, "it appears you have effectively
told Ellen to do the same thing. Shutting her out of an important
part of your life, and distancing yourself from an important part
of hers, is not a good way to begin a marriage. And if it is creating tension between you now, it will probably cause more conflict
later."

One of the qualities of compatible partners is that they say they "understand" each other—that the words and actions by which they communicate, in public or private, have the same meaning for both of them. At the simplest level, for example, if John tells Mary, "I'll be there in a moment," Mary knows fairly accurately how long she will have to wait. For John and Mary, the word "moment" connotes roughly the same amount of time. But a "moment" might mean anything from thirty seconds to fifteen minutes, depending on the couple. Similarly, if John and Mary are at a party and John notices Mary is nervously tapping her foot on the floor, if they communicate well he knows she wants to leave. In the context of their relationship, much of what they say and do carries underlying messages that are unique to them as a couple.

Therapists call this a "congruent" communication style, and a few couples are lucky enough to be on the same communication wavelength from the start, although occasionally it is the reason they were drawn together in the first place. That doesn't mean a couple can or should be totally congruent, completely attuned, all of the time. (As Dr. Sherod Miller, an expert in communication styles, jocularly observes: "It's all right to have a good argument once in a while. When my wife and I have a fight I don't want it to get ruined by communication skills!")

For many couples, being too good at communication skills is the least of their worries; instead they must work hard to learn each other's language. And make no mistake, women and men do use words differently, express their ideas differently, even have different communication styles. Two California sociologists, Don Zimmerman and Candace West, recorded conversations held in public places between couples who knew each other, and between women and men who were meeting for the first time. They found that in both situations men bend to dominate the talk, to interrupt, to change the subject abruptly, with little or no resistance from the women. Topics introduced by women are likely to be dropped in favor of topics of more interest to men. Yet men seldom interrupt other men.

Zimmerman and West believe this tactic represents a man's way of establishing or displaying control; in a sense he is saying, "I'm the boss here." If that is so, today's assertive woman is more likely than women from the past to point out the error of his conversational ways. Other experts suggest that interrupting a conversation is something a man learns in the early years of childhood, when he is vying for attention, defending his opinions, challenging other boys. At the same time a young girl is learning how to get along with other girls through more subtle and diplomatic conversational means.

In her book *Language and a Woman's Place*, linguist Robin Lakoff says that the intonation and sentence structure women use still reflect their once traditional sex role. But if that traditional role is now outmoded, Lakoff suggests, the change is not wholly evidenced by communication patterns. "Men's language may be increasingly adopted by women," she writes, "but women's language is not being adopted by men." Lakoff cites women's use of "empty" adjectives: *lovely, divine, sweet,* words few men would be caught dead using. And while females are allowed (or even encouraged, by fashion and cosmetic advertisements) to name colors precisely—beige, lavender, coral—men, writes Lakoff, "would usually be criticized for describing colors in such detail."

Moreover, Lakoff continues, "Women . . . use 'tag questions' . . . to avoid committing themselves or accepting responsibility." (Where a man might say, "Let's have dinner at seven," a woman would more likely say—with a rising inflection—"Let's have dinner at seven?") "Questions at the end of a sentence," says Lakoff, "give the impression that the speakers are unsure . . . and are seeking confirmation even though they know precisely what they are talking about."

Couples who do not have a "congruent" communication style must work to learn each other's language. But some never manage to do that: Each partner continues to expect that he or she always ought to understand (or be understood by) the other—even though what each says or does may convey vague, confusing or conflicting messages. Therapists have a word for this too. They call it "mystification"—a process by which meaning is garbled, lost, or distorted.

Sometimes a person deliberately uses this sort of mystification to manipulate a partner or a situation. Evading questions, for instance, or giving ill-defined and ambiguous responses, or retreating into silence—all are devices designed to maintain the *status quo,*

to avoid rocking the boat. But more often mystification is an unconscious attempt by one person to get or keep control of an intimate relationship.

Consider the woman who charged that her husband was so
"sneaky" in the way he criticized her that sometimes she wasn't
sure exactly what he was trying to tell her, and thus she frequently was at a loss for an appropriate response: "If I get dressed
up to go out, he'll say, 'You're going to wear that outfit?' The
other day I was planting a rosebush and he said, 'That's where
you're putting it?' Naturally I take these as criticisms. But when
I show my annoyance he says, 'Why are you upset? I was just asking a question.'"

This sort of "loaded" question is a device commonly resorted to
by someone who wants to manipulate a situation or control a
relationship without a confrontation. By couching his criticism in
an indirect way the husband was able to express his feelings—and
then turn the blame on his wife if she reacted angrily.

One way to deal with such distorted communication is for the
wife to announce that she realizes what her husband is doing. She
might, for example, say it is unfair of him to convey opinions that
upset her and then duck taking any share of the responsibility. If
he won't confront her, she may have to confront him. She could
say something like, "When you make a remark like that about
what I'm wearing I know you aren't asking for information. You
can see what I have on. I think you said that about my dress because you don't think it's suitable. Is that true?" Another possible
way of handling a loaded question is to head it off in advance.
For example, she might say, "I was thinking of planting the rosebush over there. Do you think that's a good place for it?" If he
disagrees, she could ask him to suggest a better spot. But if he
agrees, or says he doesn't care, then he should see how unreasonable it is if he later questions her decision.

The loaded question is but one of many ways some people de-
feat the purpose of communication by surrounding it with
vagueness and confusion. For instance, there was the man who
accused his lover of "deliberately misunderstanding" him when
they argued: "You only listen to what I *do* say and never to what
I don't."

A second form of mystification occurs when one person communicates only part of a message, with the rest—usually the significant part—secreted in a "hidden meaning." Having a hidden meaning (also referred to as a "hidden agenda") prevents (or sabotages) the exchange of honest information. Asking, "Do you want to eat out tonight?" may mean either "I'd like to go out" or "I'd rather stay home." Similarly, "What would you like to do this weekend?" may mean the questioner would enjoy a quiet time, or it may mean he or she has already made a plan and is only waiting to spring it on the other person.

When someone asks a question that conceals a hidden agenda it is often to find a "safe" way of bringing up a touchy subject. Answering such a question can be a dangerous venture. That's why counselors teach couples to make a "statement of intent" first, one that makes clear immediately what the speaker has in mind: i.e., "I was thinking of asking the Smiths to come over Saturday. How would you feel about that?"

Probably the most infuriating misuse of communication is the "double bind." That occurs when one partner simultaneously is given two conflicting messages that apply to the same situation. Here is an example of a double bind in its simplest form:

She: I'd like to see that new Jane Fonda movie tonight.

He: It doesn't sound interesting to me. Why don't you go? I'll stay home with the kids.

She accepts his offer, enjoys the film, but when she gets home he is in a foul mood:

She: What happened to make you so sour?

He: You know I can't get any work done and watch the kids at the same time.

She: Work? You never said you had work to do.

He: I always have work to do. You should know that. That's why *I* can't take time to see a movie!

The Catch-22 of double-bind messages is that they require the recipient to do *something*; but whatever he or she does is bound to be wrong. It's a case of "damned if you do and damned if you don't," as the dilemma faced by a recent counseling client clearly shows:

> My husband accused me of being uninterested in sex because I did not take the initiative more often in our lovemaking. But now when I do, he seems displeased. He complains that a woman shouldn't be the sexual aggressor. How can I find out what he really wants?

This is a classic double bind: The more one tries to reach an acceptable solution, the more unacceptable it seems to become. In such a maddening situation, where it is impossible to read a partner's intention accurately, one tends to start guessing; mind reading. When any response fails to please, one eventually thinks, "Why even try?" and gives up—leaving both persons dissatisfied and alienated.

How can you find out what the person who communicates a double bind really wants? Here is how the counselor advised the woman in the above case:

> Your husband probably doesn't know, himself, which behavior he prefers. People who send such paradoxical messages are usually unaware, on a conscious level, that they are doing so. Evidently your husband is extremely ambivalent about his desire for you to be sexually assertive. His insecurity in this area makes him need to feel in control, one way or the other. Unfortunately, while he is the one with conflicting feelings, you are faced with trying to figure out how to behave at any given time.
>
> There is no perfect solution to your problem, but there are ways you can try to deal with it. One is to do what you feel like doing without trying to second-guess him, and let the chips fall where they may. This may not make things better, but it will at least do something to relieve your own frustration. Another method is to ask him directly, "Do you want me to take the sexual initiative now?" By asking your husband to commit him-

self one way or the other *at the moment*, you are turning the tables, forcing him to make the choice.

A third approach is to confront your husband frankly and ask his help: "You say you want me to initiate sex, but when I do you don't seem to like it. I'm not sure what you want. You give me one message, and then switch gears and give me an opposite one. That puts me in an impossible situation since whatever I do can't satisfy you." Let him know that you want to please him but that he will have to help you. This last approach may lead to some difficult discussions, but it is the best way to work out an end to the impasse.

To overcome misunderstandings caused by these varieties of "mystification," each partner needs to be patient and sensitive to what the other says or may be trying to say. To develop as much congruence as possible in the messages that pass between a woman and a man you need to define your words clearly, to spell out your feelings frankly, and to declare your wishes forthrightly.

The Feelings Behind the Words

My woman friend has an annoying habit of telling me what I think or how I feel. For instance, she'll say that I am angry with her when, in fact, I am not. Or she will decide that I didn't enjoy our meal in a restaurant when, actually, I thought it was quite good. Why does she think she knows better than I do how I feel about things?

Therapists advise couples such as the one described above to "prove out" their version of each other's statements. The process might start with the woman restating, in her own words, what she thinks her companion feels or means. If she is wrong, he can correct her. If, even though wrong, she still insists her interpretation is right, he can gently remind her that he is the only person who really knows how he feels or what he thinks.

The sexes have always found it difficult to share each other's feelings as expressed in words. And the pace of change in sex roles has intensified the problem. Women, traditionally believed to be more in touch with their feelings than men, have not always been able to communicate them clearly (as we have seen from Robin Lakoff's comments). Men presumably can be more articulate about facts than about emotions. Recent research indicates that these characteristics are much more evident when women and men communicate across sex lines than with others of their own sex. In other words, in mixed company men suppress their emotions and sensitivity more than when alone or with other men, while women inhibit their logical, more decisive sides more when with men. Women and men react so strongly to the communication style of the other sex that both frequently seem to deny parts of themselves in reaction to the other.

Recently, however, there has been a new development. As women increasingly move into male-dominated fields of work, differences between women's and men's communication styles are lessening. Women are learning to camouflage their feelings, to maintain self-control, and to be far less passive in the presence of men. This does not mean they have become harder or more callous; it does mean they are less inhibited about speaking up, and are more decisive and persistent in cross-sex conversation. Men, on the other hand, have been encouraged (by women and other men) to be more expressive and to give freer rein to their feelings. They seem more willing to reveal themselves, and to have less need to dominate when women are present.

The new patterns of communication between the sexes are probably no less interdependent than before. The difference is that instead of being a vehicle for denying parts of themselves, the new patterns are helping each sex to realize certain potentials that were formerly inhibited.

Words have so many different emotional connotations for each of us that it is not surprising we react inappropriately to them from time to time. For instance: A suggests to B that they reexamine the household budget. B's immediate reaction is defensive: "I'm not extravagant! I know where the money goes!" But A didn't make (or even intend) that charge: "I just wanted to see if we could afford a weekend trip."

Couples in an intimate relationship speak to each other in a language—words or gestures—that is symbolic of their experiences together. From that spoken or silent communication they draw meanings that are unique to them as a couple. But there is a way for women and men who may not have that shared background still to arrive at an appropriate emotional response to each other. It is, simply, to discover the feelings behind each other's words: the reason they are being spoken; the *why* of them. Conversely, the key to *getting* an appropriate response is to ask yourself, before you speak, *for what reason am I saying this?*

Communication between intimates serves several basic purposes:

• To share experiences, no matter how mundane. Often we don't realize how important this aspect of communication is until the person we feel comfortable talking to or listening to is— through death, divorce, the breakup of a love affair—no longer there.

• To arouse empathy in the other person, so you have a sense that your feelings of the moment, whether downbeat or upbeat, foolish or realistic, are shared and understood.

• To release pent-up feelings. Women have typically felt free to vent their anxieties, and men to release anger. But as role stereotypes fade, assertiveness classes are encouraging women to express angry emotions, and the male liberation movement is encouraging men to express their personal worries, even their fears. Two recent incidents bear witness to how difficult it can be to adjust to these developments. In one instance we listened to the complaint of a woman whose brother had just found out his wife was having an affair.

"After a dreadful fight," she said, "my brother asked his wife to move out, and they are still living apart. Now, every time my brother and I talk he goes through the whole story again, down to the last detail. He cries. I can understand that he is hurt, but as much as I sympathize with my brother I am beginning to resent his calls or visits. When I try to cut him short by saying I've heard the whole story many times, he seems surprised. Why does he keep repeating it to me. Is there anything I can do to help him stop?"

Two significant things are going on here. This man, instead of stoically keeping his "emotional bleeding" to himself, feels able to lay bare his pain, even to cry in front of another person—a woman, at that. But this "unmanly" act makes his sister nervous. It is quite possible that the man has adjusted to the changing patterns of sex-role behavior better than his sister has. We suggested to her that she examine her own values to discover whether she has trouble accepting non-traditional behavior from a man. Since her brother obviously needs to share his pain, and trusts her to give him support, it could be a growing experience for her to learn how to give understanding to a man who is confronting his emotions. We explained that in a period of severe emotional distress, talking about the problem is part of the healing process: "The repetition is a symptom of the brother's anxiety—a compulsive need to relive his problems—so he represses the memory of having told the story before. It is difficult to be a patient and empathic listener under such circumstances. But the situation won't last indefinitely."

The second incident was sparked by the following letter we received:

> I have read how important it is for a woman to be able to express her aggressive feelings. But whenever I try to do that it upsets my fiancé. He accuses me of "coming on" too strong, being unladylike. Well, maybe I am, but not long ago I was passed over for a deserved promotion as a result of office politics, and I needed to share my anger with the man I'm going to marry. To me, that didn't seem illogical or wrong. But when I began to shout and pound the table he said he couldn't stand to see me act that way, and he left the room. Don't I have a right to vent my feelings the same way he does?

The answer is that some people find it hard to remain calm in the face of an outpouring of strong feelings. This man probably was not prepared for such a strong expression of anger from a woman. He may wonder what he is letting himself in for if he goes ahead and marries her. Or he may feel her emotional demands on him may be greater than he can support.

Self-disclosure of this kind can take place only in a safe emotional atmosphere. When we expose our innermost feelings we expect that the listener will understand the risk we feel we are taking in being so open: *I may sound like a fool . . . Am I being a bore? . . . Will he/she use this against me some time?* But the risks need to be run because self-disclosure can stimulate self-growth. For many years a woman we knew, a skilled gardener, dreamed of becoming a landscape designer. Because she felt herself incapable of this goal she never mentioned it to anyone. One day when she and her husband were discussing their children's ambitions, she suddenly told him about her own—even though she feared he would laugh. To her surprise, he listened attentively and encouraged her to enroll in college courses. Today she has a thriving business.

Giving and getting this kind of emotional support is what "feeling" communication ultimately is all about. You can most effectively provide that support if:

• You understand the intent behind a partner's statements.

• You avoid making snap judgments about what the other person's remarks may mean, or about what you think they may conceal.

• You focus on the matter at hand, and don't confuse it with other incidents, other feelings.

• You accept the other person's right to express feelings in any way he or she considers appropriate, whether or not that meets your sex-role expectations.

What's Your Communication Style?

Couples develop rules that govern their dialogues with each other. Most of the time they do not realize these rules exist. The pattern by which they communicate becomes a habit. James L. Hawkins, a family sociologist at the University of Minnesota, constructed a series of family vignettes to find out which communication styles women and men prefer each other to use, and which styles they actually use most of the time. He devised a set of six fictitious "critical incidents" that often come up in a relationship, along with four possible ways partners might deal with each of them. We have adapted Hawkins' survey so you can test yourself to see which communication style you would use in these situations. Check the answer that comes closest to the way you would respond in each case:

1. There are times when you would really like your partner to do something for you.
   ——a) You say what you want, and ask if he or she will do it, or if he or she would rather not.
   ——b) You tell the other person to do it, and expect it to be done.
   ——c) You hint around and hope he or she will figure out what you want.
   ——d) You bring up the subject to sort of get an idea of how your partner will react.

2. Sometimes the two of you disagree over whom to invite to your home, or what to do on an evening out.
   ——a) You don't make a fuss, but just go along with your partner's plans.
   ——b) You suggest both of you figure out something you both would enjoy.
   ——c) You say something like, "If it's going to start a fight, let's not do anything."
   ——d) You say how strongly you feel, and check to see how he or she feels.

3. Sometimes the other person seems "down in the dumps" about something.
   ——a) You ask him or her to talk about it.
   ——b) You say you are concerned, and want to know what, if anything, is wrong.
   ——c) You tell him or her to stop moping.
   ——d) You try to distract your partner, to cheer him or her up a bit.

4. You are quite angry about something your partner did.
   ——a) You don't mention the subject; instead, you busy yourself with other things to get your mind off it.
   ——b) Very sincerely, you say you *are* angry and would like to explain why.

_____c) Without letting on that you are angry,
          you ask if the two of you can discuss some-
          thing that is upsetting you.

_____d) You blow up and tell him or her off.

5. Your partner does something that pleases you very
   much.

_____a) You say how nice it would be if he or she
          did it again sometime.

_____b) You say, straight out, how pleased you are.

_____c) You say something like, "I'd better enjoy
          this while I can, you'll probably never do
          it again."

_____d) You keep your feelings to yourself.

6. You are worried about something.

_____a) You try to act as if nothing is bothering you.

_____b) You don't let on that you're worried, but
          you bring up the subject and start to say
          what you think about it.

_____c) You crab around, but don't come out and
          say you are worried.

_____d) You say you're worried and share your con-
          cern with your partner.

The responses represent the four conversational styles that
Hawkins identified. They are:

• *Controlling:* Persons who exhibit this style discourage any disagreement and seek to have their own way. Often they show little
awareness of their partner's opinions; even if they do, being right
and "winning" is more important to them than affection or having a good relationship. Implicit is lack of trust of the partner's
judgment or capabilities, or sometimes lack of respect for the
partner's personal dignity.

• *Conventional:* Those who communicate in this manner give
the appearance of talking, but the topics are superficial and the
speaker does not risk exploring issues that may be emotional or
controversial.

• *Speculative:* Involves exploration of issues and openness to new
ideas. This kind of person, however, is unable to self-disclose

readily and may spend a good deal of time asking questions of the partner to avoid talking about himself or herself.

• *Contactful:* Persons who exhibit this style not only are interested in their partners' viewpoints but are also self-revealing. They emphasize sharing of thoughts.

To find your communication style, compare your answers with the following key:

    Controlling responses are: 1-b; 2-c; 3-c; 4-d; 5-c; 6-c.
    Conventional: 1-c; 2-a; 3-d; 4-a; 5-d; 6-a.
    Speculative: 1-d; 2-b; 3-a; 4-c; 5-a; 6-b.
    Contactful: 1-a; 2-d; 3-b; 4-b; 5-b; 6-d.

Not surprisingly, Hawkins found that women prefer men to use the contactful style more, and the controlling style less, than men themselves prefer to do. "This is consistent," says Hawkins, "with the patriarchal tradition of male control over women, and with the increasing momentum toward equalitarianism. Feminists have been spearheading the struggle to eliminate the old pattern. Our data show clearly that . . . the struggle is not over. [Yet] a certain hopefulness is implicit in the data when it is recognized that both men and women rank controlling communication last."

Women see men as more controlling and less contactful than men believe themselves to be, Hawkins finds. "If men are to be believed, they have largely abandoned the patriarchal tradition . . . If the women are to be believed, the men still engage in substantial controlling behavior and not enough contactful interaction." Meanwhile, women indicate they want men to share their ideas and feelings more intimately and to risk being more vulnerable. Men, it seems, are not willing as yet to give as much of this as women would like.

Talking to Each Other About Sex

It is paradoxical that in a time of liberated sexuality for both women and men, many couples still find sexual communication troublesome. They are ashamed or afraid to discuss a partner's sexual behavior or interests, and are equally silent about their own needs or desires. But when sex is common currency in the media; when couples blithely set off together to spend an evening at an R-rated or even X-rated film; when sexual satisfaction is considered to be a personal right rather than a lucky accident—in short, when sex is no longer a man's prerogative or a woman's duty but is accepted as a mutual sharing of joy and caring, why should talking about it be such a problem?

True, most of us grew up before the so-called "sexual revolution," in families where sex talk was, if not forbidden, at least not encouraged. But neither did most of our parents or grandparents talk openly about money or conflicts among family members, or about death. We who grew up in these families find none of these topics—except sex—all that difficult to discuss. Women and men who say they can tell each other "everything" still report great difficulty in talking to each other about their sexual desires and concerns.

For example:

• A twenty-eight-year-old man is distressed because he believes he is not fully satisfying his partner. "I try, but I really don't know what she wants. If only she would tell me . . ." It does not occur to him that he could ask her.

• A woman in her late thirties, married for fourteen years, admits that sex is not nearly as satisfying as it used to be. "I still love my husband and want him physically," she says, "but there are things he does during our lovemaking that annoy and distract me. I haven't mentioned it because I don't want to upset him—and, I suppose, because I'd feel embarrassed to talk about it."

• A middle-aged man writes out his sexual fantasies, and then leaves the slips of paper where he knows his wife will find them. He is too shy to tell her, face to face, about his sexual wishes; and terrified, no doubt to face the fact that the physical side of his marriage is disappointing to him.

There are several major obstacles to constructive sexual communication. One of the most common is a sense of embarrassment. Marital and sex therapists find that both women and men are acutely uncomfortable talking about sex in general, and tongue-tied when it comes to expressing their specific personal preferences and turnoffs. But overcoming this psychological block is the first step toward better sex talk—and to better sex. Women and men who can express their sexual needs unselfconsciously usually find their love life vastly improved.

Another obstacle to good sexual communication is the feeling some people have that talking about sexual preferences and responses destroys the spontaneity of lovemaking. "If I have to tell my partner what makes me feel sexy," one woman said, "it spoils things for me. Anyway, if he really cared about me, he would know. I don't think a good lover needs instructions." Another woman expressed a fear that such frankness could be risky, "Maybe he resents being given orders in bed. Maybe what turns me on turns him off."

Statements that defend sexual silence, though they have a seeming surface logic, are barriers to intimacy. Sexual researcher Robert Bell once told of a woman who for years faked orgasms so her husband would not feel a failure as a lover. "Now I am trapped," she said. "I'd like to be honest with him because that would be a start at solving our problem. But it would also mean admitting that I've been deceiving him all this time." Like all other kinds of intimacy, sexual intimacy rests on a foundation of mutually honest communication. Still another hindrance to frankness is the fear that what one partner considers a constructive comment or suggestion will be taken by the other as personal criticism.

It is true that comments that seem critical of one's sexual competence or skill can be read as an attack on one's masculinity or femininity. "My husband never took time enough before intercourse to arouse me sexually," one woman said. "Many times I planned to talk to him about it, but I hesitated for fear of wounding his ego. Finally, I decided that if he truly loved me he would want to know why sex was not working for me. So one night I said, 'Look, there's something I have to tell you.' When I told him, he was shattered."

Similarly, men report that when they make suggestions that would increase their sexual pleasure or excitement, their partners often react with tears, anger, or anxiety. As a result, many couples simply continue to endure unsatisfying sex, preferring to suffer quietly (or hoping for some magical improvement) rather than have a talk about their sexual incompatibility. Sometimes it is the specter of self-criticism that hampers sexual communication. A woman who described her lover as "tender and patient" nevertheless worried that the man would lose patience because she took so long to become aroused. She could have relieved her mind—and, probably, his—by explaining to her lover that it was her very anxiety about the matter that short-circuited her physical response, and that it wasn't always necessary for her to climax in order to enjoy making love with him. Hesitant to raise the issue at all, she remained silent.

A significant aspect of sexual communication involves the *roles* each partner takes whenever he or she makes a sexual statement or gesture. By assuming a role, one person automatically assigns a reciprocal role to the other person. For example, a woman who assumes men should always initiate sex will project this obligation onto her partner. If he does not do so, she may be disappointed; but having defined her role as the passive one, she will not make the first move. There are many roles one can play in sexual relationships: aggressor, tolerator, teacher, pupil, critic, martyr, and so on. Good sexual communication requires that women and men be aware of which role or roles they are taking, and which they are projecting onto others.

Recent changes in the sex roles that traditionally have been assigned to or claimed by women and men, however, are complicating matters. At the simplest level, some women say they feel that speaking up about their sexual needs may make them seem too sexually aggressive. "I love my husband," a counseling client remarked not long ago, "but he is interested in sex only about once a month. I need it more often than that."

"Have you discussed this with him?" we asked.

The woman looked stricken at the suggestion. "Of course not," she said, "I wouldn't dream of hurting him."

Other women in the same circumstances (especially those who feel the old role constraints no longer apply) would not hesitate to spell out their sexual desires or demands. Therapists nowadays frequently hear male clients complain about being treated as "sex objects":

> I'm under great pressure in my job [a middle-aged man tells a counselor] and I'm concentrating all my energies to deal with it. Frankly, I haven't much energy left to give to sex these days, and my wife is giving me a hard time about it. Instead of sympathizing with my

work problems, she actually nags me about making love. But I can remember all the times *she* begged off from sex, saying she was tired or didn't feel well, and expected me to be understanding!

Here is another instance:

> The woman I live with claims that I have no right to feel rejected when she refuses to make love. She says she is not rebuffing me as a lover, but merely exercising her privilege to decide whether or not she is interested in sex at that particular time. I've told her that if she could change places with me, she might know how it feels to suggest lovemaking and be turned down. But she says I want to control everything without any respect for her feelings. How do other couples work this out?

The answer, as always, is through the kind of sexual communication that makes it possible for women and men to understand each other's viewpoint better. It is not unusual, as we have mentioned, for partners to have different levels of sexual interest and energy, or for individual levels to vary from time to time. The solution lies in finding a compromise that is based on what each person openly states he or she would find sexually satisfactory.

Men do not want to be treated as "sex objects" any more than women do. A man who feels his partner is making too many demands, or is judging him on the basis of his sexual performance, is likely to turn off. That is why a woman needs to be quite clear in her own mind of the distinction between sexual aggressiveness and sexual assertiveness.

Aggressiveness we define as being demanding *without* regard for a partner's self-esteem; it insists on personal satisfaction with little concern for the other person's feelings. Assertiveness, in terms of sexual communication, means raising these delicate issues in such a way that the result is even more enjoyable lovemaking for both partners. They must feel convinced that each is as concerned about the other as about himself or herself. The not-so-secret secret of good sexual communication is that the very act of reacting verbally almost always leads to a mutually reinforcing series of responses that bring a couple closer.

Theory is one thing; practice another. How can a woman and man actually go about initiating or improving their sexual communication? Our suggestions fall into two categories: ways of expressing your own needs and desires, and ways of finding out what pleases the other person.

Asking for What You Want

• Be positive and loving in your comments. Instead of criticizing ("Why don't you ever do what I've told you I like?"), try complimenting ("You know how much I enjoy it when you do that.").

• Make your requests in the form of "I would like" statements. Rather than criticizing a partner by saying, "You never rub my back, and you know I like that," take the responsibility for what you want by saying, "I would love it if you would rub my back." By not shifting the responsibility to your partner, you avoid putting him or her on the defensive.

• Be specific about what you want. Comments such as, "I wish you'd be more romantic," or, "Say something sexy to me," are simply too vague for a partner to interpret accurately. Says one sex therapist, "I coach a client to learn to say exactly what kind of pleasure he or she wants, and when and how. If a person says he or she wants a partner to say sexy things while they are making love, I say that I don't know what 'sexy things' means, and probably the partner doesn't either." Being specific about what one wants may be embarrassing or difficult at first, but it does give the partner the chance to say, "Yes, I will do what you want," or "No, I would rather not."

Finding Out What Your Partner Wants

• Ask questions that leave room for more than a "yes" or "no" response. To say, "Do you like this?" or, "Does that feel good?" may get an affirmative answer or a negative one, but it isn't likely to yield much concrete information. Perhaps something else would be even more enjoyable. Perhaps it felt good but not wonderful. Try to ask open-ended questions that will tell you more about your partner's reactions. For example you might say, "How could that be better for you?" or, "What else would you like me to do?"

• Don't assume that you always know what your partner likes or wants. Of course non-verbal clues—body movements, facial expressions, voice tones—are important "stop" and "go" signals during sex. But it is sometimes easy to misinterpret these reactions, so find out from the other person if his or her reaction is indeed what you think it is.

• Learn to listen carefully when your partner talks to you about lovemaking. To be sure you have understood your partner correctly, rephrase his or her statement or repeat his or her request. Another way to get accurate feedback is to act out what you have been asked to do. If, for instance, one person says, "I wish you would be gentler when you touch me," the other should try what he or she believes to be a gentler touch, and then ask whether it was indeed what the other had in mind.

• Make your partner feel as comfortable as possible about telling you what he or she wants. If you react to lovemaking suggestions by habitually becoming angry, hurt, or defensive, the chances are you will effectively cut off constructive sexual communication.

Saying It with Symbols

"For my birthday last year my wife gave me an expensive suede coat," a man told us recently. "I suppose I should have been pleased, but it was the wrong size, and in a style and color I never wear. Wouldn't you think that after ten years of marriage she'd care enough to pay attention to the kinds of clothes I like and the size I wear?" Another couple spoiled their wedding anniversary when the woman angrily rejected her gift—a week at a fancy reducing spa: "Why don't you just come right out and tell me you think I'm too fat?" she said.

There are many ways to communicate without words. Thanks to the spread of information about personal relationships in recent years, most people know that "non-verbal behavior"—a gentle touch, the smile across the room, cooking someone's favorite dish, an unexpected bouquet—can be a way of saying "I love you." But we resist the knowledge that symbolic messages often convey hostile feelings, too. Taking a particular posture, for example, may signal that one is squaring off for a fight. "Looks that kill," stony silences, slamming doors, all become clues that most partners learn to read with unerring accuracy. Non-verbal communication comes in many forms besides gestures and directly observable actions. Illness, for example, may be used to gain a partner's attention or sympathy; it also can provide a handy excuse for angry or demanding behavior.

Money is another effective tool of symbolic communication. It can be a source of power in a battle for dominance; a reward for good behavior; a device for punishing a partner. One live-together couple quarreled when he accused her of making a pass at another man at a party; the next day he took seven hundred dollars they had set aside for a vacation trip and spent it all on fishing equipment for himself. A working wife may exercise subtle control over her husband by insisting that what she earns is "hers" and what he earns is "ours"—counting on a man's traditional sense of obligation to support the family. Sex is another avenue for indirect communication. There are women and men who deliberately withhold it as a way of showing displeasure, bargaining for power, or punishing a partner. Food—perhaps our basic symbol of love—can also serve to send messages. Consider this man's story:

> I went on a diet because my wife said my weight made me unattractive. At first she was careful to prepare only food that the diet called for. But now that I've lost twelve pounds she serves me large meals of rich foods. And if I don't eat everything on my plate she is hurt.

Why do you think a woman would prepare tempting dishes for a man she has urged to diet? It is very possible that she is using food as a symbolic way of communicating her unconscious, ambivalent feelings about the prospect of having a slender husband. Perhaps she worries that he may become attractive to other women. Perhaps she has used the excuse of the man's obesity to camouflage her own disinterest in sex and is concerned that a slim husband may be more sexually demanding. Certainly the full plate is a symbol of some kind of anxiety or concern that she cannot or does not want to express in words.

Gifts, too, are symbols that can have deep psychological significance. They can delight or disappoint us, make us feel loved and understood or insulted and embarrassed. They may show that much care and thought has gone into their choice; or be so routine or inappropriate that they seem to say, "Here's a present only because I had to give you something." Also, as one sociologist puts it, "Gifts are one way in which we communicate to a person the mental image we have of him or her." A woman concerned that her man works too hard may buy him a jogging outfit or a new tennis racket. A man who thinks of his woman primarily as a homemaker is likely to give her household appliances; if he sees her as a decorative "object" that reflects his success he may give her furs and jewels.

What we say with our gifts indicates the kind of relationship we have, and also can reveal a good deal about the personality of both giver and recipient. The *compulsive* giver overwhelms by the extravagance of his or her gift. It is an extravagance that testifies to the huge emotional stake he or she has in it—unconsciously seeking to buy acceptance, perhaps trying to compensate for feelings of inadequacy. Overgiving can also be a way to establish dominance over the recipient.

Scorekeeping givers seem to balance on some mental scales what they get against what they give. A tit-for-tat exchange may indicate a desire to keep the other person at an emotional arm's length.

The consistently inept giver may also be giving a message. When someone invariably gives you an inappropriate or unbecoming present, you are entitled to wonder if he or she is acting out hostile feelings or sending a message you don't particularly want to hear. One young woman got a black lace "baby doll" nightgown from a man after she dated him once. "It was really upsetting," she said. "Was I supposed to go to bed with him on our next date? Or does he just have a talent for buying the wrong thing?"

But if givers reveal some of their attitudes and feelings by their gifts, recipients often do the same by the way they react to them. Sometimes they deliberately look for hostile messages in presents. A working wife whose husband gave her a microwave oven for her birthday took it as a snide criticism of the fact that she was seldom able to have dinner ready on time. Actually, the man honestly meant the gift to take some of the load off the woman's domestic chores.

When and How to Talk Honestly

Legend has it that a Hindu wise man tested a pupil by ordering him to bring back a "good thing" from the marketplace. When the youth returned with the tongue of an ox, the wise man said, "Now bring me a bad thing." Again the student came back with an ox tongue. The wise man nodded approvingly. "That is good, for truly a tongue may be the source of both good and evil."

The moral of that fable is even more to the point today. Total frankness between women and men has come to be seen as a worthy goal in and of itself. Asking a partner to "tell me exactly what you're thinking," or being brutally honest yourself, assumes that true friendship or real love will be automatically strengthened if it can undergo such a test.

Obviously, the degree of openness that exists between a woman and man is a key element in the quality of their relationship. The amount of genuineness and self-disclosure two people share stands in direct proportion to the amount of satisfaction each derives from being together. Under certain circumstances, frankness between spouses, lovers, or friends can be a force for good. It can help to clarify feelings, avert misunderstandings, and dissipate resentments. Under other circumstances, telling the "whole truth" may not be in the best interests of a relationship. Family therapist Paul Watzlawick puts it well when he says, ". . . a large part of communication consists in knowing what one is *not* supposed to say . . . *not* supposed to hear."

Complete frankness can be an immature and selfish act. What some "honest" folk do, in many instances, is seek reassurance for their own opinions or forgiveness for their actions at the expense of the other person's feelings. We sometimes defend this kind of frankness by saying, "But he (or she) *wanted* to know the truth." Yet not everyone does, at least not in every situation. Total truthtelling may mask a neurotic need to "dump" one's own fears or guilts on another. Or it may be a way of venting masked hostility, or be used unconsciously as a weapon or revenge. For example, a man who described to his second wife intimate details of his sex life with his former wife claimed that he did so to encourage his somewhat inhibited spouse to experiment with different sexual techniques. "After listening to his stories," the wife said, "I felt so awkward and angry I couldn't function at all." Had the husband been sincere about communicating frankly, he would have talked with his wife about their *own* sexual problems in an effort to resolve them.

The problem for each of us is to know—or at least to sense—when frankness may hurt rather than help. Since frankness is a two-way proposition—it can be information that you insist on hearing or feel compelled to reveal—let's look at it from both perspectives.

Asking a partner to "tell all" may indicate a need to control that person by finding out everything about him or her. Sometimes it may signal extreme jealousy. One man kept asking his fiancée to tell him about all the sexual experiences she had before they met. The woman was reluctant; she had had an active sex life and feared the man would be upset at hearing about it. Finally she yielded to his insistence—and the man was furiously jealous. He continued to suspect her every time she had to work late or go out of town on business. Ultimately, his constant suspicion and their arguments about it led to their breakup.

Before demanding total frankness, it is always a good idea to ask yourself, "Do I really want to hear all that? Do I really want to know the answer to my question?" A woman who repeatedly asked her husband if he thought she was overweight learned this lesson the hard way. At first he evaded the truth with remarks like, "There's just more of you to love," or, "You make such great meals I'm gaining a few pounds myself." But she would not be put off, and finally the man gave her the answer she did not want to hear. It hurt badly.

The other side of the coin—being frank yourself—raises different problems, as we have seen. In both cases therefore it is wise, before giving in to the urge to be "completely honest," to examine your motives. Ask yourself, "Why am I going to tell (or ask for) the whole truth? Am I seeking to wound the other person's ego? Am I trying to relieve my own mind of guilts?" Be sure that what you are going to say is important enough to be worth risking the consequences.

Another useful question is, "Will frankness help this situation?" In several surveys by family sociologists, couples said the biggest difference between good and bad communication was whether a partner tended to say things that would be better left unsaid. A good example of something better left unsaid was provided by the case of a young wife whose husband had a fixation on large breasts:

> He buys all the girlie magazines and makes me look at pictures of those well-endowed centerfold women. When we go out he stares at women with large breasts and makes admiring comments about them. Finally I asked him if my breasts were too small to please him. He said, "If you want the truth, I wish they were bigger. But I love you anyway."

Denigrating a partner for something he or she cannot change is unfair and needlessly cruel. Suppose, reversing the situation, this man was short and his wife wished he were taller, and therefore made uncomplimentary remarks about his height. Saying "I love you anyway" would hardly repair the damage done to his self-esteem. And that damage can boomerang—as it did in the case of the small-breasted woman. Self-conscious about her body, she began to think of herself as a poor sexual partner and lost interest in sex.

To restrain an impulse to communicate hurtful truths is not necessarily the same as being *un*truthful. It might be wise to stop making such a virtue of total honesty and replace it with the concept of "appropriate honesty"—sharing whatever information seems likely to reduce tensions and increase satisfactions while keeping mum about whatever seems likely to be needlessly damaging. The following guidelines for "appropriate honesty" are useful:

• Before you volunteer information or respond to a question, ask yourself, "Is what I am about to say really true? Is it necessary that the other person know it? Will there be a more appropriate time and place to make this statement?"

• Be as sure as you can about the other person's emotional capacity to handle a frank answer or comment. In general, someone unwilling to level with you is unlikely to want you to respond frankly to him or her.

• Be sensitive to the other person's values, and talk about matters you know are important to him or her with particular gentleness and tact.

A Few Words About Listening

Most of us think of communication as a one-way street—a street running from our mouth to the other person's ear. But if the other person can't, won't, or doesn't know how to listen, there is *no* communication going on. Dr. Carlfred Broderick, a renowned marital therapist, tells the story of a widow who sought to relieve her loneliness by advertising in a local paper:

WILLING TO LISTEN
*Will not give advice or
interrupt. Call_____.*

Within twenty-four hours the flood of calls was so enormous she had to have her phone disconnected. But not interrupting or not giving advice doesn't mean that listening is a passive process. It is (or should be) an active one, with the listener paying close attention; giving feedback that assures the speaker he or she has been understood; and listening with empathy in order to tune in to the intent and emotion behind the words. There may be no greater kind of support given by one person to another than the reinforcement for a person's feelings and beliefs about himself or herself that comes from truly listening. Social critic William Whyte pointed out many years ago that "the mere act of listening may be far more important than anything we have to say."

4—WORKING WITH EACH OTHER

Maturity can be measured, Freud declared, by a person's ability to work and to love. Achieving satisfaction in both these areas is still the hallmark of a mature individual and the prescription for a mature relationship. But the task is harder now than Freud could have imagined. In turn-of-the-century Vienna, as in most of the western world, work and love were largely separate spheres of activity. Today, with millions of women working alongside men—as subordinates, as superiors, as colleagues, as competitors—work is inextricably intertwined with emotional relationships between the sexes.

Women have always worked alongside their men, at home and on the outside. History books are filled with the very real contributions made by a few women to support themselves and their children. What is different today is the sheer number of women, married and single, who are employed during most of their adult years. Another difference is that most women today take for granted that they will work for most of their adult years as men traditionally have.

More than half of the women in the nation, about 43,000,000 of them, either have a job or are looking for one. Approximately 60 percent of these women are married and more than half have children. Virtually all childless women are employed; over half of all women with children under eighteen hold down jobs; and close to 40 percent of women with children under six years of age also work outside the home. In only one of every three families is the man the sole breadwinner. Only seven of every hundred

American families today fit the traditional picture of the "nuclear" household, where father is the wage earner while mother remains at home caring for house and children. There are today more than three million "dual-career" couples, an increase of 7 percent in the past decade.

But these statistics are merely the bare bones of a revolution that is causing a vast and sudden upheaval in the life-styles of men and women of the eighties. Change can be dealt with if we have some precedents to guide us. But the fact is that woman's new dual status as worker and nurturer, as wage earner and homemaker, has developed so quickly that most women and men are still groping for guidelines to help them cope with the practical and emotional problems that have ensued.

There are few "role models" on which to pattern new ways of relating to each other. Both sexes, for example, are concerned with questions of "fairness." In the workplace itself, is it fair for women doing substantially the same work as men to earn less? Is it fair that the assertiveness required for a woman to advance up a career ladder should be taken, in some quarters, as a denial of her femininity? In the home, partners are also concerned with questions of "fairness": Is each person contributing equally to the joint enterprise? How should jointly earned money be handled, and by whom?

In both areas—workplace and home—women and men are concerned about the effect of their new roles on conventional standards of masculinity and femininity. And the shifting balance of power created by a working woman's new-found independence and self-reliance arouses in some men feelings of jealousy, hostility, even fear.

Yet if the strains seem more numerous than the satisfactions— if the transition from old roles to new ones is as much a source of tension as of renewed self-esteem—most women and men nevertheless are finding that the ultimate rewards can be productive for both partners. In this section we will examine how couples are learning to deal with some of the problems that arise when both persons are employed, and those that occur on the job when women and men are fellow workers. To achieve a mutual accommodation in either area is not an easy assignment. But women and men seem to be finding the results well worth the effort.

When Both Partners Work

A generation of young women and men has grown up in homes where they were materially and emotionally affected by their parents' reactions to the feminist movement, and especially to the burgeoning of the two-paycheck family. This generation is also mindful of the forecast that by the end of the decade almost all single women, almost all married women, and three out of four women with children under eighteen will be employed outside the home. These young people are, therefore, well aware of the challenges they will face in meshing job and home responsibilities, and in making sure that their emotional relationships survive the strains that dual-earner couples encounter.

Women whose mothers were homemakers are for the most part unwilling to follow that example. "My parents were divorced after twenty years, and my mother has no skills to earn a living," a graduate student says. "There is no way I will let myself get in that position." Other women feel anxious about trying to emulate their "supermoms" who wore themselves out by trying to be perfect employees and perfect homemakers at the same time. "Can we really expect to have the best of both worlds?" these young women ask. "Or must we choose between working and having a family?" And, "Will my man resent my accomplishments and my independence, or will he be proud of me?"

Such questions are asked more often by women than by men, but men listen thoughtfully to the discussions that are provoked. Most young men seem pleased that they are no longer expected to shoulder the entire economic burden. They know that all but a tiny percentage of couples will need two incomes to maintain a reasonable living standard, and they do not want to be trapped, as so many of their fathers were, into spending their lives as economic drones. And for both sexes the question of when—or whether—to have children is the most perplexing and controversial issue.

What makes all of these stresses even more potentially damaging to an intimate relationship is that they tend to produce unrecognized—or partially repressed—ambivalences. For instance, an electrician whose wife works as a dental hygienist says, "It's only fair that we should share the household chores." But a while later, seemingly unaware of the contradiction, he talks with some bitterness about having to clean up the kitchen after dinner. "That's not my job," he mutters. A hospital nurse says she gets an enormous amount of emotional satisfaction from her work. "But then I feel so guilty when I have to be on the night shift. My husband doesn't say anything, but I know he hates being left alone in the evening." (This woman eventually quit her job, where she was in line for a promotion, to do private-duty nursing —a dead-end position, but one that allows her to choose her own hours of work.)

Moreover, it's not just the man who needs his wife's financial help or who merely tolerates her desire to work, who has mixed feelings. Even the most liberated husband—one who enthusiastically encourages his wife's career and willingly shares household tasks—is likely to be affected by them. One such man is a twenty-four-year-old social worker whose wife is in a bank's executive-training program. They developed a point system for various chores and drew up a chart to keep track of how many points each accumulated.

"It worked great for a while," the husband said. "Each of us did whatever needed to be done at any given time, and the point score stayed more or less even. But in the past few months I've fallen pretty far behind. To be honest, I find I resent doing housework. That bothers me because I thought I was beyond that kind of hang-up. But I guess the stereotyped ideas about 'man's work' and 'woman's work' are so ingrained that what we think doesn't always jibe with what we feel. So I hear myself saying, 'Damn it, it's my wife's job to get dinner ready!'"

Perhaps the most flagrant example of this "double message" was provided by a man whose wife occasionally travels on business. "When Helen has to go away I just say, 'Have a good time, darling, and don't worry about me.'" But Helen told a different story, "When I'm out of town even for one night, Jerry has a fit. He wants to know where I'm going to be every minute. He calls me several times a day. When I ask if he wants me to quit, he says no. Then the next time I have to travel, he complains that there's no point to being married if I'm 'always' going away."

Both of these men outwardly supported a wife's decision to work. Inwardly each hedged—or actively undermined—that support with a significant *if, and,* or *but.* Yet none seemed truly aware of the implicit contradiction in his feelings—the paradoxical ambivalence of his attitude.

No matter how much a woman earns, or how important her work, she is likely to be the one primarily responsible for keeping the home clean and the children organized. (Fewer than one in ten working wives have paid domestic help.) Studies show that men contribute an average of one and a half hours a day to household chores. Men whose partners are employed put in about thirty minutes more a day than men whose partners do not work. The demands of a man's job do not seem to be a major factor. Men who work less than forty hours a week pitch in at home an extra thirty minutes a day, while those who work fifty to sixty hours a week put in thirty minutes a day less on household tasks.

Moreover, advice from self-styled "experts" as to who should be responsible for "women's work" when the woman is employed outside the home was, at first, almost always directed at the woman herself. It was assumed that she now had two jobs, and that her options were either to try to get her partner and/or her children to "help" her, to hire someone to do the housework, or to lower her standards for how the home would be managed. (One noted female psychoanalyst advised women to obtain full-time care from "trained nurses or governesses and maids" to run their households. For women working to make ends meet, this is reminiscent of Marie Antoinette's "Let them eat cake.") In any event, the message clearly was that if a woman chose to—or had to—work outside the home, the work inside the home would still be primarily her responsibility. Both women and men seemed to buy this assumption, as the following letter and our answer show:

I'm an advertising copywriter and I live with a man who has just opened his own consulting firm. When we moved in together a year ago we agreed to divide domestic chores evenly. But I've been doing almost all of them because most evenings my partner works late at his office or brings paperwork home. He says this is just temporary —that as soon as his business is running smoothly he will have time to do his share of the housework. Friends warn me that if he isn't willing to lend a hand now, he never will be. What do you think?

Your friends may have a point. But that doesn't necessarily mean your partner is deliberately misleading you. He may have made his promise with the best of intentions. But the main factor in how much time a man is willing to give to domestic duties seems to be his psychological attitude toward them. Men who have negative feelings about household work somehow always manage to find outside commitments that make it "impossible" for them to fulfill responsibilities at home. Of course, your partner may be one of those characteristically "busy" persons who will always be overinvolved in work; overextended in commitments.

One way you can tell if this is so is to look back at his earlier work patterns. For instance, in college did he carry extra courses, hold a part-time job, *and* serve as student body president? When he joins a civic or business group, does he inevitably become a hard-working officer? Does he typically take on more work than he can comfortably handle? If such is the case, it would be naïve to assume that your friend will have free time to help you when his firm is "running smoothly." Once that happens he will no doubt find several other pressing activities that require his attention.

It may be that in his desire to please you, your partner was overly optimistic in his promise to share the chores fifty-fifty. A mutual reassessment now seems in order. If he still maintains he wants to be an equal partner in domestic duties when his business load lightens, you are going to have to wait to see if he keeps his word. Ask him to estimate how long it will be before this occurs, and have a tentative time plan of your own as to how long *you* want to wait. If he never gets around to carrying out his promise, you will have to decide whether you are willing to settle for whatever amount of help he does give.

Though most men acknowledge that times have changed and they must change with them—that any reasonable man should share tasks with a partner who also works—converting that intellectual agreement into emotional acceptance is a different and more difficult matter. "Shoulds" often give birth to resentments. And what men dislike most about sharing household chores, it seems, is not so much actually *doing* them as it is the idea that they are *expected* to do them. Men say things like:

> Of course I want to help. But she knows I hate making beds. I'd like to be able to say, "Look, I don't want to do this one particular thing."

> I'm perfectly willing to grocery shop on Saturdays, but I hit the roof when she calls me at the office and asks me to stop at the store on my way home.

> We worked out an equitable division of household jobs. But now I work at home, and my wife feels entitled to ask me to do all sorts of extra things. I didn't leave a list of my errands when she was home.

> I'll do my part of the housework. But I'll do it when I'm ready—not when she thinks it ought to be done.

Some men actually sabotage their arrangement by "accidentally" ruining a meal they are cooking, buying unsatisfactory no-name-brands at the supermarket, or doing a cleaning job they know a woman will find unacceptable.

Rhona and Robert Rapoport, British sociologists who have done intensive research on dual-career families, say that a couple who insist on "equality"—each spouse putting in the same amount of time on housework, for instance, or doing an identical number of onerous chores—may be creating rather than solving problems. For example, one husband told of offering to clean the oven after his wife had fixed a broiled-chicken dinner. "First she thanked me, then she did a double take. 'Why should I thank you?' she said indignantly. 'I cooked. I did the dishes. Now you do one little thing, and I'm suppose to be grateful?' Well," the man continued, "I pointed out that all she had to do was put the chicken in the oven and place two plates, two cups and two saucers in the dishwasher. Cleaning the oven took me thirty minutes of hard scrubbing. What's so equal about that?" According to the Rapoports, it is more important to balance duties and rewards in a way that both persons feel is fair rather than measurably equal.

The other side of that coin is that many women find it hard to give up their sense of control or "authority" over household affairs: "I asked my husband why he always waited for me to request his help," one woman told us. "Couldn't he see what needed to be done? When I was late getting home from work, why didn't he start to fix dinner, or at least set the table?

"His answer took the wind out of my sails. He reminded me of what happened the few times he did take over on his own initiative some of the chores that had always been mine. I found fault with how he did the job. That was the first time I realized that I actually resented what I saw as an encroachment on my 'territory.'"

While most working wives (or unmarried women who share an intimate relationship with a man) feel overburdened, many also feel guilty at not being able to handle the dual load. Guilt has been called the "occupational disease" of the working wife, especially if she has children. "I get silently furious if my husband doesn't help carry some of the load," one woman said. "But when I tell him how I feel he says, 'Don't worry about it. It doesn't matter if the beds aren't made.' The trouble is," the woman continued, "I feel inadequate as much as I feel angry. I think I should be able to do it all myself."

Women who choose to be employed even when it is not an economic necessity are particularly prone to develop "superwomanitis":

A friend of mine confessed recently that she was depressed for days after she had talked to me because, she said she felt so incompetent by comparison. She said, "You do so much, so well, and with such little effort." Suddenly I realized I was being terribly dishonest with my friends and family about the effort and strain my life was exacting. The truth of the matter is that I am afraid to complain, or to ask for help, or not to be superefficient, because I know my husband would say, "If

it's so bad, quit. You don't have to work." But I *wanted*
to work. So I keep playing the game I played as a kid on
my bicycle—"Look, Ma, no hands!"

A few years ago a television commercial for a patent-medicine
tonic attracted attention when it showed a man, married to such
a superwoman, urging her to avoid "tired blood" by taking the
tonic regularly. But lest it appear that men are entirely to blame
for the state of affairs, it should be said that even the most helpful and understanding man usually cannot take much of the burden from a woman because he is already under his own pressure
to be the principal provider for his family. Many men put in long
work weeks—some at more than one job—and already spend as
much time as they can with children or doing household repairs
and yardwork.

Moreover, men are also trapped by ambivalent feelings. A man
may take pride in his partner's accomplishments at work and welcome the fact that she is helping to share the financial burden.
Yet at the same time he is likely to feel that his role in the intimate partnership is somehow being subtly downgraded. "It
bothers me a lot that I can't support the family alone," a man
said. Another commented that he was being "seduced" by his
wife's income into a higher standard of living than the couple
could realistically afford: "She went to work so we could have
money for 'extras,' like a new car or a decent vacation. What
upsets me is that now we think of those 'extras' as necessities."

Old-fashioned? Perhaps. Unliberated? No doubt. Still, it is one
thing for a man to believe intellectually that he should not have
to carry the family financial burden singlehanded (most men *say*
they approve of the idea of being part of a two-paycheck household); it is quite another thing for him to *feel* that when his partner shares that burden he is abandoning his essential function and
the chief measure of his masculinity.

A Matter of Overload

Not all dual-earner couples face exactly the same pressures.
When a woman's income is a necessity, both women and men respond more positively to her employment than if she works for

personal goals. A couple's sense of unity grows from the idea that they are working as a team. Carrying out domestic duties presents a different situation for a childless couple in a small apartment than for a couple with several children who live in a large house.

The social expectations held by a couple, or their family and friends, over how they play their roles are rarely the same for childless couples, or those with grown youngsters, as they are for parents of small children. But one factor that remains true for *all* two-paycheck couples is "overload"—the pressure of having far too much to do in far too little time. Working couples increasingly report being fatigued, irritable, "burned out." When both partners are employed there is virtually no time or energy left for the simple pleasures of being together. "We have twenty minutes at breakfast, when neither of us is coherent," a woman says. "We don't see each other again till six at night. Then it's hurry to make dinner, rush to get laundry done, rush to get to sleep so we won't be exhausted in the morning. If this keeps up we just won't know each other anymore." (And this is a childless couple!)

Many of the strains from overload are due to the fact that only recently have large numbers of couples entered the dual-earner life-style, and they are just beginning to develop the outlook and the techniques they need to restructure four basic areas:

   • *Quality of family life desired:* When couples try to hold on to a standard they maintained before the woman became employed, or attempt to live up to what other couples do who have only one partner working, they frequently push themselves beyond endurance. Entertaining, involvement in children's activities (Little League, Girl Scouts, P.T.A.), and participation in community affairs all will have to be modified.

   • *Quality of domestic living:* Housework does not go away, but standards can be reduced. Some of the additional income can be invested in time-saving devices and hired help. Couples will have to modify their homemaking standards so that even if they never finish the tasks awaiting them, they will feel satisfied with the way the work is done.

   • *Task division:* When both partners are juggling several roles simultaneously, it is important that they put less emphasis on sex-typed "his" or "her" duties. There are two basic tenets for the division of household responsibilities in a dual-worker family: (1) Tasks should not be apportioned according to who earns more or less if each partner's available *time* is equal. (2) No task should be seen as inappropriate for one partner or the other by virtue of sex. Work should be divided on the basis of which partner is most capable of doing it, and which one has the time and energy.

• *Managing stress reduction:* Working couples need to learn, say management consultants Francine and Douglass Hall, that "while people can't manufacture more time, they can make better use of the time they have. Managing time does not mean working harder, it just means working smarter." Recreation and play are important antidotes for stress. They must limit the number of their obligations—realize that if a busy schedule is to accommodate one thing more, something else must be given up. It is important for those couples to acquire the ability to say "no!" As more couples follow the dual-earner life-style there must be less social pressure on them to be "superwomen" and "supermen."

Why Some Working Couples Are Happy and Others Aren't

The level of satisfaction two-paycheck couples get from their personal lives fluctuates with the shifting balance of the stresses and the benefits these couples experience together. From the dozens of studies researchers have conducted in the past few years on the effect of a woman's employment on a couple's "happiness" or "satisfaction" with each other, a few key findings stand out:

• Compared to couples where only the man is employed, couples where both partners work say they are less happy *only* when they have preschool children.

• Once her children are in school, however, the woman who works by choice rather than necessity, and who likes what she does, reports a better relationship with her partner than either the woman who dislikes her work, or the woman who is not employed.

• A major factor in the happiness of a working couple with children is how satisfied both parents are with the quality of care the youngsters get.

• Childless couples tend to blame overload or the stress of a non-traditional life-style for any dissatisfactions resulting from their dual employment.

• Most married men say they experience no more discord or stress if their wives work than if they were full-time homemakers. In fact, many say the second paycheck eases marital tensions.

• A man is likely to feel *more* stressed if his partner has worked less than a year, or if she previously had a job but is not currently employed. It would seem that a woman's transition from one role to the other, and the adjustments this requires the couple to make, are the real stressors.

Does a woman's vocational success affect a couple's happiness? It is often suggested that a man may resent his partner's having a better job or making more money than he does, and that even though at one level he may be proud of her, at another level his self-esteem is affected. Indeed, there is evidence that some women turn down promotions or refuse prestigious jobs precisely because they fear that being more successful than the men in their lives will lead to trouble at home. And for many a man that is true: He feels threatened when his partner's work achievements exceed his own.

Women, too, are troubled by the reversal of traditional roles. They may be emotionally uncomfortable in a relationship if they appear—to themselves or to outsiders—to be the dominant member of a partnership. There is even some evidence that this kind of role reversal is a factor in divorce. One study reported twice as many divorces among couples where the wife's occupation had a higher status than her husband's than among couples where the wife's job ranked lower than her husband's. Moreover, these competitive feelings are intensified when both partners work in the same field.

Fortunately, a growing number of men are *not* threatened by a successful partner. They are secure in their own right. Some of them were raised by mothers who were high achievers. Many of the younger men sat next to bright women in college classrooms and got used to the idea that women would be competing with and outdistancing them. Men who enter an intimate relationship with an already successful woman (or one who aspires to be) typically have a high degree of self-esteem. Not surprisingly, they are also less traditional in their attitude toward sex roles.

When Sandra Day O'Connor was named to the U. S. Supreme Court, her successful attorney husband described his reaction this way: "My life has become vastly broadened as a result of her appointment. I am not only happy for Sandra because she is so competent and so deserving, but I am happy for myself and my family because all our lives have become more interesting. Sandra's accomplishments don't make me a lesser man; they make me a fuller man."

What differentiates those women and men who do not handle status competition well from those who appear unruffled by it, or who seem even to thrive on it? For one thing, both sexes seem to react more positively to a woman's higher job status if she achieves it in a field of work that is primarily identified with women. Consider the example of Donna, a nursing supervisor at a large metropolitan hospital, and Bill, an aviation mechanic with whom she has lived for five years. They show nothing but admiration for each other's work. Bill feels that his job is every bit as important and satisfying as hers: "She works on human bodies, I work on airplane bodies," he says. "She may have a fancy office to herself, but I'd rather have the camaraderie of working with the guys in the hangars."

David and Theresa, both insurance salespersons, provide a striking contrast. "The tension between us has been enormous during the past year," Theresa says, "because my sales figures have zoomed and his have not. I even considered taking it easy for a while to even things up, but that wouldn't be fair, and anyway I don't want to lose my momentum." This kind of backing off, or moving to a lower-level position, is, unfortunately, a common reaction by some women when status competition gets too intense.

Couples for whom traditional concepts of masculinity and femininity are relatively unimportant have far less trouble adjusting to the success of either partner. When both persons hold to conventional ideas of sex roles—man as provider, woman as the supportive partner—the woman's job success will make them both uncomfortable and unhappy. When one partner has the traditional view and the other doesn't, there occurs what sociologists Dana Hiller and William Philliber call "reluctant wife" and "reluctant husband" relationships. The "reluctant wife" resents having to work, and the "reluctant husband" believes a woman's place is in the home. The following two case reports illustrate the patterns:

Mark is a high school teacher whose parents were both highly respected college professors. As Mark grew up he saw his mother and father cook, clean house, and raise their children with no thought for which task was supposed to be the man's job or the woman's. As an adult, therefore, Mark was equally unconcerned about "his" and "her" roles.

When Mark married Julie, she was a novice textile designer. Over the years she became successful in her work beyond either her own or Mark's expectations. At the time the couple came for counseling Julie was earning four times as much as her husband.

But what brought them into therapy was not Mark's jealousy of his wife's professional or financial success. Rather, it was her discomfort at their non-traditional partnership. Julie was a "reluctant wife." She alternated between wanting to quit and have a baby, and berating Mark for not getting into an occupation where he could make more money (so she wouldn't have to). "I've lost respect for Mark because he isn't more ambitious," she says.

The "reluctant husband" was a man whose live-in companion was immediately hired by a prestigious firm the week after she was graduated from law school. "I didn't expect that," he said. "I thought Laura was going to law school just to be doing something stimulating." Though this man was himself a successful business executive, he needed to feel that he was the *sole* provider in the relationship. And he needed to have a woman who would devote her energies to enhancing his career and making his life comfortable. Laura's new job made him feel psychologically impotent—and, ultimately, led to his sexual impotence as well.

Another kind of competition that occurs when both partners

work is the competition for each other's attention and time. One source of dissatisfaction, for example (especially when there are children also contesting for a share of the limelight), is that partners give the best of themselves to their jobs and their colleagues, leaving only bits and pieces of leftover time and energy to give to each other. It is not uncommon to hear a woman complain that when she was a homemaker she listened attentively to her husband's stories of his day at the office, but now that she is employed he doesn't offer the same sympathetic ear:

> I recently got a job as a secretary, and I'd like to have my husband ask how *my* day went. I'd like to share with him what happened to me at work. But he doesn't want to hear about it. I know my job isn't fascinating, but don't you think he ought to be willing to listen to my day just as I listen to his?

A working couple we know call their dinner-table exchange of information "show-and-tell" time. One evening the woman said to her husband, "Do you realize I ask how your day was and you tell me all about it, but you almost never ask about mine." "Do I really?" the man asked, chagrined. "I'm sorry. I'll try to be fairer about that." But the next night, as the woman began to recount an incident in her office, the husband interrupted her, "That reminds me of what *my* boss said today," he remarked, and he was off and running with his own anecdote.

The point is that while each partner *should* be interested in the other's news, old habits are hard to break. The husband of the newly employed secretary may simply be used to being the main "show-and-tell" speaker in the family. Perhaps he thinks that what she has to say about her job isn't as interesting or significant as what he has to say. Or maybe he is so accustomed to hearing the routine details of her previous days as a homebody that he simply tunes out her words. She is going to have to encourage—perhaps even *train*—her husband to be a more empathic and responsive listener.

Some of this poor listening can be a reaction to the *way* in which one person tells another about his or her experiences. One may need to examine whether, for instance, she recounts every single detail regardless of its interest or importance instead of concentrating on the heart of the matter? Or does she, without meaning to, turn the day's events into a litany of complaints and problems? If so, then perhaps one way to get her husband to pay more attention is to tell him her news in a more entertaining and imaginative way.

Danger: Conflicts of Interest Ahead

Freud probably never imagined that it would be harder for partners to mesh work and love if they pursued their goals with similar, rather than clashing, interests. But if each person is equally eager for career success, work can easily come to dominate their relationship at the expense of love—and at the expense of sex, too. Career-oriented couples are especially vulnerable to this syndrome; they can become so immersed in work, so satisfied by its rewards, that they seem totally self-centered rather than other-centered. Yet this attitude may not be as selfish or narcissistic as it appears. Dedicated workers, almost like workaholics, have a great deal of difficulty putting their work lives and their private or intimate lives into separate compartments. They focus on each segment in its own time and space. However, this usually turns into a one-way proposition: personal life is subsumed by work life. The result for many dual-career partners is that romance virtually vanishes from their relationship.

This development is not unique to two-paycheck couples. But it is a particular hazard when both the woman and man are wed to their jobs. "Life gets so serious," one such woman observed. "We saw a marriage counselor once who told us to put a little romance back into our lives. But who has time for that?" The marriage counselor was right, of course, since working couples who are satisfied with their relationship report that they consciously inject romance into their lives. They learn that romance and passion, while difficult to manufacture on demand, need not wait for total spontaneity. As busy as both partners are, if they wait until they are each free, rested, and not preoccupied, they may wait a long time. Yet being alone as a couple—having fun together, taking time to make each other feel special and loved—is (or should be) a high priority when both persons are work-involved.

Another problem endemic to dual-earner couples is the lack of energy for sex. "It's almost as much of a hassle as housework," one young woman declared. Said a man sarcastically, "If my wife were having an affair, she'd probably make love to me more often just to keep me from suspecting she was making it with someone else." If the bonds of romance and sex are not carefully nourished, it is all too easy for the working couple to suspect each other of having outside intimacies, and to become jealous. For men, jealousy can extend to the new frontiers of freedom that work outside the home has opened to women. A man may be pleased that his partner's job is helping to make her a more interesting and informed person. Yet at the same time he may fear that she is becoming *too* independent and interesting. "I know it's foolish, but I can't help feeling a little threatened," one man admitted. And in some instances those fears may be justified.

A woman's employment holds the potential for a worry that usually only women used to have to cope with—the possibility that one's partner will be sexually attracted to someone he or she meets in the course of work. This is no fancied danger. Surveys indicate that while the percentage of all wives who have had an extramarital affair is rising, almost twice as many working wives have such liaisons as non-working wives. Many employed women report a heightened awareness of their sexuality when they are around men who remind them that they are attractive and desirable.

"I had an affair," one woman told us, "partly because my husband was so busy he seemed uninterested in sex, and partly because we both had such irregular working hours it made it easy to make up cover stories. Besides it was romantic!" And no wonder. Coworkers see each other at their best: full of energy, sharing common interests, eager to make a good impression, highly visible to each other. It isn't hard to understand the ease with which an on-the-job relationship can ripen into something more. Women and men who work together often grow closer emotionally than women and men who are nominally intimate partners but actually merely coexist in a harried, cut-and-dried relationship.

"The mystery to me," one dual-career father remarked, "is how people in our circumstances find *time* to have an affair. I am so busy just keeping my head above water that there is no room to fit another woman into my life." But the riddle has an answer— where there is a will, there is a way. Some of the busiest executives, some of the most overworked of today's women and men, want and need ego-stroking romance and affection. These are powerful magnets. Such people *find* the time to get those rewards.

Consider the example of a couple we'll call Todd and Maureen. They had taken their love life for granted while they concentrated on building their careers. Rather than look to each other for the intimacy they missed, each of them sought to find it outside their marriage. Now they sat in the counselor's office hoping to put the pieces of their nine-year partnership back together. During the preceding year each had had affairs. Each wondered why. With the therapist, they explored what had been so special about their time with other partners. The answer seemed to be that it was "exciting," while their own sex life had become a perfunctory and passionless ritual:

> *ML:* I have a question for you both. When do you believe that sexual foreplay begins?

> *Todd:* Well, I know that it takes a while, if that's what you're getting at. Although, to be frank, it takes Maureen longer and longer to get turned on.

> *Maureen:* I think I know what your point is. During my affair I was thinking about our being together for hours ahead of time. I thought about wearing something special, a nice perfume. I even went to bed early the night before so I'd be rested.

> *ML:* Foreplay lasted for hours, didn't it? You know, it *is* true that our most important sex organ is the brain. I wonder what would happen if you both thought about and planned for sex with each other as carefully as you did for your affairs?

How do dual-worker couples survive the conflict between work and love? For one thing, they keep in view what Todd and Maureen forgot: The very things that make an affair so exciting are the ones that have a way of being neglected in a busy, long-term relationship. A man was recently separated from and then reconciled with his wife. As he put it, "The zing was gone from our relationship. I saw my friends with young, attractive women, so I thought, 'Why not me, too?' The funny thing is that after I prowled the bars for a while it struck me that what all those men, including myself, were looking for was what I already had in my wife. I decided to go home and spend the same time and energy on someone who already loves me."

Couples who successfully mesh work and love set aside time for each other; they take frequent breaks away from work and family pressures to be a couple; they remember to make each other feel special with both words and actions. It is not so much what they do as the attitude with which they do it. Psychiatrist Roger Gould sums it up this way: "In this heyday of life-style variations and experimentation, a successful couple knows that when love is good, it is addictive. . . . Our shared secrets become love-bonds, and we feel confirmed as loving, lovable, worthwhile, and wanted."

"More money" is cited as the most important reason for being a dual-worker couple. For some, two incomes are a necessity to keep pace with rising expenses; for others, the second paycheck means a chance to save for the future or to indulge in present luxuries. But no matter how welcome the extra income is, it does give rise to emotional conflicts.

A working woman, for instance, typically has more influence over family decisions than a non-working woman. Bolstered by the increased sense of competence and self-worth, she gains from her ability to contribute to the couple's finances, she is able to assert herself more strongly. And her "bargaining power" increases. When a woman earns enough to support herself (even if it is not enough to match the two-income living standard she is used to), she no longer feels she must give way to a man's views simply because he provides the bulk of the family resources. This power shift upsets some men.

"It really bugs me that Lori earns as much as I do," one man admitted. "I used to feel very protective of her. I can't feel that way anymore. She doesn't need me." Moreover, a working woman has the opportunity to compare her input into money matters with that of other employed women. "For a long time after I started to work," a woman recalls, "I dutifully deposited my paycheck in our joint account and asked my husband's permission if I wanted to buy something for myself. When I said I needed new shoes, he said we couldn't afford it. But I knew he had just bought a new fishing rod he certainly didn't *need*. I mentioned this to a friend at my office, and she was furious—at me! 'How can you be so uninvolved in budgeting the money you work so hard to earn?' she asked. I realized how right she was, and from then on I insisted on sharing the spending decisions."

This question of financial "control" is probably the single biggest point of conflict between a dual-earner couple. Each partner should have the right to keep some money he or she can call "mine," to spend or save as he or she chooses. It is wise for a two-income family to work out a system for money management before the issue comes to a head. It is not easy to shift financial gears *after* a woman goes to work, as this case shows:

> After twelve years as a full-time homemaker my wife has taken a job [a thirty-six-year-old telephone repairman says]. To my surprise, she is putting her entire salary in a separate bank account in her own name. She says it is my duty to support our family, but that since she still carries out her household responsibilities, whatever she earns on her job should be hers. It's not what my wife does with the money that bothers me. Actually, she spends most of it on things for the house and the children, and some on clothes for herself. What I resent is her attitude that what I earn is "ours" and what she earns is "hers."

> For a woman who has been totally financially dependent on a man for many years [the therapist explained], earning money of her own is a heady experience. For one thing, it is obviously important to your wife not to have to deposit the evidence of her new independence—her paycheck—into your joint account. For another, since she *is* holding two jobs—one at work and one at home—it is reasonable for her to enjoy some of the financial rewards as she sees fit.

> Basically, you are raising an artificial issue when you claim your wife is setting up "her money" and "our money" categories. In actuality, your wife is making her salary part of the family income since you say she spends it on items that would, normally come out of your earnings. The real issue between you, it would seem, is not

whose money is whose, or what it goes for, but which of
you is in control of it.

Perhaps this couple—and others like them—would feel more
comfortable and secure if each contributed to a joint account in
proportion to their earnings, and put the rest in separate personal
accounts. The joint account could pay household bills and other
family expenses, and the individual accounts could be used for
personal items. (This arrangement also has some practical advantages: It helps the woman acquire a credit rating of her own, and
possibly yields some tax savings by giving her a separate record of
work-related expenses.)

A third major focal point of conflict when both partners work is
the question of relocating geographically when one person or the
other is offered a better job in a different city. According to Census Bureau statistics, 22 million women and men make job-related
moves every year. In most instances the working woman takes it
for granted that she will give up her job and move with her man.
Conversely, men have usually taken for granted that a woman
should refuse a promotion, a transfer, or a better job offer that involves relocation if it means he will have to give up *his* job.

But as more and more women carry a significant part of the responsibility for earning a family's living, moving to accommodate
a man's career has become less automatic. This is particularly true
for women in professional careers as opposed to women in routine
employment. Ideally, experts suggest, a couple should make this
decision on the basis of which partner has more to gain or lose
from moving or staying. But that is a value judgment that is usually hard to make. Even though three out of four dual-career couples say they consider their jobs equally important, in reality in
most cases it is still the woman who moves—despite the fact that
even for a person with highly marketable skills, a move holds the
risk of loss of seniority, fringe benefits, and the invaluable net-
work of contacts she has built. Here is a typical example of the
conflict that faces the growing number of women who feel their
work is as important as their partners' work:

My husband is slated for an important promotion in
his company, but it means transferring from Boston to

Kansas City. I don't want to move. I would lose all the
seniority I have built up as a high-school teacher here, as
well as *my* chance to be promoted to an administrative
post in the school system. Yet if he refuses the transfer,
it could harm his future with his firm. How can we decide whether his career or mine is more important?

This woman could perhaps get another teaching position in
Kansas City, but she would not be likely to find one at her present level of income and prestige. Her attitude and involvement
in teaching have made it a career for her. How do working partners handle such a dilemma? Some agree that neither one will accept a work-related move that can harm the other's career. That
decision may well rule out advancement for one or the other.

Personnel executives (and couples who have chosen this path)
say that many companies look unfavorably on employees—men
particularly—who let family considerations affect their career decisions. Some employees are even passed over later for promotions
in the *same* location as "punishment" for refusing the earlier opportunity. Nevertheless, couples who decide to stay put at whatever career cost believe they will be happier in the long run than
if one partner rises on the career seesaw at the expense of forcing
the other to move down.

A few couples agree to take turns at career opportunities, alter-
nating whatever sacrifices have to be made. Others agree that the
person who would have the hardest time relocating successfully
has the right to make the "move or no move" decision. And still
other couples opt for "long-distance marriages," commuting to be
together on weekends if the distance is not too great or the travel
costs not prohibitive. (Some commuting couples spend $10,000 a
year on travel, to say nothing of their telephone bills.)

There are signs, however, that large companies are becoming
more responsive to the problems of dual-earner couples. In a recent survey nearly 30 percent of the firms questioned said they
would try to find a job for a transferred employee's partner. (But,
in fact, only 5 percent actually have such a policy and are actively
implementing it.) "No wonder a woman earns only fifty-nine
cents for every dollar a man earns," a business analyst observes,
"when she is the one who must almost always pull up stakes."

Our advice to dual-earner couples is to plan ahead for relocation decisions. Having a "policy" will leave you better prepared to make mutually agreeable choices.

The Difference that Children Make

Whether or not a working couple have children may make the most significant difference in their adjustment to the dual-earner pattern. We've already talked about the "overload" of stress that working partners must carry; when there are children to consider that stress is multiplied. The sources of stress are both external (such as making suitable child-care arrangements and dealing with emergencies that require sudden changes in work schedules) and internal (parental concern or guilt over a child's well-being and dealing with social pressures).

Increasing numbers of working couples have "dealt" with these pressures by the simple strategy of making sure they never have a chance to occur: They decide not to have children or to postpone having children until they can afford to hire competent child-care help. Women are more likely to make that decision than men, obviously because they are the ones most affected by the strains of having to balance the demands of jobs and children. Many voluntarily childless couples, now in their mid-thirties, are beginning to change their minds. Faced with the knowledge that the biological time clock means that births get riskier for both mother and child as a woman gets older, some couples are grappling with *when*, rather than *whether*, to become pregnant. (They are also faced with another kind of "time clock": add another eighteen or twenty-two years to their age, and a working couple could easily be nearing retirement before their child is ready to strike out on his or her own.)

Working women who decide to have children follow three main patterns. In the *delayed* pattern, a woman does not begin to work outside the home until her children are old enough to be in school, or perhaps even old enough to be trusted to be alone after school. But since more and more women are postponing their first pregnancy in any event, nearly all of them work for several years before becoming mothers.

Most common of the three patterns is the *interrupted* pattern, in which a working woman takes a leave of absence (or quits her job if she must) to have her child and to stay home with it for a certain length of time. How long the "interruption" lasts depends on several factors: the number and spacing of the children, the family's financial needs, and whether a woman can safely be away from her field of work for long without losing her skills. (An engineer told us that after staying home for five years to raise her two children, she had to be retrained before she could be rehired: "The new developments in my field were totally foreign to me.")

Nowadays the *continuous work* pattern is becoming increasingly popular. A woman does not stop working except for a brief maternity-leave period. This option is ever more commonly chosen by single mothers, and by career women who are highly committed to their work. The pattern is also adapted nicely to the needs of the woman who wants to work only part time.

No matter which pattern working partners choose, making sure a child has adequate care is the biggest problem they face. The alternatives are familiar: hired sitters, relatives who help out, working a different shift than one's partner so that one parent or the other is always at home, finding a neighborhood child-care cooperative, using a commercial day-care center, or allowing the older child to be a "latchkey kid." None of these options are entirely satisfactory, and all of them have one or more drawbacks. Most working couples with children simply grit their teeth and try to get through the most difficult child-raising years without letting the stress destroy their own intimate relationships.

One positive aspect of the situation is that men are more willing to share child-care responsibilities than household tasks. Most men enjoy the chance to be closer to their children—to know them better and to be a more intimate part of their lives. "My wife had to go to a teachers' convention in Florida for a week," said a New England husband. "This meant I had to do everything for the kids—get them dressed for school, make breakfast and lunches, help with homework, get them to bed on time. I even had to braid my daughter's hair—something I had never done before! I got a tremendous kick out of it, and so did she."

A father of three, married to a nurse, said, "I encourage my wife to work because it is good for both of us if she can get away from the kids for a while. Besides, the children realize they have two parents, not just one. Our three-year-old used to call for Mommy whenever he needed something—even when he knew she wasn't home. But after a while he started calling for Daddy. That's a nice feeling."

Some men dislike taking care of children. They are stunned by the amount of time and energy it requires. They are bored. They can't stand the messiness of changing diapers or cleaning up food spills. And even husbands who willingly share parenting have some reservations about the long-term effects on the children. "Since my wife went to work, our twelve-year-old daughter is much more independent," a man said. "But I wonder if she isn't too independent . . . if she has too much freedom and not enough supervision." And a New Yorker married to a school guidance counselor claimed that he has to give special attention to his nine-year-old to make up for his wife's apparent lack of concern. "She spends most of her time solving other children's problems," he observed sarcastically.

On the Job: When Women Work with Men

As women and men take their places together in the world of work, there have been several key shifts in the way they think about and behave toward each other. At first it seemed that women, more than men, were concerned about how they would "fit in" to what was traditionally a male arena. Seminars were organized to teach women how to deal impersonally with their male colleagues. There were courses on how to "dress for success." Women were urged to overcome the so-called "fear of failure," ascribed by some psychologists to real or imagined handicaps stemming from the idea that being efficient or competitive is not a feminine trait. At the same time they were urged to avoid the "fear of success"—a syndrome allegedly afflicting women who feel that accomplishment in a male-dominated work world marks them as something less than womanly, and will adversely affect their emotional relationships with men.

For most women—especially those working for or with men for the first time—"fitting in" becomes to some extent knowing where to draw the line between standing up for one's rights and yet not alienating fellow workers (meaning, of course, male colleagues or bosses). The following excerpt from a counseling session illustrates a typical dilemma:

> *Marilyn:* I find it harder and harder to go to work these days. I get headaches, I feel tense. My doctor says it's stress from my job, and I'm pretty sure he's right.
>
> *ML:* What's the worst part of your job?
>
> *Marilyn:* Being taken advantage of. It happens all the time. There are several men in my department, men on the same level as I am, who think nothing of asking me to help them out when they get behind on their work even though I have plenty of my own to do. They don't ask the other men—just me.
>
> *ML:* Can't you say "No"? Or is it that the men don't hear you say "No"?
>
> *Marilyn:* Some of both, I guess. I try to be considerate and help out when I can. So quite often when I want to say "No," I don't. Then when I do refuse, they more or less insist.
>
> *ML:* It's all well and good to be helpful and considerate, of course, but it seems to me you are paying a high price, mentally and physically, for doing so. Perhaps we should examine why you don't feel you can take care of your own needs.

Marilyn had been taught, all her life, that it is good to help others. But she had never learned to differentiate genuine consideration for another person's real needs from "politeness"—which in her case was a convenient disguise for a lack of assertiveness:

> *ML:* Giving help to others doesn't mean you must sacrifice yourself. In effect, you have made yourself a "victim" by being so readily available as a "rescuer." It is your behavior rather than the inconsiderateness of your coworkers that is putting you in this position. You know this in your body, because it flashes all those tension signals when you want to say "No" but do not say it.

When you don't have time to help the men out, simply refuse. Say, "Sorry, I can't today," or "I'm pressed myself right now." Repeat that as often as you have to in order to get your message across. Smile, if you must. But don't cave in.

The concept of "team play" is still another facet of work politics. Men, the theory runs, learn how to be team players from their youthful involvement with sports. Most of today's women did not have the same opportunity to learn about teamwork on the playing fields and in the gyms at high school and college. As a result, women whose jobs require cooperative endeavors often need to teach themselves (or learn from others) how to take the initiative and join "the team."

I work in an all-male office [a magazine editor says]. Never once did my colleagues invite me to join them for lunch, coffee, a drink after work. I was complaining about this to a woman friend who works in a male-dominated law firm. "Why do you have to be asked?" she said. "You could invite *them,* you know, or just ask if you can join them." I hadn't realized that I was really part of the team, and that if I wanted to join in its activities I needed to take the initiative.

Is a woman less able than a man to separate her personal self from her working self? According to the cultural stereotype, she is more likely to "personalize"—to feel more responsible for whatever happens, to take criticism more emotionally, to be more subjective than objective. Career consultant Marilyn Kennedy believes that anyone can succeed at workplace politics if he or she learns the secret of "personal distancing—saying to yourself that there are actually two of you: a professional working self and a personal self." Distancing makes it possible to put a buffer between the slings and arrows of the workplace and your personal feelings.

Personal distancing is especially important as a way of making sure that one does not mix sex and work. Of course it happens, but it almost always leads to problems. In the past, troublesome sexual relationships usually involved a subordinate woman and one of her male superiors. It was rarely the person with the higher position whose job security was jeopardized. And even today, if the woman is her partner's superior, she still will usually bear the brunt of the eventual gossip and negative reaction. Although court cases for sexual harassment are by far most often brought against men, it is not unknown for a woman to be the defendant.

When a Woman Is the Boss

A college teacher told us, not long ago, of a conversation she had with a male colleague: "He said he disliked the idea of having a woman as a department chairman or a dean. I was somewhat taken aback by this, because at the time I *was* the chairperson of his department. 'Well then, what about me? I asked. 'I always assumed that you and I got along fine.' 'Oh,' the man replied, 'I never think of you as a woman.'"

Psychologists explain the difficulty that men (and, as we shall see, women too) have in accepting a woman as a boss by pointing out that a woman often reminds us of mother and triggers off repressed feelings of adolescent resentment of female authority. Neither women nor men feel so hostile toward father-figure bosses, the theory goes, because since there are so many men in positions of authority at work, we get used to seeing them as bosses and learn to separate their power from that of a father's power.

Be that as it may, both women and men consistently place a higher value on men as bosses than on women as bosses. For one thing, characteristics associated with maleness—aggressiveness, forcefulness, persuasiveness—are the same traits we value in leaders of any kind. And while there is little to indicate that women and men who hold comparable jobs vary to any significant degree in the personality traits that are needed in managerial positions, the *belief* that men are more capable is sufficient to distort the factual picture. Our beliefs, or perceptions, can twist reality enough so that we see what we expect or want to see. A career woman is certainly told often enough that if she wants to be a successful supervisor she must be "more like a man."

Fortunately for the women and the men who work for female superiors, both sexes are slowly adjusting these views. Both find it easier to accept a woman boss if they are working in a field that is considered primarily a "female" area. The adjustment is harder if the woman is in charge of a traditionally male-oriented field. For example, a woman tells of her struggle to be accepted as supervisor of a mostly male crew clearing land for a housing development: "I was hassled every day by the teasing of men who were made uneasy by my position. I told the few other women in our group that we had to do our jobs so well that we could not be criticized, not make a single mistake. Gradually we gained the men's respect. I knew I had it made when I heard one man tell the others to 'knock it off' when they started their daily ritual of put-downs."

A woman boss is likely to win acceptance more easily if she achieves her position by rising through the ranks. That gives her the same opportunity as a man to win credibility and to gain respect for her accomplishments, and this eases the transition to a leadership role. (Of course, she has the same opportunity to collect resentments, too.) A woman brought in from the outside and given authority over other employees has a more difficult time winning acceptance than her male counterpart would. Moreover, because most women are new at management, says vocational counselor Auren Uris, "every action they take is observed and analyzed. . . . Under pressure to achieve and exert authority, they feel more stress than men in equivalent management jobs."

But the fact remains that it is still so rare to see a woman in a position of workplace authority that for many people, a woman boss may be the first female since their mother from whom they have had to take orders. "The first 'boss' of every man *and* woman was a woman," says Thomas Dolgoff of the Menninger Foundation. "That relationship may well set the tone for our future authority relationships with all women."

"Ultimately," says Auren Uris, "a manager who is a woman must succeed professionally just like her male counterpart, but she may have to cope with some special obstacles and be a bit better to get equal recognition. That's not complete equality, but it is progress toward that goal." If what it takes, then, to reduce the novelty of the idea of a woman boss is to have more women in charge in the workplace, and to increase our exposure to their capacity for leadership, then the next few years should see this goal accomplished.

5—THE "OUTSIDERS" IN YOUR LIFE

Some couples picture their relationship, in or out of marriage, as a kind of self-contained emotional universe; a snug cocoon in which they are so wrapped up with each other that they are almost impervious to outside influences. At the other extreme are couples whose personal "boundaries" are so elastic and diffuse that their intimate friendships or love relationships or marriages suffer from constant external interference. As we have mentioned, many such women and men protect themselves against feelings of emotional vulnerability by avoiding exclusive intimacy with one partner; they must have buffers—separate involvement with friends, work, or hobbies—against closeness. Studies of "open marriage" or similar sexually free liaisons, for instance, suggest that such arrangements are aimed at reducing the anxiety that often comes when one person feels uncomfortable pressure to be committed to the other.

But these two models are extremes. Most of us would agree that a "total" relationship is stifling and much too fragile for the life-style of the eighties. On the other hand, "loose" boundaries that allow outside influences to intrude too freely and too often can undermine the essential character of an intimate partnership. The ground in between—allowing the outside world to penetrate when we wish or permit it, and sealing ourselves off from it when we want or need to be alone together—is obviously the ideal compromise.

But the ground is difficult to stake out. We can become involved with outsiders, for good or ill, almost unknowingly; or we can purposefully cultivate such involvement. Some outside influences force themselves upon us; some we solicit. Even when we establish our private ground it is difficult to defend. Moreover, how we include and exclude others from our one-to-one relationships becomes more complex as changing sex roles involve women more in the "outside" world and involve men more in the "inside" world of feelings.

Who are these "outsiders" who impinge on the quality of our intimate lives? At one end of the spectrum, outsiders can be the uncontrollable impersonal social and economic forces that affect our daily lives. It is not unreasonable to say, for instance, that inflation or action taken by the chairman of the Federal Reserve Board, which results in higher or lower interest rates, has a real effect on a couple's personal life. Financial problems are well-known for putting an emotional "squeeze" on an otherwise happy partnership.

Women and men who live together are frequently hassled by those who hold a more conventional morality, not to mention the social systems—insurance companies, landlords, banks, the Internal Revenue Service, for example—that refuse to deal with them as a "couple unit." Even so-called "acts of God"—fires, floods, earthquakes—impinge on intimate relationships.

When Mount St. Helens erupted, mental-health centers in the state of Washington reported an upsurge in stress, anxiety, and depression that led to increases in physical abuse and other forms of marital conflict. Our interactions with the community at large —at school, with neighbors, at church—have a great deal to do with how we react to our partner in our personal life. (We have already seen how, in this era of dual careers, the workplace affects couples.)

But the "outsiders" who affect our intimate relationships most sharply are people whom we do not ordinarily think of as outsiders at all: our parents, our siblings, our in-laws, our children, our friends. It may seem strange or harsh to label these people as "outsiders," but in terms of partners who have primary commitments to each other, that is what they are. For the most part we do not give sufficient attention to their impact.

We like to think that we can control these "outside" influences; that we can choose to be receptive, indifferent, or even hostile to them. But the truth is that our choices are constrained by other factors that limit such control. To reject or to remove ourselves from these influences often means paying too high a price. So, willy-nilly, we put up with them. Sociologists speak of the "cost-reward ratio" in personal relationships: So long as the rewards outweigh the costs, we will usually continue to pay the price. Here is a basic illustration:

> Every Christmas my wife and I have the same problem. Her brother, his wife, and their two children descend on us for the whole day. My wife spends hours shopping, cleaning, cooking, and doing dishes, and they never lift a hand to help. By the time my in-laws leave, she's exhausted and I'm seething. When I try to get her to see how much nicer the day would be if it was just the two of us and our children, she says families belong together at Christmas. Am I wrong for wanting to make the holiday easier for my wife?

Clearly, it is hard for this woman to ignore family ties even when they are more of a duty than a pleasure. Presumably the good feeling it gives her to be with her family at Christmas is "reward" enough for the work she has to do. Significantly, the husband's reaction may indicate his irritation at having to share *his* family Christmas with "outsiders." (Need there be an either/or choice between his view and his wife's view? Not at all. Perhaps the families could celebrate by dining out and splitting the cost; perhaps the husband and wife could spend one Christmas with the in-laws and one by themselves.)

In California's courts, divorcing couples who have children are given a pamphlet titled *Parents Are Forever*. Its message is that even though a marriage may be sundered, each spouse's emotional responsibility to the children is never ended. But just as parents cannot "divorce" a child, so a child cannot "divorce"—end the psychological connection with—his or her parents.

Each generation is everlastingly linked to the other by powerful, often unconscious, bonds. As a result, when women and men form new love relationships each partner carries along a whole set of attitudes, conscious and unconscious, that reflects their earlier experiences with parents (what sociologists call our "family of origin"). In addition, each of us is affected by the acknowledged or repressed feelings our partner has about his or her parents. That takes us beyond the cliché of mother-in-law jokes. As psychiatrist Dr. Norman Paul puts it, "It isn't just the two of you against the world. Any intimate relationship involves *six* people—a man, a woman, and two sets of parents."

Friends constitute another category of outsiders who influence partners for good or ill. The value of friends' emotional support cannot be overemphasized. But if a friend dislikes our partner, we often feel that the friend's criticism is aimed at us as well (since the person with whom we forge an intimate bond becomes a kind of extension of ourself). Friends, as we shall see, can also create other problems. For example, cross-sex friendships hold a potential for trouble. What effect does it have on lovers or spouses if a man has close women friends or a woman has close men friends? When a couple make new friends together, the complexity of such relationships can lead to stress. Not only must the men like each other and the women like each other, but each person must also like the other's partner (but not too much). And if the couple become intensely involved with another couple, that very closeness can stunt the growth of intimacy between the woman and man in each partnership.

Much has been written about the impact that parents have on children. But the impact that children have on their parents' relationship has gone relatively unnoticed. While countless marriages have been held together by (or for) children, probably as many have been hurt by them. Children can contribute to disharmony for a variety of reasons: the pressure of their need for care and attention, the high cost of raising them, arguments over discipline. Youngsters sometimes unwittingly serve as triggers for latent tension between husbands and wives. Parents are reluctant to admit all this. They try to deny, or fail to realize, the extent to which children can provoke stresses between them; or, if stress already exists, to make it worse. And as social change fragments the nuclear family, we find children creating even more difficult problems for single parents and stepparents.

Outsiders' influence can, of course, be positive and supportive as well as meddlesome and disruptive. While the bulk of research shows that children tend to lower their parents' marital (and overall) happiness, clearly most parents derive great emotional rewards from parenthood. Support from grandparents, brothers, sisters, and friends is also a positive force in our lives when we find ourselves in temporary need; studies indicate that in time of stress it is family members to whom we most often turn. Close friends run a near second. Obviously we need friends, we love our children, we respect our parents. But we need to be aware, too, of the negative impacts they can have. In the following pages we will explore these impacts in more detail.

Parents and In-laws

There is plenty of evidence that the residual influence of kith and kin is a contributing, if not a primary, cause of conflict in one of every five troubled man-woman relationships. We usually think this is due to direct criticism or interference: "My father-in-law says the house we want to buy is a poor investment." . . . "We have two daughters, and my husband and I had agreed that he should have a vasectomy until his parents convinced him to try for a son." True, the generation gap does create differences of opinion. But when they can be frankly discussed, compromised, rejected, or even quietly ignored they need pose no real threat to a couple's intimate relationship.

Other more subtle forms of interference in the form of "helping" behavior are harder to combat: the father who gives his daughter money because he feels her husband doesn't earn enough; the mother (or mother-in-law) who, unasked, cooks or cleans for her employed daughter (or daughter-in-law) to imply that the younger woman is neglecting her home. And sometimes the struggle is between parent and partner for the loyalty of the third person in the triangle. The following statements highlight the problem from the two opposing perspectives:

> Sometimes I think my mother-in-law feels she is my husband's wife. If she had her way, she would go with us on every trip, join us at every gathering, and generally run our lives. Why do mothers hang on to their sons so tightly?

> My son and his family could be such good company for me if his wife would cooperate. My son says he'd like

to see me more often, but his wife is always making other engagements for them. I know she is jealous of the time he spends with me. Why do daughters-in-law behave this way?

Wives and mothers-in-law (and husbands and fathers-in-law) traditionally have faced this conflict of "territoriality"; of settling who, partners or parents, have the final responsibility for decisions affecting the welfare and happiness of the persons they both love. (Fortunately, this conflict occurs less frequently as the older generation remains active longer in careers and personal interests. As one older woman put it, "I'm delighted to turn over responsibility to my daughter-in-law. I was a mother for nearly thirty years. Now I have other things to do with my life.")

More often, however, discord arises out of a deeper and much less obvious problem. That involves the *indirect* ways in which that psychological outsider—"our family of origin"—continues to affect us even when we are grown. Its influence—in effect, an inner "rule book" that tends to govern the way we act and think, and the way we judge a partner's actions and ideas—is harder to cope with. The two areas most likely to be affected by this carryover from the environment in which we grew up are money and sex. Take money: As children, we learn how our mothers and fathers think and feel about spending and saving; as adults those attitudes remain within us; the parental voices still echo in our minds. Consider the predicament of an engaged couple (we'll call them Bob and Lisa). Since they live near a Southern California marina, Bob wants to buy a small sailboat. Lisa feels they should build up their savings account first.

> *Bob:* I can't see this stuff about having six months' income in the bank. Why save for a boat when I can get it now, and pay it off while I'm enjoying it? Lisa acts as if I'm going to be fired tomorrow and we'll starve to death. My parents used to say, "We work hard, so we deserve to have what we want."

> *Lisa:* Security is more important than a sailboat. Think of all the interest we'll have to pay if we borrow to buy

the boat. *My* folks never bought anything they couldn't pay cash for. And it scares me not to have savings . . . I remember times when I was little when any emergency expense became a disaster.

Lisa feels that if she doesn't hold the financial line, they'll be in trouble; Bob feels money is to be used for what he wants, not stuck in a bank. And both of them feel the way they do because the voices of their parents are saying: "This is how money should be managed."

Of course, a person may follow that voice or turn 180 degrees in the other direction. Bob could just as well have reacted to his parents' free-spending habits by becoming close-fisted about money, and Lisa to her financially deprived childhood by wanting to spend money when she had it. But no matter which course Bob and Lisa follow, they are still responding to the voices of those "outsiders," their parents.

Here's another example, this one involving in-laws and a bit more complicated since it pits opposing "outsider" messages against each other:

My wife's parents give us very expensive gifts and we can't afford to reciprocate. We're more comfortable with the modest presents my parents give us, but our children, naturally, favor the grandparents who give them the elaborate gifts. I'd like to put a stop to this by having everyone in the family agree to limit the money spent on presents. But my wife says such a rule violates the spirit of giving.

It may well be that this couple have a sort of "sibling rivalry" about who is loved most by each set of parents. The gift-giving contest may be arousing long-buried feelings of childhood competitiveness with each partner's brothers or sisters. It is unlikely that at this stage the couple are going to be able to change the ideas of either set of grandparents. They can, however, teach their children that the cost of a present has nothing to do with the love it conveys. But the couple themselves must believe that is true. Making a fuss over the issue merely evidences the opposite.

Sex, the other area so vulnerable to unconscious attitudes transmitted from parents and in-laws, is a frequent casualty of outsider influence.

"My husband is an enthusiastic sex partner most of the time," a woman told us, "but when we stay at his parents' home he won't even touch me." Counseling revealed the not very surprising fact that the man had been raised to believe that proper young men didn't try to have sex with "nice" girls. In his parents' house, consequently, the prohibitions of his childhood took over, his wife became a "nice" girl, and sex with her became a forbidden act. In a similar case, a woman who enjoyed sex thoroughly before marriage suddenly resisted it after marriage. The explanation: The woman had pictures of her parents on the bedroom wall and every time her husband wanted to make love, their faces looked down disapprovingly.

Still another couple, unmarried lovers, were plagued not by parental sexual values but by the unhappy sexual experience of the man's parents themselves. "Every time I get home late from work Larry asks a thousand questions," the woman said. "If I say I had a drink with a friend, which I sometimes do, he wants to know who it was, whether it was business or social, and how often I meet that same person." Larry denied being jealous or suspicious, but later admitted he was irrationally worried that his partner might be having an affair. "When I was a teenager," he said, "my parents got divorced because my mother was unfaithful. After that my dad always told me you could never really trust any woman. I *know* I can trust *my* woman; but I can't put my father's words out of my head."

Though sex and money may be the areas where the impact of parental voices is felt most, no area of an intimate relationship is exempt. One couple we know argue every Sunday because *she* gets furious at the way *he* looks on that day. ("Look at you, going around in those beat-up corduroy pants and that old sweater . . . it's a disgrace!") She cannot help making such hostile remarks. She remembers how proud she used to be, as a child, of the way her father looked when she went walking with him on Sundays, in his elegant three-piece suit, white shirt, and knit tie. That's the way a man *should* look if he has any self-respect, she thinks.

The unrecognized influence of parental outsiders caused a more serious rift between Patti and her advertising copywriter fiancé as they discussed their plight with the therapist:

> *Patti:* I can't understand David. He thinks of nothing but work. He gets to the office hours before anyone else, and stays later. He even works a couple of weekends every month, and when I complain about being alone he brings work home.

> *David:* Well, *I* can't understand *her.* I want to get someplace in the agency, get to be copy chief. You don't get promoted to that kind of job if you're a strict nine-to-five guy. Why can't Patti appreciate my ambition? What I'm doing is for both of us.

The therapist who helped the couple resolve their differences recognized the part that family backgrounds played in the dispute: "David's father was a hard driver, a high achiever. From the time David started school his father made it clear he expected the youth to work hard, advance rapidly. Success was expected and demanded. Patti's dad had also been a compulsive worker and a successful executive. But Patti had watched her mother turn into a lonely, bitter woman—a fate she was determined to avoid. When the couple were shown how those parental attitudes were influencing their own, they could understand and, more important, empathize with each other's views."

Like Patti and David, many women often unconsciously assume the role their same-sex parent played in the family, and repeat the behavior of that parent even when they may not consciously want to. Others may project onto a partner their image of the opposite-sex parent. Many of our ideas about masculinity and femininity stem from the way our parents carried out their sex roles. A woman whose father was an outdoorsman may push her man to be interested in hunting or fishing when he'd rather read or browse in a museum. A man whose mother baked her own breads and cakes may feel uncared for and unloved if he is always served frozen dinners. In an era when sex roles are no longer fettered to outdated ideas of what males and females "ought" to be or do, it is easy to see how such implanted values can lead to misunderstanding and conflict.

But we cannot put all the blame for all these problems on parents and in-laws. True, they instill their values and attitudes in us. This is not only natural; it is part of a parent's job. Whether their influence will be for good or ill—whether as "outsiders" they help or harm our own intimate relationships—depends to a large degree on how well we are able to separate ourselves from these unconscious links. For at the heart of the matter are the unacknowledged feelings we retain about our parents. Sometimes these feelings represent unresolved dependency. A woman may run home to mother—figuratively if not literally—every time she is even mildly unhappy with her marriage. A man may do the same thing, in effect. One young husband, feeling rejected because his working wife didn't have the time or energy to listen to his recital of the day's events, spent an hour on the phone every night talking to his mother. "*She*'s interested in what happens to me," the man said. "She always was."

On the other side of the emotional coin are unacknowledged feelings of hostility toward a parent. A young woman raised by an authoritarian father was never allowed as a child to talk back to him. No sooner was she married than she began to pick senseless arguments with her puzzled husband, displacing onto the man she loved the anger she had not been permitted to express to her father. Conversely, we may displace onto parents or in-laws feelings we cannot (or fear to) express to a partner. In-laws particularly, though innocent of any wrongdoing, are often used as targets or scapegoats for hostile feelings that should properly be directed from one partner to another. Or both sets of in-laws may be cast into competing roles by their married children. ("My folks offered to lend us more money for the down payment than yours did." . . . "We don't go to see my mother half as often as we do yours.") "I resent having to run their errands and drive them around," says a woman of her elderly in-laws. "My husband claims he doesn't have the time. But why should he expect me to do this, and then complain when I send some money to help *my* parents out?"

How can couples best cope with these "outsiders" who, after all, mean only to be close and loving? By developing constructive ways of dealing with the unfinished "emotional business" one generation has with the other. Here are some suggestions:

• Think back to your childhood and the upbringing your parents gave you. Seek the hidden links between your early experiences and the attitudes you hold now. This involves learning enough about yourself to know which ideas are truly yours and which are the remains of childhood experiences.

• Get to know your partner's parents better. Talk to them about the way your partner grew up. You'll probably learn a great deal about your companion's childhood that even he or she has forgotten, and as a result you will know more about what makes your partner tick.

• From time to time, try switching roles with your partner. If you are arguing, take each other's side of the debate for a while. You must then vigorously advance his or her point of view, and he or she must argue for yours. It is impossible to voice the other person's opinions without developing some insight into his or her ideas and feelings.

• If you still are hedged in by feelings of dependency or hostility toward your family of origin, consider getting professional help that will permit you to make peace with those feelings.

The goal for every couple, of course, is to build a personal philosophy of intimacy. What worked (or didn't work) for those outsiders, your parents, should no longer influence you. What counts is what will work for the two of you. But there remains one sticking point: It is doubtful whether any of us can ever become entirely free of the complex emotional linkages we have with our parents, even after they are dead. No matter how old we may be or how mature we may grow, it is almost impossible to deal consistently with our parents on an adult-to-adult level. To some extent we will always act and think of ourselves as their children. And perhaps this is not such a great price to pay for the many years of care parents give us.

Children

• In the course of talking with a counselor about the problems in her marriage a woman suddenly interrupts herself. "You know," she says slowly, "I think my husband and I would get along a lot better if it weren't for the children."

• In Minneapolis, family life expert Dr. Paul Rosenblatt

watched hundreds of childless couples and couples with children as they strolled and shopped in the city's downtown center. He found that couples who had children with them talked to each other less, smiled at each other less, and touched each other less than couples who were not accompanied by youngsters.

• "My wife has become almost a basket case since our baby was born," the young husband declares, "and I'll be one myself if things don't change. She's so involved with the child, so worried she'll do something wrong, that she is physically and emotionally drained. The baby is five months old, and we've made love only twice in all that time." Then he bursts out, "I need some attention too!"

Despite the suggestive evidence of these typical reports, it is extremely hard—to some it may seem an unfeeling distortion of family values—to label children "outsiders" in their parents' lives. Indeed, until about ten years ago research on parent-child relationships focused almost exclusively on the effects mothers and (to a lesser degree) fathers had on their offspring. More recently there have been a growing number of studies of the impact youngsters have on the primary relationship between their parents. Much of the research supports the presumption that partners will manage to weather the child-rearing period if their marriage is reasonably satisfying. Indeed, for a long time it was common for couples to believe children "keep us young" or "help us settle down." These are familiar and perhaps often true statements. But it is also true that the drain children impose on parents' time, energy, and economic resources cuts sharply into those and other satisfactions.

For example, a young man accuses his wife of neglecting him, of turning into a social recluse, of refusing to have sex. Something has gone wrong with their marriage, he says. Actually, nothing is basically amiss in the marriage itself; his wife is so fatigued and distracted by the demands of their two young children that she cannot give him the love and attention he is used to receiving from her.

A wife complains that her husband gives so much of himself to his job that he has no time for her or their family. In fact, the man feels under enormous pressure to keep up with the bills for doctors, camps, orthodontists, clothes, school tuition, and other extra expenses youngsters make necessary. By working longer and harder to do what he considers a good father should, he is becoming in his wife's eyes a poor husband. Both the accusing husband and the complaining wife are probably aware, on an intellectual level, of the reasons for their spouses' behavior. But on the emotional level they feel rejected and blame their partners for situations that are essentially caused by the pressures of child raising.

Little wonder, then, that virtually all current research on the subject indicates that children tend to detract from, rather than enhance, the closeness between husband and wife. In fact, a couple's satisfaction with marriage *and with each other* drops sharply soon after their first child is born. With minor variations, it stays at a lower level throughout the years of child raising, increasing again only after the youngest child leaves home.

Women, especially, say that children have a negative impact on the quality of marriage. Answers to a series of questions in a major magazine showed that women who had children (especially if the youngsters were under six or were teenagers) were less satisfied with their lives than women who did not. Compared to the childless women, mothers said they were "less optimistic about the future," had less control over key events in their lives, tired more easily, were irritable and angry more often, and were not only less interested in sex but enjoyed it less when they had it. All in all, just over half of the women with children said they were satisfied with their marriage; but of those without children nearly three quarters said they were satisfied. In short, if children do not actually damage the man-woman relationship, they certainly do not seem to make it any better.

The move by women and men away from traditional parenting roles has both eased and exacerbated this state of affairs. As men take on more responsibility for child care, and as they spend more time and show more interest in their children, the burden on women has lightened. But be cautioned: A man who starts out by espousing an equalitarian relationship often changes his tune once his wife becomes a mother. Many men harbor deeply ambivalent feelings. "I don't mind taking care of the kids," an auto mechanic says, "just so long as their mother's around when they need her."

A family counselor says you can always spot a man who has a

hidden reluctance about sharing child care: "He will say, 'I had to baby-sit yesterday.' That's a sure sign he sees it as a chore rather than as a pleasant or enriching experience. Did you ever hear a woman say she was 'baby-sitting' with her own children?" At the same time women, while freer now to seek a more complex indentity than being just partner or mother, are finding their independence clouded over by guilt feelings. As writer Jim Sanderson, a champion of female and male liberation observes: "Every woman who has committed herself to a career has serious questions about how . . . she can possibly do justice to [her children] and still compete in the economic world. . . . She must either add the role of mother to that of partner and worker, or try to balance all three roles in what may prove to be an almost impossible undertaking."

The impact of the child as "outsider" begins even in pregnancy. "When a couple become pregnant and have a first baby," write sex therapists Lorna and Philip Sarrel, "they experience a profound series of changes—biological, psychological, and social." And though a growing number of couples are prepared for pregnancy and birth, few are prepared for what being parents means. Indeed, the arrival of a first child is frequently described as a crisis, or even a trauma, for the new mother and father. As one family therapist has pointed out, the responsibility looms as overwhelming: "There is a qualitatively different level of commitment to parenthood. . . . Marriage vows can be broken. Parenthood is forever." At least for eighteen years, legally; and in most cases for another four or more years till a youngster is self-supporting and self-reliant. It's not surprising that deciding on how many children to have becomes more of an issue of disagreement between couples *after* the first child's birth than it was before.

The new "outsider" affects every aspect of the couple's life together. As the routine of child care takes hold, a couple (especially a younger couple) may feel trapped. Impromptu outings are mostly a thing of the past. Parents must devote at least twice as much time as childless couples to household tasks. The amount of time parents spend in intimate conversation—indeed, in *any* conversation not related to domestic duties—is cut in half. And, far from least important, a couple's sexual relationship is likely to be seriously affected. A new mother, in particular, may feel her partner's normal sexual interests and needs should take second place to the child's needs. It is but a short step for the man to blame this sexual rejection on the child.

Moreover, parenthood sometimes has unexpected effects on the way women and men feel about themselves as sexual beings:

> In the early days of our courtship and marriage my husband was openly affectionate. Unlike most men I had known, he was able to express loving feelings. And when we made love, he would talk quite frankly about what he wanted sexually and whether he was pleasing me. However, since our two children were born all this has changed. My husband no longer talks about his feelings and desires or about mine. I miss the intimate talk we used to share. What could have caused this change?

Most likely this man feels his role in the couple's relationship has changed. He may no longer see himself as a lover but as a provider. As a result, he has adopted behavior that seems to him more in keeping with his new self-image—earning a living, helping at home, being a loyal if not passionate or articulate sex partner. Remember, too, the role that our parents play as "outsiders": If this man seldom saw or heard *his* mother and father express their loving feelings, he may be unconsciously patterning himself after that marital model. But the counselor moved on to a more important point:

> ML: Having children may have made your husband think of himself more as "Daddy" than as lover or sex partner. This is a reaction to parenthood usually more characteristic of women than men. Some women, once they become mothers tend to see themselves as non-sexual. But some men also feel it isn't "proper" to be openly affectionate, or to indulge in sexual talk or activities when there are children around who may see or hear.
>
> Your husband is probably unaware of the change in

his behavior, and the reasons for it. What you can do is focus on the positive rather than the negative. Compliment your husband whenever he is affectionate or romantic. Tell him that you still like—still need—to have him tell you that he loves you. Explain that sex talk is arousing to you. And to prove your point be sure to continue expressing your loving feelings and desires to him.

So far we have been talking about the *direct* impact a child can have on an intimate partnership. Still another way in which children contribute to discord is by unwittingly serving as "triggers" for latent emotional conflicts between a couple:

> My wife and I have just had our first child after eight years of marriage. I was prepared for the fact that we would have less time for each other, and that money would be scarce when she quit her job. The really upsetting change is that we seem to argue now over every decision, when we used to discuss things logically and compromise if we needed to. She uses devious methods to get her way, and I find myself getting angry and stubborn.

Much is going on here. For one thing, a baby's arrival often changes the power balance in a marriage. In this case each partner appears to be trying to deal with that change in his or her own way. Since the woman left her job and is now financially dependent on her husband, she may well be seeking other ways to hold on to her right to have an equal say in decisions. She may feel that deviousness is her only way of coping. This is not necessarily an unusual situation. As a matter of fact, a recent University of Iowa study reported that most couples deal with disagreements differently after a child's arrival. Resolution by mutual give-and-take tends to be supplanted by arguments in which the woman either gives in to keep the peace or becomes manipulative in order to get her way. At the same time the husband may feel that since he now shoulders the entire burden of supporting his family, he is entitled to make decisions which the couple formerly made jointly. Such a situation is particularly difficult for couples after so many years of childlessness, during which both had a great measure of independence and intimate sharing.

In today's climate of equalitarianism, it is possible for such latent conflicts and power struggles between a woman and man to remain dormant so long as the scales of their partnership more or less balance. But the arrival of a child on the scene often tips those scales and allows the conflict to surface. A couple caught up in such a struggle may consciously or unconsciously use the child as a lightning rod on which to discharge the electricity of their anger at each other. It often seems safer than a head-to-head confrontation.

For example, a couple sought counseling because, they said, they were "greatly upset" when their fourteen-year-old daughter's school guidance officer told them the girl was cutting classes, not doing her homework, and was in danger of failing many of her courses. It is not usual for parents to seek professional help so quickly for a youngster's school problem, so it seemed likely there was more involved. And indeed the couple soon stopped talking about the daughter's troubles and began arguing with each other.

Husband: My wife expects too much help from Mary Anne around the house. I think her schoolwork and school activities should come first. The reason her grades are bad is that she doesn't have enough time to study.

Wife: Too much help? Mary Anne hardly does anything! When *I* was fifteen, I cleaned house, took care of my little sisters after school, even had dinner started when my mother got home from work. And *my* grades never suffered. Just because his mother waited on him hand and foot is no reason for me to have an irresponsible child!

ML: Are you saying that the way your parents brought you up produces a more responsible adult than the way your husband was raised?

Wife: No question about it! He still expects me to pick up after him. We had a terrible fight this weekend when I asked him to help me vacuum after he insisted Mary Anne do her homework instead of her regular Saturday chores. I think if he feels that way, *he* ought to be willing to help out. But he doesn't lift a finger to help!

ML: It sounds to me as if you two are angry at each other about more than just different approaches to child rearing. [To wife] What if you didn't have children? Would it still bother you that your husband didn't pick up after himself or help you?

Wife: Of course. We argued about that almost from the day we got married. His mother always waited on him, and he expects me to do the same. Now he wants Mary Anne catered to the same way.

Husband: I don't want Mary Anne catered to. I just think she ought to have a chance to do her best in school, to enjoy school. But you use this same argument no matter what. Any time you don't like what I do or say, you say my mother spoiled me.

ML: Well, the problem seems to be bigger than Mary Anne's chores *or* marks. I hear a problem of conflicting values between the two of you that has nothing to do with her.

About half of all couples who enter counseling say they have disagreements over values. That in itself is to be expected. Significantly, however, the differences do not usually create real discord until they are focused on their children. Then the conflicting ingrained attitudes—"*My* mother never let me go to school dressed like that." . . . "*My* father wouldn't stand for any back talk."—frequently turn into running battles.

Children as "outsiders" can also be used by parents to mask oblique criticism of each other. A man who complained that his wife dressed their daughter "like a tomboy" eventually admitted he felt she herself was lacking in femininity—which in turn proved to be a euphemism for the fact that she did not arouse him sexually.

Another woman used her child to attack her husband. If the

boy brought home a poor school report she'd say, conspiratorially, "Don't tell your father, he's in another of his bad moods." If the boy needed help with some project she'd say, "I'll help you; you know your father doesn't like it when you bother him." Under the guise of protecting the child from his father's irritation, the woman was conveying her low opinion of her husband, as well as offering evidence of what a good mother she was.

In virtually every survey of what women and men want from an intimate relationship, companionship ranks at the top of the list. Yet companionship is one of the areas of marriage most significantly affected by the impact of a child. Again and again couples complain (or wistfully regret) that they don't have time to talk to each other anymore, that they don't do things together anymore. Family therapists call this "emotional distancing" or "disengagement."

Granted, most couples experience a drop-off in shared activities and communication over the years. But the presence of children accelerates the process. Most parents can't take a weekend trip by themselves without making costly or involved child-care arrangements. Vacations are usually child-oriented. Even the simple pleasures a childless couple can share, such as shopping or browsing together or having a spur-of-the-moment evening out, are difficult.

Moreover, a good deal of marital conflict can be traced to the idea that children should be protected against the realities of family life. A working mother tells how for years she saved her household work until after the children were asleep, often cleaning and ironing till two in the morning, in order to give the youngsters her undivided attention. Naturally, this started many arguments with her husband. "I guess I was wrong," the woman said recently. "One day my daughter asked me to drive her to a party, and I said I was too tired. 'Why can't one of the other mothers drive you?' I asked. 'Oh, Mom,' Jane said, '*they work!*' I wondered what she thought *I* did!"

Few parents are sufficiently objective to be able to recognize and deal with all the emotional strains children can impose. Too often help comes after the fact, able only to repair rather than prevent damage. But couples can take steps to head off the stressful impacts children have on marriage *before* they reach a critical stage. Here are some suggestions:

• Keep the lines of communication open between you. For example, if you are childless but thinking about starting a family, make an honest assessment of how emotionally comfortable you both are with children, how much you think they would add to your happiness. Obviously, it is hard to gauge such reactions in advance, but one way is to look back at your own childhood. Was it happy? Did you enjoy the give-and-take of family life? How do you feel about your parents and the way they raised you?

• Make sure each of you knows the other's attitudes toward child raising. Dr. Harold Feldman, family studies specialist at Cornell University, states that the compatibility of parents' philosophies about this is one of the most crucial factors in determining whether they will avoid marital conflicts. Learning where you agree, and working out compromises where you disagree, can avoid making your children a focus for arguments.

• Try to differentiate between problems that result from the normal stresses and strains of child rearing and the problems that are created when one or both of you "use" the children as weapons in a marital struggle. One way to distinguish between these two sets of conflicts is to look for the underlying themes that run through your arguments. These represent the basic messages that are always present, no matter what the topic—money, sex, chores, or children.

• Be realistic about the expectations you have of yourself as a parent. Too many couples come to counseling saying they "have nothing in common anymore except the kids."

• Most important, establish and maintain firm boundaries between your married life and your family life. The two are—or should be—separate worlds. Being a parent does not mean you are no longer a wife or husband. "It seems selfish to want time for ourselves when the children need us so much," a mother says. "I resent spending money on my daughter's ballet lessons when my wife and I can't afford to go to a good restaurant. But how can you admit that, even to yourself?" a father asks. The upshot often is repressed anger, unconscious guilt—both of which lead to irritations parents take out on each other.

There are signs that a growing number of parents realize they are entitled to rewarding lives of their own despite the demands of children. A young couple with three children told us how they justified an occasional weekend away from their children in order to reestablish their bonds as husband and wife:

> As rarely as we went away, the children still resented it. In near desperation over their whining we hit upon an explanation that seemed to work. We told them that in only a few years they would be grown and would be leaving us, so we needed these weekends to begin to practice being alone.

Eventually, your marriage will be again what it was in the beginning: just the two of you. For the relationship to retain vitality in those later years, attention must be paid to it all along the way.

A word about couples who think they may choose to remain childless. With the evidence of all the tensions children can place upon partners, all the adjustments that must be made, there seems to be valid reason to ask, "Why have them?" Thousands of couples have answered this question by deciding not to have children. Voluntary childlessness may disappoint your own parents, who want to hold a grandchild; but that concern must take second place to your own deepest, most carefully thought out feelings. Obviously, both partners must be in complete accord on the final decision. If at first you are not, it is wiser to set the discussion aside for a while and consider it again at a later time. Sometimes couples who would like to have one child, no more, decide to remain childless on the theory that an "only" youngster cannot have a happy childhood and will not be a well-adjusted adult. Neither is true. Research shows that "only" children are as well, if not better, adjusted than those who have siblings.

We have talked with hundreds of parents about whether they would have children if they could go back and start over. Some replied that there were days when nothing went right and when their children's behavior would have tried the patience of a saint; on such occasions the answer would be a resounding "No." A few parents said they always felt negative about being parents, an admission that points up the fact that not everyone is suited for parenthood. Most parents, however, reported that they had their highs and their lows, yet even with all the problems parenthood brings, once their children become part of their lives they could not even imagine being childless.

Friends

Friends are the third major group of "outsiders" whose presence can create difficulties for a couple. Friendship—"life's noblest virtue," as it has been called—is not usually thought of as a source of conflict. Because good friends make us feel worthy, they help to strengthen the feelings we have for our intimate partner. It is natural to be pleased and proud that the woman or man we have chosen to love has also been chosen by another to be a friend. And in our mobile society, friends supply the practical help and psychological support that once-nearby family members used to provide.

Mental health experts say that having friends helps keep us healthy, physically as well as emotionally. "Friends," says one pamphlet, "can be good medicine." But while some kinds of friends and friendships can improve a couple's relationship, others can damage it. It's important to reexamine your friendships to determine which effect they are having.

Problems with friendships are likely to occur in three main areas. The first centers about those friends each partner had prior to their own relationship. Many women and men find to their dismay that they must choose between the partner and these old friends. A California physicist told us that his fiancée (who never went to college) was so ill at ease with his friends that he had to stop seeing them. "Now we mostly see people she chooses," the scientist said. "They bore me, but I suppose I don't mind being bored as much as she minds feeling dumb."

A young married couple can come to resent the relative freedom and affluence of single friends from their former lives, especially if the couple are tied down with small children or large mortgage payments and, in turn, blame each other for their "entrapment." (We'll look more deeply into the potential conflicts between partners and their friends from earlier times in Section 6, under the heading "Troubles Out of the Past.")

Difficulties can arise, however, even when partners make new friends together. It is a peculiarly American concept that friendships are (or ought to be) formed on a "couple basis," two by two, in linked pairs. (Happily, this idea is slowly giving ground. Many of today's young women and men resist the notion that couple friendships must always exist as a foursome. However, as we shall soon see, this change can lead to other tensions.)

But it's not easy to form friendships in foursomes. The women must like each other, the men must like each other, and each man and woman must be able to get along reasonably well with the partner of the opposite sex. Instead of two linkages, eight must be worked out. The complexity of the friendship pattern often proves a source of conflict. Strains develop if each member of the quartet cannot feel equally comfortable with all the others:

> When my husband doesn't like someone he just sits there, silent, making no attempt to disguise his boredom. It humiliates me.

> A man was astounded when his companion finally said she hated his best friend's wife: "We see them almost every week, and you never notice how she criticizes me!"

> Every time I visit my old college friend I get furious. It's not Jenny's fault that she married well, but when I see how she lives I can't help feeling cheated. My Bill is just as clever and hardworking as Jenny's husband, so why do we have to scrimp along while they have so much? I know it's ridiculous, but I honestly think I have to stop seeing Jenny if I want to keep my marriage.

Certainly friends inject a variety of interests and personalities into a couple's experience that enhance their relationship with each other. But on occasion a couple may become too involved, too close with friends. In one such case two couples who had become devoted friends were trapped in an unpleasant situation when one of the men made a sexual pass at the other woman. "I tried to rebuff him tactfully," the woman said. "But his feelings are hurt, and of course things between the two of us have changed completely. I can't tell his wife—she's my best friend. And if I told my husband, he'd blow the whole thing wide open."

Even when sex does not intrude, being intensely involved with one other couple, or with a group of couples, can narrow one's horizons and stifle personal growth. Such closeness also has the potential to overwhelm the intimacy between partners. Not long ago a woman in her early thirties came to us with this problem:

> We're fortunate, I guess, to have three other couples we feel quite close to. But I would like to spend some time alone with the man I live with. When I tell him this he gets annoyed and accuses me of being antisocial. I can't seem to make him understand that it's important for us to have some emotional privacy—some conversation, some experiences that only the two of us share.

We hear many similar stories. The fact is that having friends around *all the time* can be an unconscious device to avoid facing the conflicts or tensions that exist between the partners themselves. At the very least the presence of outsiders—no matter how much you like them and they like you—usually chokes off personal conversation between partners. It puts a stop to intimacies, to practical discussions, and especially to honest debates that get problems out into the open.

Here is a rather extreme example (but not so atypical as one might think) of how overinvolvement with friends can camouflage the difficulties in a couple's own relationship. Two couples in a small midwestern city spent several evenings together each week, shared nearly every weekend, and usually took their vacations together, too. At one point they even linked their homes by wireless intercom so they could talk to each other at will. This continued until a job change caused one of the couples to move to another city. The transplanted couple soon made friends in their new community, but the couple left behind could not shift friendship gears so easily. For one thing, they had cut themselves off from most of the other people in town. With time and effort they might have found new friends, but they had gone so long without doing so they didn't know how to go about it. Moreover, the closeness of their friendship with the first couple had overwhelmed their marriage. Alone, they virtually did not know what to say to each other or how to enjoy doing things by themselves.

We all need someone we can tell our troubles to—and friends make marvelously sympathetic listeners. It is comforting to be able to get things off your chest without fear of reproach. But confidences to third parties can be damaging. Revealing such intimate problems as sex, money, children, or in-laws to an "outsider" can be a partial betrayal of your partner. Receiving a confidence can be dangerous, too. As one expert observed, "In talking intimately with a friend you risk not only revealing something you'll regret, but also hearing something you really don't want to know." Accepting a friend's confidences may also involve you and your partner in the problems they represent. Research shows that when a friend's troubles intrude too far into your own life there can be a "contagion" effect:

> A number of our good friends have gotten divorced recently. My husband says we should stop seeing them, and spend more time with happily married couples. Is there any truth to the notion that our friends' troubles can spread to us?

Some years ago a researcher found, to his amazement, that when he plotted the geographical incidence of divorce in a midwestern city, "clumps" of divorces occurred in small, self-contained areas. It was as if one couple's divorce opened up the floodgates for other couples in the neighborhood, flushed out suppressed differences, and made divorce itself more "thinkable." Of course a couple with a reasonably solid relationship should not fear that a friend's divorce will be catching. But it is possible to be affected by too close a connection with recently divorced or divorcing friends *if* you as a couple are currently having problems. Divorce itself is not contagious, but emotional reaction to it can be.

A unique and thorny issue facing women and men in the eighties—especially for those who place a high value on personal choice and freedom—is how best to integrate "cross-sex" friendships with an already existing intimate partnership. Despite the progress and growing maturity of the liberation movement for both sexes, it is still common to question whether it is acceptable for a man to have a woman friend his spouse or lover does not

know well, or if it is right for a woman to have a close male
friend apart from her lover or husband. The French have a word
for such a relationship. They call it *l'amitié en rose*—a loving
friendship. It is not overtly sexual, although there may sometimes
be a sexual attraction. Yet women and men are finding that there
are rewards in transcending sexual feelings in order to relate to
the opposite sex on a platonic basis.

There always have been people who say such loving friendships
cannot successfully coexist with a couple's own intimate relationship. In a reader survey on the topic conducted by *Psychology
Today* magazine, 75 percent of the women and men who responded agreed that "sexual tensions" are a complication; that
friends of the opposite sex "have less in common" than same-sex
friends; and that—the hammer blow of hidebound tradition!—
"society does not encourage such friendships." Proponents feel
just as strongly that cross-sex friendships not only can exist, but
actually serve constructive ends. (Women are likely to be more
positive about such friendships than men; perhaps, psychologists
believe, because women tend to be more comfortable in person-
to-person exchanges and more skilled in non-sexual intimacy.)

People with business and professional careers adapt to the idea
of cross-sex friendships realistically. In the words of a woman
banker, "I work with men all day. If I couldn't be friends with
them, I'd miss out on many important insights and contacts." Another woman said, "I know my husband has many things in common with his women colleagues, business matters he cannot talk
about with me."

Writer Scot Haller points out that "In a world where the role
of women has changed so much in such a short time, a man
comes to value someone who can keep him informed as to the
prevailing sentiment and sensibility . . . The women's movement
has also created a sexually relaxed atmosphere in which [such
cross-sex friendships] are more likely to occur . . . There seem to
be more and more of these relationships in which sex is not a factor or a determining characteristic. Whether or not all these platonic affairs are a by-product of the women's movement, they are
fulfilling one of its goals: the disintegration of sexual barriers and
the dismissal of sexual stereotypes."

Close friendships between women and men are not without
their problems, however. There are few guidelines for forming or

maintaining such relationships, and those that exist are frequently misinterpreted. Also, gossip, jealousy, and the fear that a platonic cross-sex friendship will inevitably lead to a sexual adventure are still quite real concerns for many couples, especially married partners. Conversations on the subject yield such typical comments as, "A woman can't really be friends with a man in her own age bracket without there being sexual overtones," and "You can't draw a line between friendship and something more intimate. One minute it can be fine, the next minute—look out!"

Some therapists believe that couples who are happily married, or who have a satisfying sexual relationship with one partner, should have the fewest problems with cross-sex friendships. The reason: These individuals are likely to have so little ambivalence about what they want from the friendship that they are less likely to raise doubts about it in others. Thus, a married man with several close women friends says, "It's not a problem for me because I'm not interested in an affair. I don't worry about being misinterpreted because I am in control of my own feelings." (Yet even when there is no likelihood of sexual intimacy, one partner may feel threatened if he or she views the closeness the other shares with an "outsider" as some sort of emotional rejection.) Friendships formed within clear-cut boundaries—the office, the classroom, the community theater group—present fewer problems for most women and men. It's when one or both parties want to expand the relationship into other areas of their lives that problems can arise.

For many couples the decision to avoid friendships with members of the opposite sex is based on the feeling that one's sexual partner deserves all the love one has to give; that another close friendship takes something away, as if a person has only so much emotional energy to invest. "I know they've never been to bed together," a woman said of her husband and a female colleague, "but they might as well be having an affair because he's cheating on me emotionally anyway. I know they share experiences that I don't share with him. He probably tells her things about himself he wouldn't dream of telling me. How do you think that makes me feel?"

What this wife doesn't understand is that her husband needs a woman as a friend precisely because he can confide in her in ways he cannot or does not want to with his wife or with his male friends. Men seldom share intimate feelings with each other; it is often easier and more helpful for them to talk with women about their problems or dreams. Nor would this husband necessarily confide in his wife, for many men are still afraid of appearing weak, dependent, or indecisive to the woman they love.

In turn, women recognize that a man friend can offer a perspective or guidance they cannot always get from their partners or from their female friends. "I can ask my friend how he thinks another man would feel or react in certain situations," one woman said. "Men have different ideas about love and work from those of women." (Of course, some male-female friendships do have their origins in initial sexual attraction. After all, platonic love does not mean an absence of emotion—merely an absence of physical sex. But men and women say that what makes these relationships so special is that they aren't complicated by sex.)

Other working women report that developing a friendship with a man in the same field helps them to advance professionally. "I made good friends with the men in the office," says one. "Their advice has been enormously helpful. But the last thing I'd do is get sexually involved with any of them—our friendships are too valuable for me to take that risk!" In short, though office romances are usually recognized as being hazardous to one's occupational health, office friendships are seen as valuable assets.

In spite of the advantages they offer, platonic cross-sex friendships aren't easily formed. Quite simply, women and men have to learn how to go about making friends with one another. Rarely are we taught to view someone of the opposite sex as a friend or potential friend. We may have an occasional "brother-sister" relationship during childhood, but it rarely survives once the adolescent dating games begin.

A man who is the product of a time when any close relationship with a woman was automatically defined as being romantic or sexual, may not know how to interpret a purely friendly overture from a woman. Nor are women much more adept at making friends with men. Some, consciously or not, use their femininity to seduce a man into friendship, which is surely a contradiction in terms. Or they may romanticize a friendship as it grows more close. Other women are suspicious of men who want to be their friends; they look for hidden sexual motives. And some, still confused about changing sexual roles, find it difficult to take the initiative in cultivating a friendship with a man for fear they will seem too aggressive.

If you feel comfortable being friendly with someone of the same sex, there is no reason to feel uncomfortable about doing the same with someone of the opposite sex. If you understand and are open about your own feelings, it is unlikely that a friendly advance will be misjudged for a sexual one. But:

• Don't conceal your status if you are married. Mentioning a spouse or lover is one way to make it clear that your intentions are friendly rather than romantic.

• Let any friendship develop gradually. Wait until you know each other well before you feel free to talk about intimate matters.

• If a friendship takes on sexual overtones, promptly clear the air with a frank discussion. Similarly, if your spouse or lover is unhappy because you enjoy the company of a friend of the opposite sex, discuss those jealous feelings. Silence only increases suspicion. It's also sometimes helpful to include the friend in social plans with your partner so they can become acquainted.

• Know what you expect from a friendship with someone of the opposite sex. To cultivate a friendship with the secret aim of having it turn into a romantic relationship is dishonest and usually unsuccessful.

Unless you are an orphan, a total misanthrope, or are willing to live as a hermit, it is virtually impossible to escape the stresses that the "outsiders" we have talked about—parents, in-laws, children, friends—can create. But it *is* possible to deal with them rationally. The task for every woman and man who wants to have a truly committed relationship with an intimate partner is to sort out the emotional tangle between parent and partner, child and partner, friend and partner. Only then can you begin to function as an independent and responsible adult.

6—TAKING THE HEAT OUT OF CONFLICT

"I remember the first time Lynn and I had a fight," one of our friends told us recently. "It wasn't long after we fell in love, and I thought it was the beginning of the end. But in a day or two we forgot the terrible things we'd said. A few weeks later it happened again. This time I was sure the rift would never heal. But somehow we got over that one, too. It took many of these fight-and-make-up sequences before Lynn and I realized some conflict was inevitable, and we might as well learn how to handle it."

Finding a way to take the heat out of conflict so that it does not do lasting harm is one of the most important challenges intimate partners face. That is particularly true if you believe, as many family therapists now do, that intimate relationships are essentially "conflict systems." The very nature of a partnership that brings together two persons with unique backgrounds and individual needs makes some conflict almost inevitable. This does not mean that couples are destined to be constantly at odds. But realistically, total unselfishness is a rare commodity, and most of us are at best ambivalent when faced with the need to sacrifice our desires for the sake of a partner.

The idea that discord may be the rule rather than the exception flies in the face of what we think a close relationship should be. But if that is true—and there is strong evidence it is—it may answer an important question about why so many people in intimate partnerships are unhappy. For if we unrealistically continue to expect harmony and unselfish caring, even women and men who truly care about each other are going to be disillusioned and disappointed. True, there are some couples who seem to enjoy fighting; conflict is their main emotional link. George and Martha, in Edward Albee's *Who's Afraid of Virginia Woolf?* were such a couple. The heat of their vicious battles in a perverse way stoked the fire of their feelings for each other.

But most of us would rather find a more pleasant way to live. When we do fight, we are at some level fighting to find a way to get along better. That is what we mean when we say that the difference between successful and unsuccessful relationships is not whether conflict exists, but how well we can manage to deal with it. And that skill will be all the more crucial in the decade of the eighties, when changing sex roles and changing rules for relationships are creating new arenas for conflict. The old "power struggle" between women and men is taking on new (and sometimes almost ludicrous) aspects. One young woman, for instance, tells of a male friend "who actually lectured me on why I should go to Washington to lobby for the Equal Rights Amendment. It was the old male domination dressed up in equalitarian clothes!"

For the most part, how a person deals with conflict follows the pattern that characterizes his or her basic personality or temperament. Therapists have identified four primary patterns that govern the roles one plays in conflict:

- *a mover* is a person who initiates action, makes things happen;
- *a follower* goes along with what a mover starts;
- *an opposer* challenges the action;
- *a bystander* watches what is going on but remains detached from the action.

When a couple consists of a mover and a follower, there is by definition likely to be little conflict. Obviously, a mover and an opposer can expect a great deal of disagreement. The aloof bystander frustrates both mover and opposer; he or she gives free rein to a mover, and offers the opposer no one to oppose. A couple made up of a follower and bystander may have little overt conflict but are likely, out of joint inertia, to become stuck in the process of resolving hidden conflict between them. If one partner *always* (or consistently) plays one role—opposing all suggestions, say, or complying with them—it is extremely difficult for the couple to deal with their differences.

Within these roles, what tactics do women and men generally

use to try to manage conflict—if not to resolve it, then at least to prevent it from escalating? Basic techniques include *authority, control, influence,* and *manipulation.* Those who use "authority" to settle a disagreement assume that they have the right or power (by virtue of special expertise, or just by virtue of their role in the relationship) to make a decision binding on both persons. "Control" involves the use of threats, rewards, or punishments to get the other person to do what you want regardless of his or her wishes. Using "influence" to deal with conflict involves persuading a partner to agree by adducing new information or trying to reason with him or her. Finally, "manipulation" is a way of trying to win agreement covertly—by making a partner feel guilty, putting him or her in an expansive mood, telling white lies, making promises, shedding tears, etc.

A research experiment testing how married couples used these strategies and their outcomes, reported in the *Journal of Family Issues,* showed that husbands win arguments far more frequently than wives regardless of the tactic used. The most effective strategy for women is the use of influence. Significantly, influence was used as frequently by men as by women; men reported using it more than they said they wanted to, which indicates to the researchers that changing sex roles are gradually forcing men to take a more even-handed approach to resolving conflict. "It is possible," says sociologist Janet S. Chafetz, "that wives define authority and control by their husbands as demonstrating a lack of respect and love. . . . The fact that many men use a strategy they do not like—influence—probably reflects either a substantial degree of spousal equality . . . or a general understanding that spouses are supposed to be equal in their decision-making rights, or both."

When conflict occurs, how do we respond? A person we call "reality-oriented" tends to react in a way that aims to take the heat out of conflict. Such a woman or man may not always have a solution at hand, but by keeping the problem in focus he or she can at least isolate the areas of difference and work toward some agreement. A "defense-oriented" person habitually attempts to reduce emotional discomfort by "explaining" the behavior that appears to be causing it. These explanations (or defenses) can take a variety of forms: after-the-fact rationalizations; intellectualizing the conflict by discussing "principles" rather than actions; denying what happened; "forgetting" previous agreements on the issue; or, like Pollyanna, insisting that some future benefit will come out of the present unpleasantness. Although such "defenses" may temporarily take the heat out of conflict, they are rarely useful in resolving basic differences.

As a result of these different styles of dealing with conflict, the nature of conflict itself can take different forms. What usually brings a couple to counseling, for instance, is *current and open* conflict in the form of a crisis. In this section we will explore some of these crisis situations: an explosion of anger, sexual infidelity, a violent act by a "mover" that has set in motion a seemingly irreparable state of affairs. *Chronic* conflict is still another form usually traced to a stalemate between a "mover" and an "opposer," or to static enmeshment between a "mover" and a "bystander." We will look at such chronic conflict situations as continued disappointment with a partner, simmering jealousies, and long-standing disagreements sparked by past events.

The fundamental lesson we learn from all conflict is that neither partner in an intimate relationship can afford to be sidetracked into a position of having to "win" the argument. Conflicts must be managed as problems to be solved rather than battles to be won or lost. Fortunately, though changing roles increase the potential for conflict between women and men they also have the potential to stimulate new ways of reducing tensions and putting conflict to good use. Partners seem more likely than ever before to have an equal say.

Breaking the Love-Anger Cycle

Anger, whether rational or irrational, is perhaps the most studied and least understood of all our emotions. It often frightens both the person in its grip and the person at whom it is directed. As a result, it can breed retaliatory anger in others and self-reproach in ourselves. Even when anger seems justified we often feel ashamed of it or shocked by it. A honeymooning couple had just such an experience:

> *Stephanie:* It was the fourth day of our trip in the Caribbean. Paul asked whether I'd mind if he went

deep-sea fishing the next day. I was a bit hurt that he would want to take a day of our honeymoon for something he knows I don't enjoy, but I told him to go ahead. Next day I sat by the hotel pool, all by myself, and I could feel anger building up inside.

By the time Paul came back I was furious. That evening we had an awful fight. He finally apologized and of course we kissed and made up. But it changed the whole atmosphere of our honeymoon. Both of us were really shaken by the experience. It was scary that we could get that angry at each other.

Some women in Stephanie's place might have kept their anger in; been afraid to risk an argument. "I try my best to keep the peace" is a phrase counselors often hear from men as well as women. Unfortunately, we "keep the peace" at the price of feeling cheated and resentful. At the same time we deny ourselves and our partners the chance to learn how to defuse anger and then to deal with the conflict that caused it. Moreover, letting negative feelings accumulate only makes us angrier in the long run; even small things grow large. As therapist Paul Vahanian points out, "The issue does not lessen or grow clearer with time . . . it merely becomes more obscure."

Angry feelings are at times inevitable for intimate partners. Intimacy makes us vulnerable. An affront or a disappointment—real or fancied—from a loved one provokes anger more intense than if the hurt came from a stranger, whose words or actions are not so important to us. How can we deal most effectively with angry feelings caused by or aimed at someone we love? To begin with, couples need to understand the nature and function of anger as a healthy emotion—a biological survival kit that helps us function in a crisis. Anger is triggered less by fear than by attack or frustration. Getting angry as a response to frustration is a normal reaction; witness the baby squalling in fury when he or she isn't fed or changed on time.

Most people tend to deal with angry feelings in one of two ways. *Suppressing* anger is, as we have pointed out, one of them. *Releasing* anger with no holds barred is another. This "venting" theory, which achieved wide popularity a few years back, was based on the classic concept of catharsis. It holds that bottled-up animosity only grows more intense, while expressing one's anger lessens hostility, clears the emotional atmosphere, and presumably enables one to deal calmly with the underlying issues.

But after such a gut-level exchange can partners really move on to settle their differences rationally? According to sociologist Murray Straus, who has done intensive research on fighting between lovers and spouses, the answer is no. Venting anger verbally tends to increase, not reduce, hostility; it inflames conflict rather than takes the heat out of it. And releasing angry feelings full force at someone we care about can create enormous anxiety. Some people can emotionally accept a lot of screaming during a quarrel, others are dismayed or overwhelmed by it; hurling pots or invective may not be overly upsetting to one partner, but to the other words or actions that go beyond certain limits can be shockingly hurtful. Such discrepancies can create a "secondary conflict" between spouses that cause more antagonism than the original dispute.

The result of an experiment conducted some years ago by the National Institute of Mental Health is a case in point. Researchers wanted to find out how young married couples communicate with each other in typical conflict situations. The experimenters staged scenes in which the couples found themselves arguing over how to celebrate an anniversary or what television program to watch. A main finding was that both wives and husbands almost always responded to harsh and hostile statements with others in the same vein. Only gentle, thoughtful, and loving words produced conciliatory replies.

Other studies show that when a person is encouraged to unleash aggressive emotions, he or she is increasingly likely to continue such behavior. Catharsis, it seems, has some unexpected psychological side effects. For some people the feeling of well-being that comes from the release of tension is an immediate emotional reward that reinforces aggressive responses. In other words, when we do something that makes us feel good, we want to do it again. And some people are likely to raise the ante—to go from verbal fighting to physical aggression. Consider the not unusual case of Ellen and Jerry:

> *Ellen:* We always said what we felt, no matter how harsh, and enjoyed making up afterward. One night,

when we had both worked late, Jerry picked me up at my office. We stopped to buy hamburgers and French fries to take home for a quick dinner.

Jerry: Ellen started to nibble the potatoes and I asked her to wait until we got home. She just laughed and said, "But I'm hungry now." I said, "So am I, and you're eating all the potatoes!"

Ellen: It was all so silly. I suppose we were tired, or bugged by something else, but it just felt good to say mean things. Jerry kept calling me selfish and finally tried to take the box of potatoes away. I held on to it, and he squeezed my fingers hard. That hurt. I got furious. "All right, here are your crummy potatoes," I said, and threw them at him. Ketchup sprayed all over. Jerry cursed and threw the box back. For about ten seconds we swerved around in traffic. It was only when we nearly sideswiped another car that we stopped. We didn't say another word until we got home. Later Jerry and I admitted we'd both been scared by the way our anger had flared so fast and so viciously.

Somewhere between suppressing anger and venting it lies the territory of sarcastic "humor," where an angry person can take verbal potshots at a partner and at the same time deny that he or she is doing so. Here is a good illustration from our case files. The client was a serious-minded accountant, once-divorced, and now engaged:

The woman I'm going to marry has one habit that upsets me very much. She's always making jokes and sarcastic remarks to ridicule me. When I get angry, she says she was only kidding, that I have no sense of humor. But her sarcasm is not funny to me. Can you suggest some ways I can get her to stop doing this?

Perhaps this man's fiancée *was* only kidding and didn't realize the impact of her words. But anyone who uses sugar-coated hostile remarks to put a partner down probably fears the imagined consequences of being openly angry. Indeed, the frequent use of sarcasm often conceals chronic anger. Here's what the counselor said:

> Before you can deal with your fiancée's habit, you need to determine if it's something she does with everyone or just with you. If it is a trademark of her personality, you may not be able to do much about it. But if *she* wants to change, she can ask you to help her by pointing out each time she uses ridicule or sarcasm to belittle. She may not be consciously aware of what she is saying. If you are her only target, however, she may be trying to tell you she is angry with you or feels inadequate about your relationship. She may fear you will not love her if she is openly angry. She needs your sympathetic encouragement to be frank about her feelings.

The most constructive way to understand and deal with anger lies somewhere between the extremes of holding it in and venting it freely. It may help if you can visualize angry feelings as existing on a scale ranging from *annoyance* to *irritation* to *anger* to *rage*.

When annoyances and irritations are not dealt with promptly, they tend to gather momentum, to push us toward anger and rage. What we need to learn is how to discharge ill-tempered feelings a *little* at a time. For the most part, that means coming to grips with vexations or resentments promptly—bringing them out into the open before they have a chance to snowball. Unfortunately, many people prefer to avoid this kind of confrontation, not realizing how effective it can be at defusing a potentially threatening situation.

Sometimes anger flares suddenly. It is often hard to respond calmly in the heat of an argument or in the face of what you may feel are unfair accusations and attacks. It takes practice to control your feelings, to guard against flying into a rage. The intelligent thing to do is to release the angry pressures immediately, but *indirectly*. Walk away until you have cooled down. Get rid of your fury through vigorous physical actions—hit some tennis balls; pull up stubborn weeds. Write out your angry feelings and then tear up the paper.

Once you have harmlessly released the immediate emotional pressures you will feel a lot better, and you will be able to deal with the causes of the anger in a more realistic and constructive way. Finally, in reflection, ask yourself *why* you got so angry. Were your feelings misplaced? Were they out of proportion to the words or actions that triggered them? Did you take as a personal affront something that was not aimed at you at all? Did you jump to wrong conclusions? Did you get more upset than the incident warranted?

Therapists who use videotape playback equipment during counseling sessions to help couples see themselves objectively report an unexpected reaction. Women and men who watch themselves arguing angrily usually say, "That can't be us." For the picture on the screen graphically reveals the contradiction between their anger and their image of themselves as a loving couple. Veteran therapist David Mace has identified this contradiction as the "love-anger cycle." Intimate partners, he explains, seek to become even closer to each other. As they do, however, the differences between them loom larger. Disagreements that at a distance seemed unimportant become sources of discord. Loving feelings are temporarily replaced by hostile ones. If partners withdraw emotionally from each other for a while, the anger dies down. But this means backing away from their desire for intimacy. This love-anger cycle baffles partners until they learn how to break it before it does serious damage. Mace suggests three steps:

First, acknowledge your anger. Simply tell your partner, "I'm getting angry," instead of communicating this indirectly with a sarcastic comment or an outburst of rage. It does not occur to most women and men to take this direct approach. Yet it is as realistic to say, "I'm angry" as it is to say, "I'm excited."

Second, disclaim your anger as an emotional but not logical response. This does not mean you do not have just cause to be angry. It means, instead, that your anger is not to be viewed as totally rational. To acknowledge that you are emotional, and that your partner is not your enemy, leaves room for an invitation to negotiate the conflict. You can say something like, "I'm angry, but I don't like being angry with you. I don't think it solves anything, so I will try to cool down."

Third, ask your partner for help in finding out why
you (or both of you) are angry. In other words, recast
your angry reaction as a problem to be solved. Such a
request is hard to turn down. And once the search for an
explanation begins, anger almost always drains away.
Breaking the love-anger cycle is one way to take the heat
out of couple conflicts.

Two seemingly paradoxical aftereffects of an angry confrontation between intimate partners are depression and sexual stimulation.

After a fight with the man I live with [a twenty-nine-
year-old woman reports] I feel depressed for days . . .
not angry, just tired, frustrated, uninterested in anything. My companion thinks I am sulking on purpose,
but believe me these moods are no fun for me. Is my reaction normal?

Depression is a common reaction to anger. For one thing, the
argument highlights the conflicts between this couple. For another, their failure to resolve them leaves "unfinished" anger, a
sense of pointlessness about the confrontation. When not admitted, these feelings can turn into apathy and fatigue. Certainly the
woman's reaction is normal. Equally certainly, it might well be
avoided if she and her companion could enlist in a mutual effort
to resolve their conflict in a more direct way.

Unlikely as it may seem, anger can also be a sexual turn-on for
some people:

Almost every time we fight, my husband wants to
"make up" by making love. After being so angry I'm not
in the mood, but if I refuse he gets mad all over again.
He says arguing makes him feel sexy. Can you really
shift emotional gears that fast?

There is valid psychological backing for the fact that so many
torrid love scenes in fiction (and in real life, too) follow angry exchanges between lovers. For one thing, many of the physiological
changes that accompany anger—increased pulse rate, irregular
breathing, muscle tension, pupil dilation—also occur in sexual

arousal. Thus, it is possible to feel physical excitement and label it either as anger or as sexual desire. For another, anger often leads to heightened aggressive feelings. When these are not discharged in a direct way—such as throwing something or hitting someone—they may be channeled into another (and more socially acceptable) form of aggressive behavior.

Many people unconsciously see sex as an aggressive act. For others, who see sex as a tender way of relating, anger is incompatible with lovemaking. In this particular instance, the man may not so much be "shifting gears" as looking for reassurance that the argument has not damaged the affectionate bond between the couple. If he needs sex as a sign that he is still loved, then it isn't surprising that a sexual rejection rekindles his anger.

When Someone You Love Lets You Down

The literature of relationships has some peculiar blind spots. Not so many years ago, when women and men were still locked into their traditional sex roles, studies and reports on parenting focused exclusively on a mother's responsibilities; the word "father" appeared only as a rare reference in an index or footnote. This myopic approach has, of course, changed as men themselves changed from being mere begetters and breadwinners to emotionally involved parents. But another blind spot still exists. Family-life researchers continue to study and write at great length about such conflict-prone emotions as anger and jealousy, while feelings of *disappointment* go virtually ignored.

Oddly enough, laypersons seem to ignore it as well. Though most of us probably are disappointed by a friend or lover far more often than we are made angry or jealous, and though the single feeling that most often mars our emotional relationships is the hurt that comes from being "let down" by the person we love, still disappointment with a partner is seldom mentioned by women or by men as a serious problem or a cause for conflict.

One reason may be that as children we were criticized for dwelling on disappointments. When our best efforts failed or our fondest dreams were dashed, we were told not to sulk, that life isn't always fair, that we can't always have everything we want or the way we want it. As a result, we are still embarrassed to admit to being disappointed. It seems too trivial a thing. So we tend to

hide our hurts not only from others but from ourselves as well—
and in doing so we never learn how to deal effectively with disappointment.

But women and men had better learn how to deal with it because the paradoxical nature of intimacy makes disappointment
between partners virtually inevitable. Disappointment is a matter
of unfulfilled expectations. The closer two people grow, the more
they come to expect from each other; and the more they expect,
the greater the chance of disappointments. In the long run it is
how two people manage these emotional hurts that holds the key
to their success as a couple.

The first step in learning how to handle disappointment is to
recognize that there are two kinds. One stems from unrealistic expectations. We all have them, partly because we are largely ill-
prepared for the give-and-take of intimacy and emotional vulnerability. We also have them because we illogically believe that the
person we love will be able to meet all our needs and wants. We
become disenchanted when that image proves flawed. Listen to a
young husband whose image of his wife's sexual nature did not
allow for realistic change. The man, a sandy-haired architectural
draftsman in his early thirties, came for counseling more in sor-
row than in anger (as is usually the case when disappointment
strikes):

> My wife and I lived together for a year before we got
> married, and our sex life during that time was exciting.
> So you can imagine my surprise and disappointment
> when, practically right after the wedding, this woman
> who seemed so passionate became uninterested in sex.
> She finds excuses to avoid making love, and when we do,
> it is perfunctory, at least on her part. I've tried to get my
> wife to see a sex therapist but she refuses. I feel really
> cheated. What can she do to get over this problem?

While the man's disappointment is understandable, the way he
was trying to deal with it was not. The therapist's task was to
help him uncover all the factors involved:

> ML: You seem to be reacting to your sense of disap-
> pointment by giving all responsibility to your wife. If

she would just "do something" about the situation, everything would be fine; is that what you really mean?

Husband: Well, it's not *my* problem, is it?

ML: In most cases these problems stem from the relationship, rather than just from one or the other partner. Sometimes, of course, women do see themselves in a different sexual light, or have different sexual expectations, when they marry, but it's also possible you are romanticizing your memories of that earlier time. In any event, you're not likely to make matters better while you still blame your wife. If she has developed a block to sexual or emotional arousal, that's something *both* of you need to work on. Maybe your approach to lovemaking has changed since your marriage. Perhaps *you* don't approach sex with the same enthusiasm you once did. But so long as you keep placing all the blame for your disappointment on her, you will only make her feel guilty and resentful. If that happens, she may disappoint you even more.

Unrealistic expectations also contribute to our disappointment through the images of our own past experiences—experiences that give us fixed ideas of how a partner should behave. Often these "life scripts," as counselors sometimes call them, are based on what we learned in earlier relationships with other people: our parents, relatives, friends. The well-known family therapist Carlfred Broderick tells in his book, *Couples,* of such an impasse in his own marriage. Whenever he got sick as a child, Broderick's mother would bring him an endless supply of tall glasses of fruit juice. She did the same for his father when he was ill. Soon after his wedding Broderick caught the flu. He went to bed and waited for his fruit juice, but none was forthcoming. Eventually—and with what he thought was great tact—he said to his bride, "Honey, I didn't realize there wasn't any juice in the house." Taking the hint, she brought him one small glass of orange juice.

"That was all," says Broderick, "I couldn't believe it. I was so hurt that if I hadn't felt so badly I would have left." The same sequence of events happened every time Broderick got sick. Finally his wife said, "What is this with you and juice? I don't think I can stand to go through another illness with you constantly grousing about juice. Even when I get it for you, it doesn't seem to do any good."

Broderick explained how he grew up believing that no matter what ails you you get well in direct proportion to the amount of fruit juice you drink. But the more Broderick examined his theory about illness and juice, the sillier it began to sound. "It spoiled sickness for me for good," he says. "I have rarely missed a day of work since."

Since our expectations usually are based on what seems to *us* a sensible set of rules, it is hard to fathom why our partner disappoints us by calling them unreasonable. But there is a simple formula for analyzing whether one's expectation is reasonable or not.

The first step is to ask yourself, "What did I really expect?" and "Did my partner know I had this expectation?" It is surprising how often unclear communication can leave one person confused and/or the other in the dark. But if a partner *does* know, then we need to ask ourselves, "Did he or she *agree* to fulfill my expectations?" If not, we are simply setting ourselves up to be hurt.

The second kind of disappointment grows out of *legitimate* expectations. In this case, one person's need or wish has been clearly voiced and agreed to, but the other doesn't follow through. For example, a couple agree that when she travels on business she will call home when she reaches her destination so that he won't worry about her. She fails to do so because immediately upon arrival she has to attend an important meeting. Is the man's hurt or disappointment justified? If the woman was prevented from fulfilling their agreement by extenuating circumstances, the answer is no. If, however, she repeatedly neglects to make the agreed-upon call, the answer is yes. Willfully disappointing a partner is a serious breach of trust.

Sometimes a reasonable expectation can lead to disappointment because *too much* has been agreed to, and a partner finds it impossible to carry out his or her part of the bargain. A woman may want her man to be more affectionate, or (like our architectural draftsman) a man may want his woman to be more passionate, and the partners may promise to do so. But changes in feelings are easier to promise than to effect. A man who promised his fiancée he would be more thoughtful about special occasions tried to make up for his lack of sentiment by giving her expensive presents. He could not understand why she was disappointed when he gave her a gold bracelet on her birthday but scheduled a business trip that kept him out of town that day. When "too much" has been agreed to—and this man's promise to change a basically entrenched attitude *was* too much—it's wise to renegotiate.

There are times when it is not possible to renegotiate, and when other options for dealing with disappointment must be followed. Here is a woman (we'll call her Mary) whose partner evidently did promise "too much" without realizing it at the time:

> *Mary:* I am thirty-one, and when I got married eight years ago my husband and I agreed I would keep working until he finished law school, and then we'd buy a house and start a family. But my husband has since changed his mind about wanting children. I don't know what to do. Is there any good way for me to handle this kind of disappointment?

> *Counselor:* Your first option is to wait and hope your husband will change his mind. Use the waiting period to try to find out why he resists having a child, what his real objections are. Perhaps he fears competition from the child for your love. Perhaps he worries about the responsibility of being a parent. Perhaps he thinks it is wrong to bring a child into a world threatened by nuclear destruction.

> A second option is to reexamine your own motives. Do you really want a baby, or do you just want to hold your husband to his promise? Are you sure you wouldn't regret giving up a life-style you've become accustomed to —with personal freedom, time for your own interests, money for your own wants? You may come to see merit in your present way of life. If you cannot change how *he* feels, you may find that you can change the way *you* feel. Finally, if having a baby is that important to you,

and if *not* having one is that important to your husband, the two of you may have to decide whether or not you want to stay married.

When disappointment strikes it is futile to nurse the hurt. Partners who cannot forget or forgive usually grow increasingly bitter. The worst thing this wife could have done was to give in unwillingly to her husband's wishes. Almost certainly her rancor would have corroded their life together.

To be open to new satisfactions we must bury old disappointments. Nor does it make sense to deny disappointments. That simply cuts us off from any awareness of the real cause of our distress. If we trust the ones we love to do what they reasonably can do to meet our realistic and legitimate expectations, and if we can be as open as possible about our needs and desires, we are far less likely to be disappointed by our partners, or by ourselves. We can make disappointment work for instead of against us if it leads us to explore what our relationships really offer.

Jealousy: When the Green-eyed Monster Sees Red

Imagine, for the moment, that you are at a buffet dinner party. You and your intimate companion (mate, lover, live-together, it makes no difference) have been chatting with old friends and meeting new acquaintances. You wander off in your separate ways for a while, and then you spot him (or her) at the other side of the room talking animatedly with an attractive person of the opposite sex. They smile at each other. As you watch, he (let's settle on the male pronoun) jumps up to replenish her plate. You can't recall when he last was so attentive to you. Then he reaches into his pocket, searches out a pencil and, on the inside of a matchbook cover, writes something. What else can it be, you think with a sinking in the pit of your stomach, but her phone number? Suddenly you feel the stirrings of anger, anxiety, wounded pride, a thrill of fear—that combination of emotions to which we give the name of jealousy.

Jealousy . . . the very word seems out of fashion. Many sociologists and counselors proclaim that jealousy—and the conflicts it provokes—is dead. How can emotional possessiveness exist in a time when relationships are free, open, and equal? they ask. As arguments for their position, the experts cite the changes that have realigned the male-female axis: woman's new right to sexual freedom; married and live-together partners who, theoretically at least, give each other *carte blanche* to have other close relationships; the growing acceptance of cross-sex friendships. "Jealousy in the traditional sense," concluded the eminent sociologist Dr. Jessie Bernard not long ago, "is hardly salient at all today."

But counselors report that more and more people are seeking help to deal with conflicts that grow out of jealous feelings. Some of the very sex-role changes that were supposed to have dealt jealousy a death-blow are in fact the generators of jealousy. The woman who once wondered what her man might be up to with his secretary when he worked late at the office, or who wondered what he did at out-of-town conventions when the business sessions ended, is now herself working late at the office or making business trips. Not a few men are now wondering what kind of relationships their women may be having with male colleagues. (And it's realistic for some men to wonder. While the total number of women who have extramarital affairs is rising, surveys show that working wives are sexually unfaithful at a rate double that of non-working wives.) Indeed, as we pointed out in talking about live-together couples, the very fact that one is no longer supposed to feel jealous—that a person may actually feel guilty about being jealous—makes it all the harder to cope.

Most of us find it extremely difficult to accept the idea of emotional (much less sexual) intimacy between the one we love and someone else. If we read it as a hostile act—rejection or abandonment—we are pained and angry. To believe that the person we are closest to is equally close to another arouses deep anxieties: "What if she leaves me?" . . . "Maybe I'm not woman enough for him?" . . . "What does *he* have that I don't?"

One problem with jealousy is that it embodies such a wide range of emotions and situations. It can be totally irrational, unrealistic, almost a form of paranoia. Or it can be a valid, normal response to an actual threat to a love relationship. For most couples jealousy falls between these extremes. It is best defined, perhaps, as suspicion or resentment of someone (or some condition —a demanding job, a consuming hobby) that looms as a rival for a loved one's time and affection.

There are a few women and men who see a "reasonable" amount of jealousy as a sign of love. Sherry, a twenty-five-year-old teacher, summed up this attitude when she told us she would be disappointed if her man didn't act a bit jealous occasionally: "It's a compliment to know that he acts as though I'm still attractive to other men. It means he isn't just taking me for granted. And it's certainly good for my morale!"

Of course, the key word in Sherry's comment is "acts." Playing at sexual jealousy may be harmless, even stimulating, as long as both persons know that it is a game—and as long as neither sets out deliberately to provoke the other. But it can be a risky game if the partners aren't communicating their motives clearly:

> Can you explain why my fiancé gets so upset when I flirt with other men [a young woman asks]? It's all done right in front of him, so I'm not hiding anything. And he knows I don't mean it. It just makes me feel good to know I can still get men interested in me.

"Are you *sure* your fiancé 'knows' what your flirtations mean or do not mean?" we asked this woman. He may have quite a different view of her behavior. She intends it to be harmless, ego-boosting flirting; he may think her intentions less innocent. He may believe this woman is really looking for sexual excitement or involvement. He may fear the flirtation will lead to a new relationship that will end the one they have. Or he may just be embarrassed by her actions. Since only he knows the answers, it is important for this woman to ask, directly, why her flirting bothers him. We also suggested that the woman examine more closely her own motives; she may be flirting out of spite or repressed anger.

At the other extreme, we knew a woman who was quite upset because *her* man never seemed to be jealous even when she went out of her way to provoke that reaction. "Isn't it normal to be a teeny-weeny bit jealous of the person you love?" she asked. The answer is: No. It does not necessarily follow that where there is love there must always be some degree of jealousy. This woman was confusing love with possessiveness; she wanted to feel "owned" by her man. What kind of a person *needs* a partner's jealousy to reassure herself, or himself, of being loved? The answer frequently is: a person who is emotionally insecure.

Jealousy can be a powerful manipulative tool. In one psychological study a group of women and men were asked why they intentionally provoked their partners to jealousy. Forty percent said they wanted to test the relationship; 30 percent felt it would make the partner more attentive; 10 percent wanted revenge for some real or fancied offense.

Almost everyone experiences jealousy's pangs at some time or other. "I can't stand it when she tells me about the affairs she had before we were together," a man says. Or, "I wish I understood his work better," says a wife. "He has more in common with the women in his office than he has with me." A young woman feels jealous when she meets her fiancé's old friends: "I don't know them well enough to join in when they talk about old times. I feel like an interloper, and I feel dumb!"

A few people do not accept the cliché of jealousy as an inevitably negative reaction to an emotional conflict. "I try to examine my jealous feelings in a realistic way," one young woman said thoughtfully. "Then sometimes I can find out what the feelings are trying to tell me." Indeed, if you can control the fury and self-pity long enough to ask, "Why am I jealous?" it is possible to turn the feeling to constructive use.

Jealousy is far more often aroused by inner doubts than by outside dangers. And it can best be dealt with by concentrating on making a relationship grow from the inside rather than on defending it from real or fancied external threats. If jealousy goes unquestioned, it can become a source of trouble; if it is analyzed rationally, it can become a source of growth. If you can examine jealous feelings the latter way, you can learn what they are trying to tell you.

Basically, jealousy stems most often from a gnawing sense (rightly or wrongly felt) of personal inadequacy; a lack of self-esteem. To convert jealousy from a negative to a potentially positive reaction requires that we stop concentrating on what the other person is doing. "It requires," says psychoanalyst Dr. Rollo May, "turning one's attention to oneself and asking 'why is my self-esteem low in the first place?' I quite understand that this question may be difficult to answer. But at least it turns your concern to an area you can do something about." The following letter we received recently, and our reply, illustrates how this approach can work:

My bride (we've only been married a year) is an accountant who travels with male colleagues to audit the books of out-of-town clients. They are on the road two weeks at a stretch, staying at the same motel, and eating their meals together. My wife says it is "all business" and I believe her. But I can't stop imagining that she might be sleeping with one of these men, or even falling in love with him. Why do I feel this way when I *know* I can trust her?

Anything that disturbs a person's sense of stability and certainty in an intimate relationship—especially one of such short duration—can be seen as a threat to it [we replied]. Women whose husbands make frequent business trips have been worrying about this sort of thing for years. Now husbands are in the same boat. There are several possible reasons for your feelings. In a relationship as solidly trusting as you imply yours is, jealousy is often due to a sense of abandonment. You may be reacting to a childhood experience when you felt deserted or rejected by your parents. Or perhaps to an earlier love affair when you actually were thrown over for another man. You may simply need more reassurance from your wife that she loves and misses you.

Then again your jealousy may spring from loneliness, particularly when you envision your wife having a pleasant time with companions. If your wife's out-of-town trips inconvenience you, you may be more angry than jealous; anger can also trigger the kind of fantasies you're having. Another possibility is that you are attributing to your wife things you imagine *you* might be tempted to do if you were in her place. It seems to us you may be letting your feelings of self-pity or loneliness lead you into unwarranted jealousy. Get busy and fill the time your wife is away from you with activities that will make you happier with yourself.

Some women and men are jealous of their partners' time. One woman grew jealous of her husband's regular Sunday afternoon tennis match:

> *She:* Jerry has been in the habit of playing with his bachelor friends. I don't want to ask him to give up his game, but isn't it accepted that once you're married you spend Sundays with your wife?

> *He:* I work all week and go to business college at night. Is it also accepted that just because you're married you give up the one thing that's fun and relaxing? How can she be jealous of two hours?

Unrealistic? Of course. But real enough to the women and men caught in this situation. A twenty-seven-year-old woman we'll call Ann Watkins tells how jealousy of her husband's work almost broke up their marriage. Bill Watkins, a chemical engineer in a plastics factory, was put in charge of a special experimental project only a few weeks after he and his wife had moved into a new home in a rural community. Soon he was working late several nights a week, and many Saturdays as well.

"I worried about his health at first," Ann recalls, "but he thrived on the schedule. I was the only one who suffered, I felt. There I was, stuck in a country town with nothing to do. And as I saw it, Bill didn't even want to come home to spend the evenings with me. I was jealous—he had something interesting in his life and I didn't."

Ann expressed her jealousy in small, resentful gestures—she stopped bothering to keep dinner warm; she took no pains to look nice; she either went to bed before Bill came home or sat up only to argue with him. "Things reached the point where it was either break up or get help," she said, "and we weren't prepared to break up."

They went to a marriage counselor who after two sessions challenged Ann with some sharp questions: Did she make an honest effort to understand the job pressures on her husband? Had she ever really believed that he worked late because he had to? Did she try to develop any interests or resources of her own, rather than expecting her husband to provide the stimulation in her life?

"The answers—when I was able to face them—were unpleasantly revealing," Ann admits. It turned out that Bill's special project—running a series of several hundred complicated tests on synthetic compounds—was not all that fascinating to him. "It's donkeywork," Bill said. "It was given to me because I'm the junior man on the staff. But if I finish it on schedule and come up with some useful findings, I'll probably get a raise and a promotion. I know Ann would like that." And Ann came to see that part of her jealousy of Bill's involvement with his work was actually discontent with herself and her dependency on others.

Psychologist Gregory White, who has done considerable research on jealousy, found several sex differences in the way women and men respond to the emotion. White discovered, for instance, that women tend to become depressed and immobilized by jealousy; men tend to become angry, sexually aggressive, or even physically abusive. Another researcher, Professor Bram Buunk of the University of Nijmegen, in the Netherlands, found that women and men favor different styles of dealing with jealousy, especially when it has a sexual element.

Buunk asked couples (where one or the other spouse had had an extramarital affair) how they coped with the discovery of the partner's unfaithfulness. He offered three choices: avoiding the issue; rationalizing the situation; or having a frank talk with the spouse about it. Most said they discussed the matter with their partners to try to find out why the infidelity occurred. About half of the group sought to "reappraise" the circumstances—that is, to find a valid reason for the incident and thus dismiss their jealousy as unreasonable. One out of five persons cut themselves off from the "guilty" partner, experienced a desire for revenge, and had feelings of self-pity and self-doubt.

More women than men turned to reappraisal and avoidance as coping techniques. Whether the difference between the way women and men handle jealousy will melt away with the changes in sex roles remains to be seen. We tend to believe that as women increase their resources and achieve more equality with men in their personal lives, they may use avoidance less while men may come to use reappraisal more.

Defusing the Most Painful Conflict—Infidelity

In an earlier section we discussed the new meaning that women and men are giving to the concept of sexual fidelity, and explored some of the values that support it. However, there are those who say that if an act of infidelity enables a couple to confront and deal with a sexual problem between themselves, the relationship may be improved rather than damaged. Not infrequently infidelity results from one partner's lack of interest in sex or a difference in the partners' needs for physical signs of affection. Sometimes infidelity is sparked by an identity crisis, a man's need to reassert his virility, a woman's need to reassert her sexual attractiveness. In such cases, some therapists hold, there is usually no intent to threaten the relationship—only to feel better about oneself.

But whether or not the average woman or man can maintain a healthy intimate relationship with one person at the same time as an extra-curricular sexual liaison with another, one thing is certain: A partner's unfaithfulness can be one of the most emotionally painful experiences we can suffer. It hurts to know we have been sexually deceived by the person we love. That is true despite the fact that we live in sexually liberated times; despite the fact the changing role of women is gradually replacing the old double sexual standard with a single one. And it is that hurt that prompts the classic questions: *"Who is she/he?"* . . . *"How often did it happen?"* . . . *"Is he/she better than I am?"* Some people seem to enjoy probing the wound. For example:

My wife found out I was having an affair. I stopped seeing the other woman, and my wife said she forgave me. But now she insists on knowing all the details—how we met, what we said, what we did. My wife says she won't be able to forget the incident until she knows all there is to know. But why would she *want* to know these things? And should I tell her?

This wife may believe that once she knows all that happened, she will be able to come to terms with it, to "close it out" in her mind, to forget as well as to forgive. (The latter is often easier to do.) But total frankness in these situations seldom has that result. Indeed, it may make it harder for her to forget the incident if she has those painful images to deal with. It is more likely that this wife is, without being aware of it, "injustice collecting." But that only keeps the emotional wounds open. The therapist's advice to the husband, in this case, was to talk to his wife about *why* he had an affair:

> It may help each of you to learn what was lacking in your own relationship, what made you vulnerable to infidelity. If your wife continues to press for details, it might be sensible for you both to seek therapy jointly, so she can work through her angry feelings. Meanwhile, it is important to reassure your wife of your love until she can feel emotionally secure again.

Probing for details is pointless precisely because infidelity has less to do with the affair itself, or with the third person involved, than it does with the conflict between the original partners. "It used to be common to view an unfaithful spouse as someone who couldn't make a lasting commitment," sex therapist Dr. Helen Kaplan has said. "But now we see people unfaithful in one kind of marital situation who are perfectly capable of fidelity should they remarry."

In times past a woman, particularly, tended to swallow hurt feelings. She needed her partner's financial support; divorce was not socially acceptable; she submitted to the double standard that permitted "boys to be boys." But times have changed. Today's woman, with her new social and economic alternatives, is far more willing to confront her unfaithful partner. And confront she does, for even in an era of liberated relationships there are still few women who can easily accept a partner's sexual disloyalty. Men, who have been said to have larger but more fragile egos, are even less likely to tolerate that betrayal. Yet if none of us could forgive a partner's unfaithfulness, there would be a lot more divorces than there are. The fact is that if infidelity is not blatant or chronic, most couples manage to defuse the conflict eventually, and to survive.

What enables one couple to survive an affair while another is shattered by it? In some instances, the offended partner may deliberately turn a blind eye to the facts. Four out of five persons who say they have had an affair believe their spouses do not know about it. But sometimes the offending partner's guilt is such that he or she *wants* the other person to know about it. The motives for revealing one's infidelity can be complex, as this man's question and the counselor's reply show:

> I've had several affairs my wife does not know about. Our marriage is good, our sex life satisfying, but I occasionally want the variety of a different partner. Yet I dislike the idea of keeping secrets from my wife. On the other hand I'm not sure how she would react if I told her. Should I tell her, or leave well enough alone?
>
> *ML:* "There's another question you need to ask. That is whether what appears to be a noble gesture on your part is in fact simply a way to rid yourself of the burdens of secrecy and guilt. Self-disclosure is preferable to having your wife find out about your affairs some other way. But in all likelihood you will merely be trading one kind of emotional discomfort for another—assuming, that is, that she reacts with the usual feelings of hurt, anger and loss of trust.
>
> If you really want an honest relationship with your wife, rather than just confessing your infidelities, you might consider stopping these affairs for now. Instead, talk to her about your ideas and feelings concerning sexual exclusivity—or the lack of it—in marriage. You may find they upset her greatly. Or you may find she'd like to have the same freedom you've already taken. Will you be able to handle it if she does?
>
> In any event, you can't drop all this on her suddenly and expect her to absorb it without some distress. Making such emotional adjustments often takes years, and you may find that the price you have to pay for sexual variety and excitement just isn't worth it.

Chances are that some "unknowing" partners *are* aware of—or at least suspect—what's happening. They choose, however, to ignore it for reasons of their own. They accommodate to the situation. For example, a woman or man who fears being alone; who has few emotional or economic resources; who will put up with anything "for the sake of the children"; or who is so committed to the façade of the relationship that *nothing* is worth breaking it up for—such a person often is afraid to provoke a confrontation. But it is open to question whether a relationship that survives an affair for any of those reasons is fundamentally healthy or mutually rewarding.

On the other hand, there are women and men who are able to deal more constructively with the emotional fallout of an affair. Instead of concentrating on their own feelings of pain and betrayal, they try to find out: "Why did this happen?" The key to what may occur next lies in one partner's ability to answer that question honestly and the other's willingness to understand and accept the answer.

True, reasons for infidelity are not usually clear-cut or easy to explain. But we do know that most often it is unplanned, even casual; most affairs are short-lived. Physical unfaithfulness is frequently the result of curiosity combined with opportunity. Infidelity for these reasons usually has little or nothing to do with feelings about one's partner. Indeed, relatively few affairs are the result of deep emotional dissatisfaction with one's partner. Most affairs do *not* develop into long-term emotional (as well as physical) involvements. When they do, of course, they are truly threatening and difficult to deal with.

Ultimately, whether a couple can survive an affair depends largely on two factors. First, survival depends on how a person interprets the reasons for a partner's infidelity. Some women and men say that reasons do not matter: "I do not care why he cheated on me; the fact is he did cheat, and if he could do that he does not really care about me." Some persons can accept certain reasons (loneliness, a momentary attraction) but not other reasons. And some persons cannot understand a partner's reasons because the couple are operating under incompatible sets of rules —as the woman in this case revealed:

I have been living with a man for nearly two years, and we plan to marry in two months. I haven't slept with anyone else during that time, and it infuriated me to learn that he's had sex with another woman while away on a business trip. When I accused him of infidelity, he said there was no such thing as being "unfaithful" so long as we aren't married. What do you think of his attitude?

ML: Your view, obviously, is that since the two of you have had a long-term intimate relationship and plan to make it permanent, you are as good as married and should accept the obligations that go with it, whether the relationship is formalized or not. His view, evidently, is that until a wedding ceremony takes place he is still single and free to live by the rules—or lack of them—for the unmarried. If you haven't already talked with each other about your differing definitions of fidelity, it is something you should do right away.

It is also possible that your demand for sexual exclusivity makes your friend feel "trapped." By sleeping with other women, he is in effect saying, both to you and to himself, "See, I'm still free, I'm not really locked in yet, I still have choices." But if this is so, and your friend is not willing or able to commit himself fully to you until he is actually standing at the altar and saying "I do," it raises the question of whether there is any commitment in his mind and heart at all.

The second survival factor is how well a couple can reestablish trust (a topic we will be exploring in detail in the next section). For the offending partner this is often a slow, painful, but vital process. And the hurt partner must learn to view the infidelity as an isolated act (if that indeed is what it was) that need not automatically contaminate their total relationship. Easy to say, of course, but hard to do. It requires probing into one's real feelings.

Not long ago a couple, wed eight years, came for counseling after the husband discovered his wife was having an affair with a man at her office. When the husband issued an ultimatum— "End the relationship or I'll file for divorce!"—the woman did break off with her lover. "So," the husband said, "I forgave her. But now she hardly talks to me and we almost never have sex."

The therapist pointed out all the unanswered questions, all the unknowns in this marital equation: Did the man really forgive his wife, or is he still punishing her without realizing it? Is she frozen into herself by guilt? Does she secretly resent having yielded to the ultimatum? What problems in the marriage may there be that first led the woman into her infidelity? What is missing in the marriage? Shouldn't both partners take the situation as an opportunity to examine their ideas of what their relationship should be like, and perhaps redefine the ground rules for it?

> I've recently found out that some of the men in our circle of friends are having affairs [a young woman says]. The man I love assures me he would never do such a thing. Can I be sure of that?

Nobody can give anyone a guarantee that a partner will never, never be unfaithful. But since most of us are reluctant to admit that possibility, we seldom take the logical step of asking: "How can I guard against my partner's being unfaithful?" There *are* practical safeguards against infidelity and the conflicts that it brings—precautions that a couple can jointly take.

A key factor in building a climate conducive to faithfulness is, as we have said, for each person to know what causes a woman or man to seek sex outside their relationship. Beyond the obvious reasons—insufficient sex, sexual boredom, low self-esteem, middle-age crises, and so on—are the not so obvious ones: a need for sympathy or an attentive ear, or for someone who can share a community of interests. One of the best safeguards against infidelity, therefore, is for a couple to be able to turn to each other for emotional support and sustenance.

Another safeguard is for both partners to realize that the struggle to remain faithful is harder for some persons than for others. Some women and men may have greater opportunities for outside liaisons, or a lower threshold of guilt, or a more demanding sexual drive. For such persons the primary relationship must offer and provide extra rewards. An insightful person who senses that his or her companion may be tempted to infidelity will at that juncture draw the other person closer by offering acceptance and support, rather than pushing him or her farther away with threats or demands.

Here are some additional suggestions for couples who want to use preventive techniques to protect their relationship:

• Make it clear that you consider fidelity a significant value. These are times when the influences *for* having an affair are so strong that some people are ashamed to admit they have *not* had one. A businessman reports that when one of five colleagues he was lunching with asked how many in the group were faithful, no one raised a hand. "Not even me," he said, "and I've *never* strayed. But under the circumstances I was embarrassed to admit it." In such a climate it is important to assert your feelings about the value of fidelity.

• Recognize any special circumstances in which a partner may be especially susceptible to the idea of an affair, and make an extra effort to counteract them.

• Make sure you and your partner are meeting each other's psychological and physical needs well enough to ward off temptation. No relationship can meet all the needs each person may have. But too often we do not express these needs clearly, or our partners lack the emotional antennae to be aware of them. Psychologist Robert Seidenberg tells of a man who scandalized his community by carrying on a seemingly intense affair almost openly. No one in town would believe that he and the other woman spent their time reading and discussing poetry. "The man's infidelity to his wife was a verbal one," writes Dr. Seidenberg. "He chose to *talk* to another woman." That does not mean partners need to share all interests, or exclude close relationships with all other women and men. If one person has certain non-sexual needs or interests the other cannot meet, an effective way to guard against potential infidelity is to give him or her the freedom to form outside friendships based on shared interests.

• Be alert for the early warning signals of a potential affair. It's possible to detect a person's growing interest in another woman or man before sexual or emotional involvement occurs. The signals can be a sudden concern with appearance, unwarranted irritability, unexplained absences, a change in routine. But remember that seemingly suspect actions can be quite innocent. Be realistic, not paranoid.

• Try to avoid friends and acquaintances who treat infidelity lightly. Their attitude can be contagious.

• Reexamine your relationship periodically to reinforce what is good and repair any weak spots.

• Realize your own worth and make sure your partner is aware of it too. There is nothing wrong with saying, "What we have together is too good to destroy," or "I think you'd be foolish to risk losing me." Some people cannot make such statements because they lack the self-esteem to believe it themselves. Yet don't most of us want to share our lives with a partner who is emotionally secure, and acts that way?

Troubles Out of the Past

"Four things do not come back," wrote the poet Omar Khayyám. "They are the spoken word, the sped arrow, the lost opportunity, and the past life." There can be little doubt about the first three, but where relationships are concerned the past is often a recurrent and unwelcome intruder. Former friends, past lovers, ex-mates, old hurts, long-established but now unserviceable habits and attitudes—all can continue to insinuate themselves into the present, carrying with them the potential for conflict.

Many women and men have difficulty in divorcing themselves emotionally from past events. Therapists use terms such as "replaying old tapes" or "battling with ghosts" to describe the way some of us permit—or even encourage—the past to intrude on and affect our current relationships. It would be one thing if we retained just the pleasant memories. But many times what stays with us most vividly are the words, actions, and feelings that remind us of old guilts, regrets, moments of bitterness. Nor does there seem to be any statute of limitations. A woman we know continues to nurse a grievance against her husband because he went off on a business trip when their infant son was ill—thirty-eight years ago!

But though the past is a very real aspect of the present, that does not mean we have to burden ourselves with its accumulated baggage forever. Rather, we need to learn how to integrate the past into our current lives—to deal once and for all with the unfinished emotional business it represents. That is, of course, easier said than done.

Perhaps the most pervasive intrusion from the past consists of the remnants and relics of our growing-up experiences—the imprint of one's "family of origin" that we talked about earlier in discussing the influence of "outsiders." In addition to idealized concepts of the way male-female relationships should work, there are also usually leftover feelings about "right" and "wrong" attitudes, "proper" and "improper" behavior. Such rules characterize the way we tend to feel about roles in a relationship: what a woman or man is expected to do, or "ought" to do. We see this kind of intrusion from the past at work in ongoing tensions over rigidly held values:

> My husband objects to every plan I make and every penny I spend for Christmas. He says the holiday is nothing but a commercial rip-off. But I like to make a big thing of the season, and we can afford it.

Counselors are confronted with this sort of conflict quite frequently. Usually it is because the Scrooge-like partner had unpleasant experiences with Christmas or similar holidays early in life. In this specific case the man was raised in a home where money was scarce and seldom spent for pleasure or "frills." Although reasonably well-off now, he still carries in his unconscious the fear that financial hardship may strike again, and the belief that there are more important ways to spend money. "Arguing with the man is not going to resolve this conflict," we told his wife. "Instead, help him to bring out and recognize the real reasons for his attitude."

How can you deal constructively with the ghosts of the past? By learning to put them in a workable perspective. One way to accomplish that is by *accepting* the past—accepting all the events that cannot be changed and whose only tie to the present is in the mind of the person obsessed with them. Many disappointments and losses are handled in this way, almost without our being aware of it. The death of a loved one, for instance, leaves a huge gap; yet most of us, with time, come to accept the reality of the event—and go on from there to work gradually through our grief and adjust to our loss. What has happened has happened, and to belabor what might have been or to anguish

over what cannot possibly be changed is purposeless. At some point it is necessary to accept reality and move ahead, clearing the way for the positive aspects of the present.

In a somewhat similar way we can learn to live with past indiscretions in a partner's life, even though they have hurt greatly at the time:

> Several years ago my wife left me for another man. She intended to divorce me and marry him, but changed her mind and asked me to take her back. Because I still loved her, I did. But for a long time I was so hurt and angry at what she had done that I let that one incident dominate my life and our marriage. I keep dredging it up, using it to make her suffer. Finally, I realized I was making myself suffer too—and probably creating a situation where she would decide to leave me again. Eventually I was able, not to forget, but to forgive. I've learned there is a big difference between what a person thinks he or she can live with and what he or she can actually live with.

Some past events, however, continue to be an ongoing reality in the present whether you like it or not. It often surprises young women and men—married or otherwise intimately linked—when friends from the days before they knew each other come to be seen by one partner or the other as an "intrusion" on the couple's relationship. "I see no reason to keep putting up with my fiancé's old buddies," a woman says. "They're always calling him to go bowling or fishing. If he declines for my sake, he feels I've pressured him. And if he leaves me alone to go with his friends, he feels guilty. It's a no-win situation for me. Why can't his old pals realize he has a new life now, and leave him—and us—alone?"

This is not to say that couples do not or should not try to involve each other with friends who predate the new relationship, or try to convince each other of these friends' sterling qualities. But most people find this seldom works out. When a new partner is not attracted to an old friend, some couples adapt by arranging for each to see friends from the past separately—at lunch, or for an after-work drink, or any time when the meeting will not in-

volve both partners. Others, assuming that all social activities must be shared as a couple, develop a more elaborate technique for dealing with a partner's disliked friends. "First, we listed each other's friends we couldn't stand," a woman told us. "Then we listed the ones we didn't like but could tolerate. The first group we arranged to see singly. The second group we see together, but only once in a great while."

Millions of women and men in second marriages have to confront a number of intangible intrusions from the past: memories of the old love; comparisons (spoken or unspoken) of the new spouse with the previous one; a host of free-floating and unresolved regrets, resentments, and love-hate ambivalences that drain energy from the second marriage. There are also tangible intrusions—realities rather than "ghosts." For instance, integrating old friends into a remarriage can be a source of conflict since they often are friends of the ex-spouse as well. Some of these friends may still be on good terms with both divorced partners. This can lead to conflict with the new spouse. Here is what a recently wed woman said of friends inherited from her husband's previous marriage:

> I hate it when I know that people are also friends of my husband's ex-wife. Sometimes they let something slip into the conversation about her. Or they forget and start to reminisce about old times. One man even called me by her name once. I sometimes wonder if they are comparing me to her. I'm afraid I might say the wrong thing and they'll let it slip when they're with her just as they get careless around me.

Former spouses themselves become (sometimes deliberately) irritants to the new relationship. "When one remarries," a woman says, "one is never alone with the new mate." She reports how her ex-husband always manages to pick a fight or drop a sarcastic remark when he comes to claim their children for his visitation weekend. "I tell myself I won't let him upset me, but after he leaves I'm a nervous wreck. To make matters worse, my present husband is annoyed with me for reacting this way." Of course it's

natural to be irritated by a former partner's hostile behavior. But
to be a "nervous wreck"? It is possible this woman is unconsciously
perpetuating the old relationship, keeping up some sort of perverse
emotional contact just as her ex is evidently doing. She and he
have "unfinished business" and may need professional help to
close out the emotional books.

For some remarried women and men, stepchildren are the
intruders from the past. They are the physical reminder of a
partner's emotional and sexual involvement with the former mate.
And they are often seen as interlopers who deprive the stepparent
of his or her new love's time, attention, and affection. The great
majority of remarried persons seem able to absorb these symbols
of a past relationship into the new family framework. They
manage to assimilate stepchildren into their lives, neither resenting
them nor wholly accepting them. By simply going along with a
situation they *knew* they were getting into, they make the best
of conditions as they now exist. Therapists refer to such families
as "blended." They have constructively incorporated the past into
their present, much as the separate ingredients of a recipe are
merged into a new whole.

It isn't too surprising when past hurts or fallout from earlier
relationships create difficulties in the present. To some extent we
are prepared for this to happen, and may even have contingency
plans for dealing with it. But every once in a while the past rises
up in strange and convoluted ways to affect our current relationships. One of the most unusual cases we have had to counsel
was that of a man, thirty-five, a research chemist, who was almost
literally confronted with a "ghost intruder." This is the story he
told:

> Before my wife and I were married she was deeply in
> love with another man. He contracted leukemia and
> died shortly before they were to be married. During the
> man's illness my wife grew very close to his parents, and
> after his death they treated her like a daughter. My
> problem is that though all this happened four years ago,
> my wife still calls and visits this older couple almost
> every week. They somehow think of our son as "their

grandchild," and he sees them as much as he does my own parents. Frankly, the whole thing is creepy, and most uncomfortable for me. My wife says she is fond of the old couple, doesn't want to hurt them, and I understand that. But I also think it is time she let go of the past.

This man's discomfort was certainly understandable. What man (or woman) would want to have a marriage haunted by the idealized memory, or image, of a partner's former but now deceased lover? Nevertheless, this husband had to consider the feelings of four other persons besides his own.

If you feel [the therapist said] that your wife's loyalty to an old love interferes with or diminishes her feelings for you, you must share this concern with her frankly. She may not realize how much the situation upsets you. If she is keeping the other man's memory alive out of compassion for his parents, discussing this with you may help your wife see the extent to which she has gone to preserve their feelings.

Are the parents unconsciously trying to deny their son's death by keeping alive a link with his life through your son? If so, it might be kinder for your wife to put their relationship with the boy in a realistic perspective now, to prevent future pain. On the other hand, to ask your wife to cut off all contact with the older couple would be unfair; each has been a meaningful part of the other's life for a long while.

Since you are the person most uncomfortable about all this, it seems reasonable to ask you to consider what kind of relationship among the older couple, your wife, and your son you *could* accept. Perhaps visits and phone calls could be curtailed gradually. If you told the older couple how you feel about the situation, they might be able to understand and go along with whatever changes you had in mind.

Whichever course we choose for dealing with intrusions from the past and defusing their potential for conflict—whether we accept or deny them, assimilate or distort them, adapt to them or use them as self-punishment—the advice of the poet Longfellow can hardly be bettered: "Look not mournfully into the past . . . but wisely improve the present."

7—MAKING A RELATIONSHIP GROW

If there were illustrations in this book, the artist might have decorated the heading of this section with, say, a drawing of two plants, their tendrils lovingly entwined, receiving regular rations of nourishment and care so they would thrive and grow. While a relationship is scarcely analogous to vegetation, it does require much the same attention. In one sense, when a woman and man form a union, whether it be as friends, lovers, or spouses, their relationship faces the formidable challenge that nature puts to all things—grow or perish. In its most elementary use, the word "growth" denotes physical development and changing dimensions. We measure growth by the height of a cornstalk, the leafing of a tree, the division of cells. But when we speak of the growth of a relationship another meaning is implied. Development and change take on qualitative as well as quantitative aspects. For at stake is nothing less than a couple's capacity for sharing emotional intimacy, and for creating the character of that intimacy.

Few women and men today are willing to settle for the routine, devitalized, and often sterile patterns of living that so often characterized relationships in earlier times. If there was growth, then it was often of an uneven sort. Women who worked to put their men through college, for example, sometimes had to watch helplessly as those men moved ahead—and moved away. Women today, busily growing in terms of their own educations and careers, often grow beyond men who cannot be open to such positive changes in a relationship. But along with a real yearning for shared growth there is confusion as to how to go about achieving it. Relationships, unlike Topsy, do not "jes' grow." They must be nurtured. Change must be encouraged. Risks must be taken. There must be a common definition of goals. There must be the ability to meet a crisis head on, survive it, and learn from it. There must be a willingness to explore new ideas and to let go of old or unworkable ones.

Many of the most interesting and mutually productive partnerships we know have been able to do these things—even under most unusual circumstances. For instance, a couple who have been together for nine years spend only half of each year together. The man (call him Martin) is an importer who must make frequent trips, each of several months' duration, to the Far East. At first his wife (call her Geri) traveled with him, "so I know what it's like where he is, and I know the trip is exhausting and often boring." Both agree that the long separations, which other couples might find damaging to their relationships, make Martin and Geri's all the more rewarding.

"When Martin is away he becomes more thoughtful of me," Geri says. "He writes long letters that in many ways help me understand him better. To some extent, of course, I wage a constant campaign against loneliness; but each time I am alone I find I am more self-reliant. This makes me feel better about myself, makes me a better woman for Martin to be with when he comes home."

As for Martin: "Though we are separated physically by thousands of miles, emotionally we feel even closer. I spend a good deal of time *thinking* about our relationship, planning its possible future shapes. Geri does the same. When we are together we have so many ideas to exchange. We are fresh to and for each other—not only physically, but intellectually and emotionally as well."

Another couple we know, faced with an almost diametrically opposite set of circumstances, took advantage of the avenues that were open to them to grow together. The woman, stricken with polio only a month before the first Salk vaccine was made available, was to be restricted for the rest of her life to a "rocking" bed, an electric wheelchair, and an assortment of life-preserving apparatuses. Yet by learning to manage her disability with dignity and grace, and by firmly eschewing self-pity in favor of a sincere interest in those around her, she and her husband built one of the most fulfilling and, yes, happy, relationships we have ever been privileged to share in.

Some women and men look for miracles; one day, they say, I'll wake up and things will be better. Others look for a change of scene to produce the same result. But we do not leave our relationship problems behind by moving to a new town, going on vacation, buying a fancier home. The problems go right along with us. Still others opt for unilateral growth. A woman writes:

> I'm thinking of leaving my husband because I feel confined, overpowered. Is it so terrible to want to be out of a marriage that gives me—and him, too, I believe—nothing to look forward to?

No, it isn't terrible. But it might be a case of foolish overkill. There are so many things this woman, this couple, might do *within* the relationship that could give each partner more satisfaction, more of a sense of self. No one can stop a person (except that person) from growing as an individual. Similarly, no one can stop a couple (except the couple themselves) from growing together as equal partners—surely a more rewarding form of growth.

In this section we will be talking about many of the qualities that are essential to that man-woman adventure: mutual trust; the ability to give and to receive emotional support; the tolerance to accept change in one's partner, and the skills to deal with it; the strength to surmount crises; the desire to keep sexual passion alive; the courage to take growth-enhancing risks.

A tall order, you say? True. But there have been few times in history when women and men have needed as much emotional strength and intellectual creativity as they need today to make personal relationships grow. Identities are undergoing change; roles are changing; horizons are expanding. All this intensifies the demands we make of ourselves, and of those we love. The goals are worthy, but the road maps for getting there are sketchy. What we do have are options—more options than ever before. They make it possible to tailor our relationships to the unique needs and desires and expectations of today's women and men. They make it possible—if we act on them wisely—for our intimate relationships to grow.

Trust: The Foundation Stone of Growth

A friend recently went on her first rock-climbing expedition. "I was terrified when the instructor tied me into a rope harness and told me to go over the edge and climb down the rock face," she recalled. "But the instructor said, 'There's nothing to be afraid of. I'll be anchoring the other end of the rope so you can't fall.' My fear disappeared once I was able to put my trust in the instructor. It formed as much of a bond between us as the rope itself."

Trust is the basic link that holds two people together, whether for the brief adventure of a rock climb or the longer one of an intimate relationship. Most women and men usually think of trust as a quality that is honored—or betrayed—in a crisis, or when the stakes are high. But trust is not something reserved for isolated dramas. It is a thread that must be woven throughout the entire fabric of a relationship. Partners trust each other in dozens of small ways each day—to be reliable, to be honest, to act in each other's best interest, to *care*. Mutual trust means counting on promises made, agreements reached, expectations shared. It is feeling secure when we give our partner the right to make decisions that affect us. It is feeling safe when we let him or her know what is going on deep inside.

To build and maintain mutual trust is an even greater challenge in the face of changing attitudes about sex and sex roles. This letter, from a young woman who has been separated from her husband for several months, is a case in point:

> We see each other frequently, and hope to work out a reconciliation—but meanwhile I have become sexually involved with another man. My husband knows I date other people, but I'm worried that he may ask if I have been unfaithful. I know he has been loyal to me during our months apart, and I don't want to lie. But, if he asks and I tell the truth, won't that destroy his trust in me and make our reconciliation impossible?

Of course the truth will hurt, and of course this woman's husband may find it hard to reestablish trust. On the other hand, nothing—not even a harsh truth—erodes trust so much as a lie. The counselor suggested a possible way out of the dilemma:

> ML: See if you can make an arrangement with your husband that, if you do reconcile, neither of you will press the issue of what the other did during the time you lived apart. You seem certain he has been faithful, but you could be as wrong about him as he is about you. He might be just as pleased as you to wipe the slate clean. But wouldn't it make sense to spend your time and energy working out your marital problems rather than carrying on an affair? By introducing another barrier to reconciliation you are merely making it more difficult to resolve matters.

Partners who do not wholly trust each other are not likely to risk reaching out for mutual growth. Mistrust makes us raise into place the shields we use to protect our emotional vulnerability. And unless both partners clearly understand what each of them means by "trust"—and it does mean different things to different people—misunderstandings can occur. "During the past few months I suspected my husband was having business troubles," a woman says. "He kept telling me everything was fine. Last week, out of the blue, he declared bankruptcy. I was shocked, but even more shocked that he did not confide in me earlier. He says he didn't want me to worry. Now I wonder if I can trust him to be honest about anything?"

Here is a clear difference of opinion about what "trust" means. The key factor in this situation would seem to be the man's *motive* for not admitting the truth. Certainly before there is any talk about "mistrust," this woman needs to know more about why her husband withheld the facts. Perhaps it was to protect her from anxiety. Maybe he thought if he could avoid bankruptcy she would never have to know about his business crisis. Still, if you withhold the truth for a partner's "own good," you must weigh that decision against the possible damage when the truth finally does come out.

When trust is or seems to be broken in one area the disappointed partner often feels, "I'll never be able to trust him (or her) again." For instance, Bob and Karen, who have lived together for five years, are on the verge of breaking up because, Karen says, Bob "never lives up to his word":

> *Karen*: I can't believe anything he tells me anymore. I get promises, but they're never fulfilled. He says he's going to get a raise or a promotion, and the next thing I know he's quit that job for another one.

> *Bob*: There you go, exaggerating again. I've had three jobs in five years, but each was better than the previous one.

> *Karen*: What about your latest promise—about asking for a leave of absence so you can finish graduate school? It's been three months, and nothing's happened.

> *Bob*: It's a busy time at the office. I have to wait for the right moment.

> *Karen* (*sarcastically*): And when will that be?

Disappointed in her expectations for Bob's career, Karen had reached the point where she no longer trusted her man—even though she admitted he was quite trustworthy in other respects. This reaction is particularly likely to occur when trust is betrayed in an emotionally significant area of the relationship. That is why it is important for couples to isolate the area in which trust has been violated from all the others in which a partner is still dependable. A relationship need not be shattered just because one part of it is broken.

Not long ago an engaged woman was upset because, while helping her fiancé move, she came across intimate letters to him from a girl both of them had known in college: "He swears the letters mean nothing, that he broke off with her when we became engaged. But I can't pass over the fact that he never told me about her." Obviously, this woman needs either to exorcise her suspicions, or to separate out this bit of the past from the essence of the couple's relationship. The counselor offered these suggestions:

> *ML*: To begin with, look at your fiancé's record for trustworthiness in other areas. If he has often been less

than honest, you may have grounds for doubting his story about the other woman. But if he has been generally truthful, chances are he is now. Secondly, ask why he did not tell you about the other relationships. Perhaps they were not as important to him as the letters imply. Perhaps he feared that if you knew about them you would be unduly hurt or angry—that you would react exactly as you have. Or, if the letters did indeed "mean nothing" to your fiancé, he may have seen no reason to discuss them. Has he asked you to tell him how intimate your earlier relationships may have been? Perhaps you have different definitions of one's right to personal keepsakes.

What seems most important in your situation are the answers to three questions: Is your fiancé basically honest? Are you convinced that he really loves you? Is he being faithful to you now, and has he said he intends to continue to be faithful in the future?

Relationships involving remarriage seem particularly susceptible to questions of trust and mistrust. "I'm in love with a divorced woman and want to marry her," a man confides, "but I know she was unfaithful in her previous marriage. She says she would never do that again, but can I really trust that? If she was unfaithful once, why not twice?"

Women and men who have been unfaithful in one kind of a marital relationship are quite capable of fidelity in another. Infidelity is not necessarily a character defect or an emotional flaw that will continue to surface. Most people who get involved in such a liaison do so because of a unique set of circumstances. For instance, this woman's previous marriage may have been filled with conflict; it might have been sexually unsatisfying for her; her infidelity might have been an impulsive act of revenge for her partner's infidelity. Whatever prompted her affair(s) may never occur again. Indeed, if she ever did think infidelity was unimportant, or justifiable, her experience may have changed her mind. The very fact that the woman told of her previous indiscretion indicates she wants to start this new relationship on a basis of total honesty. The key point is that the man to some degree mistrusts himself and his judgment. If his doubts continue, they can poison the new relationship and bring about the very things he fears. If he cannot wholeheartedly trust his fiancée, he probably should reconsider his plans to marry her.

The previous case history was an example of trust being haunted from the past; the next is an instance of mistrust shadowing the future:

> My first wife left me two years ago to marry another man. I've met a woman I care about, and she wants us to get married. But I'm afraid my past experience has scarred me too much to trust any woman again. Is it possible to get over this feeling?

Divorce often sets in motion unconscious fears about being abandoned and betrayed. Some people "protect" themselves by refusing to open up again to intimacy. One way to change this is to work on developing self-trust. The man in this case had an unhappy experience: He was hurt, but he survived it. Someone else now finds him desirable, and worth trusting. It makes little sense to guard himself so carefully against a second disappointment that he closes off the chance of a new and better relationship. Trust of another, after all, exists only to the extent that one is willing to risk something of oneself.

Once trust between partners has been broken, nothing is so difficult and delicate as rebuilding it. It's crucial, therefore, to lay a firm foundation of mutual trust and to act promptly if it seems in danger. Here are some suggestions:

• Be clear about the difference between what you want or hope for, and what you can reasonably expect. And make sure your partner *knows* what you do expect and agrees to fulfill this expectation. Otherwise, what seems to be a betrayal of trust may be merely a lack of communication.

• You are entitled to be able to rely on a partner's promise or agreement, and vice versa. But if partners promise (or are pushed to promise) *more* than they can deliver, it's wise to own up to the situation by admitting that "I promised too much, and I'm sorry I can't do what I said I would."

• To trust another person, we must be able to trust ourselves— and to act in ways that make it easy for others to trust us. If you can depend on your own inner resources—self-confidence, self-reliance—you will be less wary about opening yourself up to the vulnerability that accompanies trusting another.

The Art of Giving Emotional Support

When partners trust each other they are able to fit into place another building block of mutual growth: the exchange of emotional support. That exchange—the promise that you will "be there" when needed, that you will not only accept your partner's feelings but also help him or her to deal with them—should be implicit in an intimate relationship. It is vital to have what you are, what you think, what you feel, and what you do confirmed by the person who is closest to you. This is not to say that emotional support always implies agreeing with one's partner. Constructive criticism can be supportive in its own way. But emotional support does imply a mutual respect between partners that allows them to sanction, if not endorse, each other's thoughts and actions. This is not primarily an intellectual exercise. The operative word in "emotional support" is "emotion":

• A woman who placed her ailing seventy-six-year-old mother in a nursing home is plagued by guilt for having "abandoned" her. "My husband keeps telling me that Mother will get better care there than we could give her. I suppose that's true, but his saying so doesn't stop me from feeling bad. Logic doesn't help. If only my husband would just put his arms around me and hold me and say I didn't do anything wrong!"

• A young attorney recalls the "loneliest moment" in his life: "It was when I graduated from law school and Diane, my fiancée, wasn't there to share the thrill with me. Her sister had just had an operation and Diane felt she should be at the hospital. I said I understood, and I tried to. But I've always felt she let me down."

Almost everyone has had the experience of feeling let down emotionally by the failure of someone we love to be with us in a time of joy or to support us in a time of trouble. Sometimes we may want only the sense of physical closeness: a handclasp, an embrace. At other times we may need the psychological sustenance of a sympathetic listener, or objective advice to help us make a difficult decision, or just someone to stand by our side and comfort us. It hurts when the emotional support we seek is lacking. "You weren't there when I needed you," we say—or think. And for some people the aftereffects of that disappointment can last a lifetime. A successful novelist cannot forget that when his early manuscripts were regularly rejected, his wife kept urging him to give it all up and get a job. "She didn't show any faith in my ability to make it as a writer," he says.

The responsibility for being emotionally supportive in a woman-man relationship traditionally fell upon the woman. By social convention she was supposed to be man's main buffer against the world, and the one expected to help celebrate his successes. But this assignment has grown increasingly arduous in a time of role change and role conflict. Women today have many roles of their own to fulfill: partner, parent, worker, self. All too often there is not enough energy left to be as supportive as a woman might like to be; all too often she herself needs support from her man. That may be one reason why many women nowadays say they feel emotionally exhausted so much of the time.

Is the woman as chief sharer of joys and sorrows an anachronism? Should she consider throwing that emotional torch to men? Not if a relationship is to grow. For that to take place, *both* partners must give—and get—emotional support to and from each other, in whatever measure each needs it or can offer it at any given time.

> Every December [a man says] my wife goes through the same scenario. As the holidays start she is full of cheer and enthusiasm. But once the gifts have been unwrapped on Christmas day she becomes depressed. She says no one appreciates her. Is there something I can do to head off her change of mood?

The simplest explanation for this woman's letdown is that she is exhausted from trying to make the day a success for everyone else. But more likely she feels, consciously or otherwise, that she does not get enough emotional feedback for the effort she has put out. When so much of the giver is invested in giving, the recipient's response is crucial. And when the response isn't up to expectations, it can be a source of keen disappointment.

Giving emotional support to a partner is a complex skill that requires sensitivity to his or her needs. For example, it is not easy to know what particular *kind* of support he or she wants, how much to offer, or when to offer it. A large part of the problem is that the person expected to provide emotional support frequently does not get any clear signals from the person seeking it. Most of us tend to feel that if we have to ask (or even hint) for encouragement or comfort, it somehow makes the response less authentic, less meaningful. Indeed, one of the most staunchly held beliefs—and one of the most erroneous—is that "if you loved me you'd *know* what I need!" Here is an example:

> *Client:* The man I'm going to marry is very demanding. He constantly asks me to do things for him. He claims that if I really loved him I would never refuse to do what he asks. But I don't see that love has anything to do with this. Sometimes I'm just too busy or tired. Could this be a serious problem in our marriage?
>
> *ML:* Yes, it could. "Self-sacrifice" for a loved one has been overromanticized. When it is carried to unlikely extremes it often leads to resentment. It is important that both of you clearly understand the difference between love and support.
>
> Providing emotional support is certainly a key element in loving someone. There may even be crucial times when it should take precedence over your own activities or fatigue. On the other hand, love does not require you to give in to your fiancé's every whim. The unromantic fact is that people's needs often conflict even if they *do* love each other. So when he says, "If you loved me, you would do this . . ." you can reasonably counter with, "If *you* loved *me*, you wouldn't ask me to . . ."
>
> Be open about your warm feelings for your fiancé and generous with your honest praise. This can go far toward relieving any insecurity he may feel. Then, if you cannot always be supportive when he asks you to be, he can't claim that it is because you do not love him.

But love does not make one a mind reader. Most of the time we just have to guess at what the other person wants in the way of emotional support. And when those guesses too often prove wrong (or when we stop guessing entirely), a relationship can be seriously damaged. Under these circumstances most of us tend to do the next best thing: We offer the kind of support we ourselves would like to receive. But this often misses the mark, too—not for any lack of good intentions but because of a failure to distinguish between what *we* think will be helpful and what the other person actually needs:

> Whenever I tell my man about some minor household problem, he lectures me on what to do about it. And no matter what I've done, he has a "better" idea of how I should have handled each situation. How can I make him realize I don't need his advice—but would like a little sympathetic listening?

Giving unsolicited advice or offering "better" solutions for a partner's problems is a common response when two emotionally close people use each other as sounding boards. It's a bad habit—but an understandable one, for it usually reflects the listener's concern, as well as his or her desire to be a helpful partner. There are some people who find it hard to hear about a problem without offering their analysis of the situation. That doesn't necessarily mean they feel the other person is incompetent. It is more a sign of their own emotional need to be supportive, to make everything run smoothly. Usually they don't realize their attitude is annoying until it has already begun to cut off communication—as seems to be happening here.

The best solution is to announce at the outset what kind of response you are hoping for. If you mainly want a sympathetic ear while you get your troubles off your chest, say so. If you want to share information or feelings, announce that ahead of time too. By telling your partner exactly how you would like him or her to listen to you, you stand a better chance of getting the kind of emotional support you want or need. (Some of us also have unrealistic ideas about the ways in which emotional support should be provided. Frequently, we feel that unless our partner comes through absolutely on target—unless he or she meets *exactly* the unspoken specifications we've set up in our own minds—then whatever support is offered is little better than none at all.)

It is difficult for many of us to offer emotional support even when we would like to. Some people are simply unaware of how negative their responses are. Some are so insecure as to have few positive resources on which to draw. Some find giving support too risky, for it leaves one open to rejection. To offset these liabilities, here are guidelines that can help to enhance the ability to be supportive:

• Try to be alert for the clues that indicate when your partner needs support but cannot openly ask for it. With some people this can mean irritability, silence, physical withdrawal, even a sudden eating or drinking or spending splurge.

• Listen attentively. This can often be more supportive than any words we can say.

• Being supportive does not mean totally subordinating your own values or good sense. Nor does it mean overreacting and being overly solicitous and sympathetic, or joining in to fuel the flames of a partner's hurt or anger.

• Essentially, giving support is a matter of being able to share the feelings of those we love.

Helping a Partner to Change

A friend, perhaps a bit more neurotic than the norm, admits to a sense of mild distress because he cannot once and for all tidy up with a neat knot all of the loose ends in his life. He would like to keep his personal world in a sort of permanent holding pattern, more or less undisturbed by any change. Obviously, it is not possible for him to achieve his goal. But even if it were, it would not be a wise or healthy goal. Without positive changes, things do not merely stay the same; they eventually deteriorate. Change is not only endemic to life and to relationships; it is an essential and powerful engine of personal growth.

In an earlier section we talked about the effect of one person's change on his or her intimate partner, and how that partner can adjust to it successfully. Now we want to talk about how one person can encourage and aid another to make changes that improve their relationship.

Philosophers tell us that nothing in life is permanent except change. Yet to many women and men the only thing that seems permanent is a partner's unwillingness or inability to change. "If only he would be more affectionate," she says. "If only she would make an effort to understand my problems," he complains. The stalemate is likely to continue, for few things are more difficult than to change the way we habitually think, feel, or act.

The prospect of having to make a change in our attitudes or behavior is distressing, and most of us tend to resist it with varying degrees of vehemence. Some take an unyielding stance: "I am what I am; take me or leave me." Others want not so much understanding as surrender: "If you really cared for me, you'd love me just the way I am." Still others retreat to the defensive: "I simply can't help it; I can't change"—without ever facing up to the fact that they won't or don't want to change.

Why do so many people resist personal change so fiercely? There are four fundamental reasons.

First, a person may need to be the controlling partner in a relationship. Making a change at the other person's request is seen as a loss of power and control. For instance, a divorced woman, recently remarried, came to us recently with this problem:

> I always considered myself competent and independent—I've traveled alone, earned, and managed my own money. But my new husband does not want me to do anything by or for myself. He makes all decisions for both of us, has taken charge of our finances, and, most irritating of all, insists on accompanying me when I go shopping, on errands, even to the doctor or dentist. When I tell my husband I'd rather do things by myself he says that shows I don't need him. I do need him—to talk to, to share ideas with, to love me. But I don't need him to escort me everywhere or to run every aspect of my life. Why does this man act this way? And how can I get him to change?

Living with someone who constantly "needs to be needed" can be frustrating. This man's reluctance to allow his wife personal freedom probably stems, first from his mistaken notion that love is based on dependency, that if he isn't "needed" he isn't loved; and, second, from an inner insecurity that he can deal with only by feeling in total control of the relationship. How can the woman encourage her husband to change? Here is what the counselor suggested:

> ML: Presumably you have already tried conventional ways to make him understand your feelings and to get him to change his attitude. If so, you might want to try a new technique for encouraging behavior change that some therapists are using nowadays. It is called "paradoxical" therapy. It is based on the theory that when common sense or logic fail to have any effect, seemingly "illogical" or "unreasonable" approaches may succeed.
>
> In your situation, the paradoxical approach would be to play the dependent role to the hilt. Ask your husband for help with everything you do, no matter how simple or insignificant. Make incessant demands on him to go with you everywhere, to take care of all your needs. After a week or so of this treatment, he may be sick and tired of your total "helplessness" and constant claims on his time and attention, and urge you to start doing some things for and by yourself. This may not automatically cure his insecurities, but it may wake him up to how burdensome dependency can be.

A second reason people resist changing is that change can be troublesome. Most of us are creatures of habit, and making changes means that we have to think about the new behavior, be constantly aware of what we are doing. This takes willpower, energy, and conscious effort. It's easier to do things the old way (even if we can see that the old way may not to be the best way).

Third, change makes some people anxious. To embark on something new and different is a challenge some women and men find too dangerous, or at least too uncomfortable. Maybe life will be better if I change, they think, but it could get worse, too. Why risk rocking the boat? Such anxieties can prevent a partner from changing a habit or a way of life even if he or she realizes that the change would, in the long run, enhance the relationship. Here is a typical instance:

> Nine years ago I married a slim, attractive, sexy woman. But with each of her three pregnancies, she put

on a lot of weight—and never lost any of it. Today my
wife weighs nearly two hundred pounds and is still gaining. I've tried nagging, bribing, going on diets myself—
everything to get her to change. Nothing works though,
and I am increasingly embarrassed and sexually turned
off by her appearance. How can I make her see what her
stubbornness is doing to herself and to our marriage?

The most helpful thing this husband can do is to stop pressuring his wife about her weight. For one thing, weight-reduction experts tell us that such programs are successful only when the
obese person freely chooses to lose pounds. For another, the husband's criticisms are probably making his wife even more defensive about her eating habits. Change in this situation is most
likely to be initiated when the man asks himself *why* his wife has
let herself become so heavy. As the counselor put it:

> ML: You make it sound as if she deliberately put on
> those pounds to upset you. But obesity is often due to
> complex psychological causes. Your wife may be bored,
> anxious, lonely, unhappy. For some people food, espe-
> cially fattening food, represents a form of comfort and
> self-love. It would be useful to talk with your wife to
> explore her feelings about your marriage and about her
> role as a mother.
>
> It is not unusual for women to put on weight during
> their child-rearing years in an unconscious effort to
> resemble the traditional "maternal" image. Such women
> feel that being sexually attractive is somehow incom-
> patible with motherhood. Obesity serves as an uncon-
> scious protection against being physically desirable to
> men. Fortunately, as their children grow into adulthood
> these mothers discover a renewed interest in their ap-
> pearance and experience a sexual reawakening.
>
> The insight both of you would gain from a frank dis-
> cussion could trigger change far more effectively than
> keeping the focus on her appearance.

Lastly, some people resist making a change because they feel it
implies that whatever they were doing before was wrong. They
see change as an admission of fault or error on their part. "My

friend is always after me to stop telling jokes at parties," one man defends himself. "She says she is embarrassed by my behavior. But everybody else says I have a great sense of humor. So why should I change when obviously she's the one who is wrong?"

In recent years behavior modification has become a popular technique for encouraging change and growth in relationships. Essentially, one person "modifies" another's actions by giving some reward for each instance of the desired behavior. To some people this tit-for-tat process seems artificial and manipulative. But it is useful in achieving simple or highly specific behavioral changes.

When the desired change is a more subtle and complex one, however, *quid pro quo* bargaining is not likely to be as productive as negotiation between partners. Often there is no way, in such situations, of making an "exchange" that both persons can perceive as "even." Something more on the part of both—understanding, empathy, a willingness to give more or ask less—is required. Negotiation, therefore, depends for its success on the degree of trust and respect two people have for each other, and on the extent to which they genuinely want to improve their relationship.

There are some important steps involved in helping a partner change through negotiation. For one thing, both persons need to talk honestly and calmly about the changes involved: why one seeks the change, why the other objects, what goals the change would help to achieve. The person who is asking a partner to change must be highly specific about just what he or she wants the other person to do. Suppose John resents the fact that Mary, with whom he lives, brings home a briefcase full of business papers every evening. Instead of attacking her by saying something like, "You don't pay any attention to me when you're home," John might say, "I really wish you could spend a little more time with me in the evenings. I enjoy talking to you."

Negotiating a change in behavior is more easily accomplished if you can show a partner how he or she will also benefit from it. For example, John could spell out to Mary some advantages she might enjoy if she did not bring home work every night. "We'd be closer to each other than we've been lately," he might say. "Besides, you need to relax more. I bet if you didn't work at night, you'd have the energy to get more done at the office the next day." Mary might agree, "You're right, we should have more time for each other." Or she might ask for time to think about what John said. Or she might suggest a compromise, "I don't mean to ignore you, but you have no idea how the paperwork piles up. Suppose I bring home only as much as I can do in an hour, and save the rest of the evening just for us?" Don't expect such negotiations to work immediate change. People need time to readjust their ideas and feelings. But the real breakthrough usually occurs when a partner believes he or she is gaining something, too —and feels better for having made the change.

In some of these scenarios the negotiation process is left unfinished. If one partner asks for more time to think over a situation, both should try to establish exactly when they will talk about it again. An offer to compromise should be accepted and encouraged—but not necessarily viewed as a final step. Once a person has made even a small move in the direction of change, he or she often finds that other or larger changes become easier to make.

Moreover, when we talk about helping a partner to change, it is important to remember that we are talking about behavioral change only. It is extremely difficult, if not sometimes impossible, to change another person's way of thinking or feeling about a long-standing habit. A woman may persuade her man to put his clothes in the hamper rather than strewing them about the bathroom floor, but that does not mean he will enjoy doing it. We may negotiate successfully for more loving actions from our partner, but we cannot ask him or her to *feel* more spontaneously loving.

Similarly, change cannot be forced upon anyone. The humanistic therapist Fritz Perls used to say, "You can't push the river." Trying to force change in another person is something like trying to "push the river." One can, however, divert the river into new channels by damming it in one place or deepening it in another. So can we encourage change in our partners. That influence, when wisely applied, can be the catalyst for growth.

Renewing the Pleasures of Sex

Every couple has secrets known only to themselves, but one of those secrets is shared by many couples. It is the ebbing of sexual desire that one or both partners experience from time to time. Sexuality, like other powerful needs and feelings, normally waxes and wanes in intensity in accordance with biological rhythms. Moreover, it can be heightened or inhibited by a wide variety of outside influences—work pressures, family problems, fatigue, illness, moods, even the weather. But no matter how often we are told that some slackening of sexual desire is to be expected over time, couples rarely are willing to admit that it is happening to them. When they do talk about it—usually to marital or sex therapists—they tend to say such things as:

I used to enjoy sex but lately I don't seem at all interested.

I never would have believed I'd feel this way, but sex is getting to be more of a duty than a pleasure.

Sometimes three or four weeks will pass when neither of us wants sex. I know there's no normal frequency but —can there be something wrong with us?

We've been married only four years, but my husband makes up excuses to avoid sex. He won't talk about it, and I can only think he's bored with me . . . or bored with making love with me.

These women and men still love their partners and have no serious physical or emotional problems that could adversely affect their ability to function sexually. They suffer only from a sexual malaise that afflicts millions of couples at some point in their relationship—a progressive dulling of passion that is due largely to sexual familiarity with each other and to the habitual patterns into which their lovemaking may have fallen.

It is possible that recent efforts to help couples improve their sex lives have put too much emphasis on frequency. Now that sex is discussed so often and so frankly in the media, we may have the mistaken notion that "everyone else" is doing it constantly. Some people have the idea that one's sexual capacities may wane if they aren't exercised often enough; but there is no irrefutable evidence that one ever really loses the ability to be aroused even after a long period of abstinence. Nevertheless, the intermittent wanings of passion almost always create anxieties about the strength of the intimate bond. "Isn't there some way," women and men ask, "that we can rekindle our sex lives?"

This search for sexual renewal as a reaffirmation of continued growth can lead down many byways. Some couples try to keep desire fresh with an almost desperate attempt at variety. They spend a weekend at the seashore, making love on the beach under the stars. They sip wine in front of the fireplace and make love on the living room rug. They experiment with new times, new places, different positions—and, for a while perhaps, the novelty works. But the trouble with these devices is that they turn into just that—devices arranged to keep sexual boredom at arm's length.

Unless supported by a deeper understanding of what is happening, the devices lose their usefulness. On occasion—particularly if expectations are not communicated well—they can boomerang completely. A man took his wife to a lush South Pacific island in the secret hope that the exotic atmosphere would reawaken their sex life. But the island women seemed to the wife so beautiful and sensual that she felt unattractive and sexually inadequate by comparison. She refused any lovemaking the entire time they were there. The couple were so angry at each other that their sex life continued to deteriorate after they returned home.

Sometimes one person wonders whether he or she might be sexually reawakened by a different partner. Most people who test this theory find that while such an adventure may indeed be exciting, sex without a loving relationship is disappointing. What they really want is sexual excitement with the person for whom they feel an emotional attachment as well. The fact is that external aids are not the answer, at least not for very long. Sexual renewal is quite possible, but its source lies within ourselves.

Those women and men who say sex is boring often mean (though not always realizing it) that they have lost interest in sex because of what they see as their partners' failing. *If only he or she would do this or that*, they think, *the boredom would vanish.* But in actuality, making sex interesting again is a goal for which one must take personal responsibility. What specifically can a person do to reawaken the enjoyment of sex?

• Sometimes sexual renewal is simply a matter of looking closely at what we have allowed to happen to our sex lives. People often let a preoccupation with work take precedence. Others devote so much time and energy to children, home, or hobbies that there is little left for real intimacy. Even an overactive social life can be the culprit. Then, too, sex becomes routinized because couples tend to take each other for granted. One woman, now seldom aroused by her husband's advances, realized why when she watched him play with their children. "He laughed with them, hugged them, tousled their hair," she said. "I remembered that he used to do that with me, too, but somewhere along the way he stopped. I guess I resent that he no longer thinks he has to bother to be affectionate with me." Couples who maintain their sexual enthusiasm for each other have special ways of showing that they care outside of bed as well as in it. Though it has been said many times, it cannot be repeated often enough: Sexual arousal begins in the mind, not in the glands or the genitals.

• Don't leave time for sex to change. Plan for it. Spontaneity is fine, but it isn't everything. As our lives get busier it may be harder to find the right moment for sex. The risk is that such a moment may be a long time coming. "It's ironic to think how elaborately we planned to be together before we were married," a woman said, "and how we almost never plan for it now."

• One road to sexual variety is to develop the ability to express physical love in different ways. Couples who can shift from tenderness to passion and back again are able to create a constantly changing sexual atmosphere. Tenderness offers each partner the chance to play a "giving" role by reaching out to the other with gentle touches and soft words. Passion lets each take part in a drama of more heightened and turbulent motions and emotions.

• Take personal responsibility for bringing sexual desire back to life. Even in the best of relationships, as we have pointed out, sex does not always remain at a peak pitch. If your own sexual life seems dull, it is easy to imagine that other couples are constantly experiencing ecstasy. Not so. An important lesson can be learned from those couples who say that sex is as good or better than ever. They may actually have sex less often than couples who are dissatisfied. The crucial difference is that they accept any temporary loss of interest or lessened excitement as a normal variation. And neither partner blames the other for it.

As one woman puts it, "I know these sexually quiet periods are bound to occur, but that's no reason to go into sexual hibernation. I know I need extra stimulation at such times, and I take the responsibility for doing something about it. I might take a perfumed bath and put on a special negligee. I might encourage my sexual feelings by imagining that I'm a heroine in a romantic novel." It is not so much the added inventions themselves that make the difference, but the new aura of interest and excitement. These are not new approaches, to be sure. But what is different— and effective—about them is that this woman is not using them merely to stimulate her lover but to reinvigorate her own sexual feelings. Instead of blaming him for her sexual blahs, she is taking responsibility for her own sexual renewal and creating an atmosphere in which change can occur.

Couples can agree to share in taking responsibility for reawakening sex. Recently we recommended that a couple arrange a rendezvous at a hotel, make believe they do not know each other, meet "by chance" at the pool, and role-play a romantic "strangers in the night" weekend. The couple said they felt foolish at first, but soon got into the fun of the adventure. More important, it worked for them. Another couple spend an occasional night at a motel that features water beds and mirrored walls and ceiling in its honeymoon suite.

The use of fantasy is still another method for refreshing a tired sex life. This may involve mentally envisioning yourself in a sexual scene with a movie star, a fictional character, even someone you know. Couples whose sex lives have been enriched by fantasy see no disloyalty or mental infidelity in this. Some couples, though, feel that thinking about another person during lovemaking is the same as having sex with that person. If they do, the result may be guilts and resentments.

> *Husband:* During the past year I've had trouble becoming interested or aroused. Recently I discovered that reading a sexy book or looking at sexy photos helps to excite me, but when my partner found out I was doing this she got terribly upset. She says it is perverted. Am I wrong to use a book to "turn on"?

> *ML:* Many sex therapists recommend the use of books or pictures to spark and enhance excitement. Nevertheless, there are people who continue to believe that using such a technique is immoral. One reason for your

partner's reaction may be that she feels anyone who does this is sexually depraved. Or she may think, "If he really loves *me* he wouldn't have to look at pictures of other women."

Reassure your companion that your use of books and photos as erotic aids is neither perverted nor disloyal, but a practical and legitimate way of dealing with your problem. Of course, such fantasizing can become dangerous if it makes you feel guilty; or if it eventually no longer serves its original purpose of arousing your interest in lovemaking but becomes an end in itself. As long as you know what is real and what is not—and use moments of make-believe to enliven your experience—fantasy can be a useful tool in lovemaking.

• Couples may forget that sex can be fun. Some years ago an academic journal published a lengthy article titled, *Sex as Work*. It pointed out—quite accurately as things turned out—that the growing emphasis on technique and performance outlined in sex manuals was not only making sex itself a chore, but creating the impression that lovemaking was a grim business. Playing at sex is one way to revive it. Sex can be many things besides intercourse.

• Talking freely to a partner about one's sexual needs and desires, hang-ups, or turn-ons is an important way of helping to renew sexual interest. Sometimes explicit sexual conversation can be arousing in itself. "If I think about my partner sexually during the day," a man says, "I tell her about it when I get home. I may even call her from the office." Letting such thoughts and feelings go unspoken can be a symptom of a sexually deteriorating relationship. Talking openly about sexual feelings without fears of being rebuffed is a way of keeping sexuality alive.

Sometimes sexual boredom leads partners to seek excitement with other partners. But what happens when they hesitate, for obvious reasons, to introduce into their primary relationships the new techniques of arousal they discovered in casual relationships? This situation is cropping up more often in these sexually free times. Here is how one woman described the problem, and what the counselor suggested the couple do about it:

My husband and I were separated for seven months, and during that time we both became involved with

other people. But we decided we really love each other
and now we are back together, working hard to make
our marriage succeed. Everything is going smoothly except sex. Even though we learned a lot, sexually, from
our new partners during the separation, we seem to have
fallen back into the same kind of routine sex that was
part of the reason we broke up in the first place. I think
we are each reluctant to do anything different for fear
the other person will wonder, or actually ask, "Where
did you learn that?" Do you have any suggestions for
getting over this hurdle?

ML: Because you are not the same person you were before you separated and neither is your husband, in many
ways you are meeting with each other as a new couple.
The experiences each of you had during your separation,
sexual and otherwise, have changed you both. Once you
realize this, you can accept the fact that you are not so
much resuming an old marriage as starting a new one.
This includes beginning a new sex life—which naturally
would draw upon whatever experiences you both have
had up to this point—ideally without creating suspicion
or resentment. Moreover, since one reason for your separation was sexual boredom, the fact that you both
learned "something different" can only be an asset to
you now. Rather than blame each other, or feel guilty,
why not reap the benefits of your new experience? Since
you were presumably both free to do as you wished during the separation, there can be no valid ground for re-
crimination.

Ultimately, one inevitable fact must be faced: Sex cannot forever keep on being as new and as fresh as it once may have been.
When the novelty wears off some couples see it as a "failure" either to arouse the other or to arouse oneself. To avoid future
"failure," they set in motion a behavioral cycle that feeds upon itself. By avoiding lovemaking they simply accelerate their loss of
sexual interest and response, and make it even more difficult to
break that deadening pattern. If sex that once was sharply satisfying has become routine and unrewarding, one must ask oneself:

What was I doing to make it so good then? What has happened to change it? What can I do now to revitalize it? How can I help my partner to share my interest and concern? The source of sexual renewal—and the growth of the loving relationship that accompanies it—lies within every person. Each of us can take the first steps to make it happen.

Taking Risks to Grow On

In a discussion with several young couples, some married and some living together, we posed a hypothetical question. Two seats are suddenly offered to you on an inexpensive charter flight to Paris. You have just enough money in your bank account to pay for the trip. Would you go or not? At first all of the couples said they would grab the chance to travel. But soon one couple—call them Jim and Alice—decided they'd have to pass it up. "Using our savings to take the trip would ruin all the plans we've made for our future," said Jim. "You see, we're saving every penny we can for the next four years, and then buying a house."

"We plan to have our first child in three years," added Alice, "and we want to move to the country when the baby is a year old."

One of the other men challenged that thinking, "All your plans are fine. But do you have to be so strictly bound by them? A million things can happen in four years. Maybe you'll have a child sooner, or decide to have one later. Maybe you won't buy a house at all."

"Or you could get a big raise, or win a lottery, or—or *anything!*" another woman said. "You might not even need your savings to buy the house. How can you let this chance to see Paris go by just because it doesn't fit a theoretical schedule?"

Jim and Alice stuck to their guns. They admitted traveling would be great, but they just couldn't see giving up their plans. The other couples admitted they might eventually decide it didn't make sense to blow their savings on a pleasure trip—but said they would certainly do a lot of thinking and talking before they made up their minds one way or the other.

Social scientists tell us that most relationships tend to fall into one or the other of two main patterns. One—based on orderliness and fixed goals—is described as "maintenance oriented." The other is called "growth oriented." This life-style allows a couple to accept new ideas and to consider new opportunities as they arise. In this decade of innovation and change in relations between women and men, couples who are growth oriented cope more easily with sex-role conflicts and the problems they bring. More important, perhaps, growth orientation is conducive to risk taking.

Many couples cling to the *status quo* even if it is not especially rewarding; its predictability makes it familiar and, therefore, comfortable. Preferring the known to the unknown, even if the known is unsatisfying, may feel "safe." But taking risks is one of the most effective ways for a relationship to grow.

Women and men who incorporate sensible risk taking into their lives—who are willing to face the possibly unsettling but nevertheless stimulating aspects of new experiences and ideas—differ in several important ways from those who play it safe. For one thing, risk takers expect more from their relationships. The most significant difference between couples who get into serious trouble and those who are able to resolve their problems is that those in the latter group demand more satisfaction from their relationships and are willing to take calculated risks to achieve it. These couples have a dynamic rather than a static concept of their life together.

A static partnership is fixed and rigid and likely to be more vulnerable to stress or change. A dynamic one is willing to accept the risks that go with new opportunities and able to handle them without fear. We are all familiar with the idea of individual potential. It implies that a person has untapped skills and talents, a capacity for growth. We say such things as, "Sue has the potential to do anything she chooses," or "Bob never lived up to his potential." In much the same way, each relationship has its quota of potential with which to call upon new resources, find new rewards.

Another quality that characterizes risk-taking couples is a sense of adventure. This is often missing in couples who lock themselves into routine ways of relating to each other. The late psychologist Sidney Jourard was struck by what he saw as "the incredible lack of creativity in partners. When it comes to altering the design for their relationship, it is as if their imaginations had burnt out. For years, spouses go to sleep night after night, with their relationship patterned one way, a way that perhaps satisfies neither. . . . There is nothing sacred to [a woman] about the last way she decorated her house: as soon as it begins to pall, she shuffles things around until the new decor pleases her. But the way she and her partner interact will persist for years after it has ceased to engender delight, zest and growth."

A critical situation that calls for courageous choices is often described as a crossroads where danger is joined with opportunity. Some couples see only the danger; others are not blind to the danger, but they are alert to the opportunity. Those who are reluctant to take the risk often defend their decisions by saying something like, "We'd rather not gamble by taking a chance."

But risk taking, as we define it, is a far cry from gambling. Gambling can be almost entirely a matter of luck; only those who study the odds and remember the cards can bring a modicum of skill to bear on the game. Risk taking, on the other hand, involves a significant amount of experimentation that can be intelligently controlled. What you are doing is thinking about how to rearrange the ways in which you and your partner interact, or how to change the way you deal with the world to reach your shared goals. We wouldn't call that gambling. We'd call it working to make a relationship grow.

What can couples do to foster the kind of sensible risk taking that can help relationships grow? Here are some suggestions:

Begin by being open to small changes in routine patterns. This will help you to become more at ease with the idea of risk. One couple received an invitation to join a Sunday-evening book discussion group. It was something the woman had long wanted to do. When she told her husband about it, he grumbled, "We always spend Sunday nights at home together." The wife pointed out that it was more by habit than by choice. "And anyway," she said, "we're not so much 'together' as just in the same room— usually watching television. If we join the book group, we'll still be with each other, but in a more stimulating way."

Of course that is a minor risk to take—and one that can be

reversed if it doesn't work. But the argument holds for larger risks as well, such as the one this woman faced when she sought the counselor's advice:

> My husband has been offered an important promotion, but it means we'll have to move to a city where we know absolutely no one. We've lived in our present community all our married lives; our friends and family are here. Both of us dread the thought of being in a strange town and having to start a whole new social life. On the other hand, if my husband turns down the new job, it will probably wreck his future with his company.

The fixed pattern in which this couple lives may represent security and stability to them, but it certainly offers few chances for personal or relationship growth. For one thing, as we mentioned in an earlier section, it is not necessarily a good thing for a woman and man to surround themselves so closely and for so long with family and old friends. Some couples unconsciously disguise (or escape from) tensions between themselves by spending most of their time with other people. The constant presence of friends and family, no matter how supportive, can short-circuit the kinds of intimate discussions every relationship needs to share.

In any event, this couple realistically has only a choice between two risks: on the one hand, a temporary time of anxiety and loneliness if they move; on the other, the potential foreclosure of career hopes if they don't. If they can be patient and persevering in pursuing new acquaintances and able to accept that it will take a while to form a new social circle, they can probably make a good adjustment to a new community. Most people do.

Women in business today are finding that transfers are as endemic to their climb up the corporate ladder as they have always been for men. As a result, a woman's partner is increasingly confronted with the choice of moving to enhance *her* career prospects. The stakes may be higher than they are for non-working wives; a man may have to give up his job and find another in the new community. But the options—whether or not to take a risk that can lead to mutual growth in many areas of their relationship—is still the same.

A second way to foster sensible risk taking is for partners to give each other the freedom to change some of the "rules" of their relationship. On the simplest level, let us suppose that a couple has agreed that each of them will have one night a week out. She uses her night to take an aerobic dancing course. He plays tennis. When he is asked to fill in as a fourth in a series of doubles matches, meaning that he will have to play several evenings in a particular week, she objects: "We made a deal, and now you're breaking it!" She is determined that the "rules" of their relationship are going to be observed strictly. That might provoke a mild argument, nothing more. But when that same attitude is carried over to major issues the situation can be more critical:

> My husband and I are in our late thirties. We've been married sixteen years and have two sons. For the past twelve years my husband has been a minister, and I'm proud to say I worked hard to support us while he went through the seminary. Now my husband says he wants to leave the ministry and become a psychologist. This means more years of study, during which I'll have to support us all again. Moreover, there's no guarantee he'll succeed in a new field of work. He says I am being unfair in refusing to let him make this change. Do you agree?

Obviously both persons have a major stake in this proposed change. The decision cannot be left entirely to the husband, for it affects his entire family; but neither can the wife "refuse to let him" switch careers. As a responsible adult, he must make his choice after carefully considering all the possible consequences. The only area in which she can exert real control is the extent to which she would be willing to help out financially. In this situation the counselor thought it was most important to look at how each partner saw the risks involved, and how each felt he or she could deal with them:

> ML: Your husband may have committed himself to the ministry when he was too young to be fully aware of his

interests and goals. Some men in this position—
especially when they have taken on the responsibility of
a family—cannot find the courage to risk making a
change. They accept "what is," even though it means
being locked into work that is no longer satisfying.

Other men, like your husband, seek to break out of
the mold they have cast for themselves. Your wisest
course is to tell your husband exactly how you feel about
his desire to change careers—particularly as far as your
financial role is concerned—and at the same time offer
to help him find a solution that will meet his emotional
needs without forcing you to sacrifice yours.

You might jointly explore ways in which your husband could combine study with work so you would not
feel you had the entire burden of support. Has he considered teaching or counseling a few hours a week at a
seminary? Filling in as a Sunday substitute for ministers
who are ill or on vacation? Has he thought of applying
for a fellowship or a grant? True, it may prove necessary
for you to take a part-time job as well, or for your family
to reduce its standard of living temporarily. But in the
long run, finding a compromise between your desire for
the status quo and his risk taking may be less costly than
having a husband who blames you for his discontent.

The thing about literal "rules"—whether the limits refer to evenings out, or to how much money partners should be free to
spend on themselves or to how often a couple make love—is that
you may find yourself defending them even if they are foolish, im-
practical, or a recurrent source of argument.

Once boundaries are established they tend to take on a power
and authority of their own. That's why they should be constantly
reevaluated to make sure they serve a reasonable purpose, and do
not set arbitrary restrictions on new experiences. Be aware of—
and try to avoid—statements that consistently and negatively reinforce things as they are. Many women and men close off conversations that might otherwise lead to the possibility of constructive risk taking by saying things that perpetuate traditional

ways of reacting—"I don't want to hear any more about that. You know it always starts an argument," or, "You already know how I feel."

The taking of risks is not limited to external events. From time to time situations arise that offer the opportunity to take risks with our feelings. For instance, there is risk in revealing your deepest needs or fears. There is risk in declaring what it is you really want out of a relationship, and then holding your breath to find out if your partner is able or willing to provide it. There is risk in putting aside superficial convention for emotionally honest talk. You may be rebuffed or rejected. You may discover that your partner is not the woman or man you thought—or even the person you want for a partner. But not speaking out is the greater risk, for it signifies a retreat from the impulse to growth. As we have said repeatedly (but it is worth repeating), intimacy is achieved only at the expense of being willing to risk your vulnerability.

This kind of risk taking is a way to seek new answers to old problems. For some couples this can be as basic as actually dealing with conflicts rather than sweeping them under the rug. For others it may mean discarding old "solutions" (which may never have worked anyway) and trying new ones. Ordinarily, such risk taking occurs when a couple is faced with the choice of improving their relationship or watching it wither:

> My wife and I have been trying to resolve problems that have been with us since shortly after our marriage eight years ago. While some things are much better, others haven't improved at all. Recently, a minister, an old friend to both of us, suggested we have a trial separation to see how we feel away from each other. This scares me because it seems as if we would be taking an awful chance. Wouldn't separation be likely to be the first step toward divorce?

In general we would be extremely cautious about recommending separation as a way to work on marital conflicts. However, under the right conditions, a separation can indeed work *for* rather than *against* a relationship. Even happily married couples know they can profit from an occasional vacation from each other. It gives both partners a chance to find out what they miss in the other person, as well as how they manage their lives without the kind of companionship they may have taken for granted. In this case, the counselor told the couple the conditions of such a separation would be critical to its outcome:

ML: First, the intent of the separation must be clearly defined and honestly agreed to by both of you. If one partner believes the separation is to find out what it's like to be alone and the other believes that it is a chance to sow some wild oats, trouble is coming. Both of you must be sure in your minds that you want to stay married and that you are separating only to achieve certain constructive goals.

The second condition is that you must both continue to act as a married couple even though you are temporarily apart. The separation is not to be used as an opportunity to be "single" again. There are some rules that minimize that risk. Each of them is based on the way happily married couples who are involuntarily separated by work, military service, or family crises manage their lives.

First, decide in advance how long the separation is to last and have a target date for when you will resume living together.

Second, the one who moves out does not set up a new "permanent" home but rents a modest, furnished, temporary place to live. Finances should be handled as they always have been, with no divisions of money or property.

Third, neither of you will date new people. This is not the time to become emotionally or physically involved with anyone else. But you may, of course, "date" each other. Finally, continue your counseling sessions together. If you do these things, and you both sincerely want your marriage to work, this risk of a trial separation may well result in a better partnership in the long run.

Remarriages often encounter a similar intimacy-vulnerability dilemma that requires a couple to take a different kind of emotional risk:

> Both my husband and I have been married once before. Each of our previous marriages ended after years of bitter arguments. As a result, though there are times when we are really irritated with each other, we avoid any kind of confrontation. We don't want to fall into that old pattern of quarreling—but steering clear of arguments doesn't seem to solve our problem either.

In their "second time around" many women and men go to great lengths to avoid making the same mistakes over again. Unfortunately, this sometimes leads them into making new—and perhaps equally damaging—errors.

It isn't surprising that this couple wanted to keep from repeating the pattern of their previous marriages. But to suppress feelings and differences out of fear, or for the sake of a surface calm, is no more productive than arguing would be. While it is not possible to block out the past completely, it is important not to let it affect the present so as to create a new set of difficulties. When this couple refused to acknowledge their differences openly they made it almost impossible to reach any reasonable resolution. Moreover, buried or avoided differences eventually come out in other damaging ways. For this woman and man, the answer was to stop wasting energy by worrying that old patterns will repeat themselves, and to put that energy into working out ways of dealing with the irritations that inevitably afflict every relationship.

Using the Past to Build the Future

Janus, the Roman god of beginnings, was pictured as having two faces, one looking backward and one looking ahead. We preserve his memory briefly every New Year's Day when we review the year that has passed and plan to be a better person in the year to come. Though some believe that making resolutions has gone out of style, most of us find some satisfaction in this personal stocktaking—some sense of knowing where we have been, where we are, and where we expect or want to be. But have you ever considered joining with your partner to take a similar inventory of your relationship? How it has been or is working? How you want it to work in the future?

Couples seldom do this kind of stocktaking. Questioning the state of a relationship is threatening. Women and men who know there are problems between them are usually reluctant to examine the realities of their life together. They prefer to keep an uneasy peace. Nor are couples in good relationships any more eager to take stock. They are as unwilling to probe their satisfactions as other couples are to examine their dissatisfactions. Both groups have plenty of reasons to offer for their attitudes. We're busy earning a living, they say; or raising a family, running a household, keeping up with friends, serving the community, finding some time for relaxation. "Who has time or energy for introspection?" they ask.

Yet if couples did take inventory from time to time they could use the past to build growth into their future. Without looking backward, women and men often lose sight of what originally brought them together. They are likely to be less aware of changes that have taken place within each person or within their relationship. And without looking forward a couple cannot hope to keep in touch with each other's hopes and goals. Remember, taking stock does not mean looking for trouble; it is simply one of the most effective devices for getting in touch with the quality of a relationship.

Looking Backward—One way we suggest that couples go about stocktaking is to set aside a chunk of time when they will be undisturbed and thoughtfully answer a series of questions. They are not designed to change anyone's life on the spot, or to provoke arguments. Their main purpose is to help a couple evaluate what has been happening in the areas that are most critical to the growth of a relationship: trust, communication, sharing, sex, companionship, feelings of being accepted and understood.

During the past year:
• Did we usually laugh and have fun when we were together?

• Did either of us too often criticize or correct the other?

• When I was away from my partner all day, did I feel good about returning home to be with him or her again?

• Was it easy to agree on things to do together?

• Was I always able to show my true feelings to my partner?

• Did I get—and give—enough sympathy and understanding?

• Did we touch when we felt warmly toward each other?

• Could I count on my partner to do what he or she promised?

• Compared to a year ago, is my satisfaction with myself less, greater, or unchanged. Is my satisfaction with our relationship less, greater, or unchanged?

• Compared to a year ago, is our ability to communicate and to handle disagreements better, worse, or unchanged? Is our sex life better, worse, or unchanged?

Ideally, you and your partner should answer these questions independently and in two stages—first, as *you* feel about them, and then as you believe your partner feels about them. (Often two people get into difficulties because of false assumptions they make about each other's feelings.) Another way of determining whether you are accurately reading how your partner sees your life together is for each of you to list three things about your relationship that are pleasing, three that could be better, and three things that each of you could do to make it better. Then compare your answers. This can be an excellent basis for growth-producing discussions.

When you have both finished answering these questions—or any other questions you both agree would be useful in taking stock—share your responses with each other. Read each question aloud and then take turns saying: "I answered yes/no because . . ." or, "I thought you would have answered in another way because . . ." Explore your thoughts and feelings about any disagreements that occur. Are you angry, disappointed, relieved, encouraged? No matter what you may feel, having emotional reactions of *any* kind is a healthy sign. It means you are emotionally involved with each other. What do you both see as problems, if any? What can each of you do to make your partnership more rewarding? (You may even want to tape-record your conversation for future reference.)

At this point in stocktaking some couples get into difficulties. When a weak area is pinpointed, each person may be eager to find a solution and, as a result, in many cases he or she tries to do too much too fast. It makes more sense to begin correcting a problem situation gradually, taking small but definite steps to improve it rather than trying to overhaul it in one fell swoop. The message implied in a series of minor but effective changes is: "I care about our relationship and your feelings matter to me."

Next, it's important to discuss the implications of changed attitudes or behavior *before* you put the change itself into effect. By the time some couples finish taking stock they are often "talked out." In an effort to end on a positive note, they grasp at a solution, any solution. But they are likely to forget that not all new approaches turn out to be constructive. Change made in one area inevitably produces often unexpected reactions in another. That's why any problem-solving changes need to be carefully and realistically planned, gradually introduced and regarded with flexibility.

Taking stock is not just an occasion for exploring your relationship; it can also be a time for discovering who your partner really is. Most couples, even those who have been happily together for years, do not know each other as well as they think they do—or as well as they should. Even in the most intimate of relationships there are areas we keep secret, purposely or unwittingly. Yet no relationship can truly grow if partners do not know—or make no effort to explore—each other's innermost feelings. "I daydream of meeting my husband in disguise and staying up all night talking to him," one woman says. "If we could talk about things that really matter, I think we could mean so much more to each other."

Oddly, many couples overlook the simplest and most productive way of "looking backward" to know each other better: asking questions. For instance, do you know what your partner's childhood was like? Does he or she know yours? Not the surface facts, but the feelings about them.

We have talked about how our own behavior is so often rooted in the behavior of our parents and others with whom we grew up. Knowing a partner's favorite childhood memories, or the memories that are most painful, can sometimes shed helpful light on current problems. (In one instance a couple repeatedly argued over how much the man spent on clothes, hair stylings, skin lotions. When he talked about how ill-dressed and unattractive he felt as a teenager, his partner could understand that unconsciously he was still trying to compensate for his former feelings.)

Did your partner enjoy family holidays when he or she was a child? If not, that may explain why he turns into Scrooge at Christmas, or she abhors large family gatherings. There are no "right" questions, and there are no "right" or "wrong" answers. The trick is to keep asking questions until one of them opens up a significant area for discussion. Here are some typical questions that prove useful in "looking backward":

• What most attracted you to each other? (You may be surprised to learn what qualities you have that he or she values.)

• What would each of you miss most if it were lost or taken away? What are your greatest fears? (Questions like these are difficult to answer because they reveal vulnerabilities. But in times of crisis it is vital to be aware of a partner's fears if you are going to be able to deal with them.)

• What childhood fantasies did you each have? (The answer can help you make contact with his or her secret desires.)

• What are you and your partner most proud of? Most ashamed of? (Such questions stimulate talk about a person's values and self-concept—and often reveal the gap between image and reality. If a man says he wants to be remembered as a loving husband and father, and then works sixty hours a week and plays golf on weekends, the discrepancy between fact and fancy becomes obvious.)

• What makes each of you feel truly loved? Many women and men have trouble giving and accepting love because they rarely mean the same thing by "love." Only when we know a partner's definition of what love is can we be loving in a meaningful way.

The questions suggested above are just a few examples of the kinds of dialogue a couple can use to enrich their relationship. Which questions are most significant to you is something you will have to discover. But equally important is knowing when and how to ask these questions, and how to listen to the answers:

• Choose a time and place conducive to private and thoughtful discussion; you should give yourselves time to pursue a topic to a reasonable end.

• Phrase your questions to yield truly revealing answers. If, for example, you ask, "What do you value most?" the reply might be a generality: "Success . . . loyalty." But if you ask, "What would you most like to be remembered for?" the answer is more likely to disclose your partner's aims in life. Similarly, don't say, "What was your childhood like?" but, "How did you feel about yourself as a child?"

• Set sensible ground rules: honest answers, careful listening, no interruptions, not using what is revealed in your partner's responses to make hurtful judgments or accusations.

• Don't make your questions sound like demands. And don't expect instant answers. This exercise is not intended to be a parlor game or a quick quiz. It is intended to stimulate intimate conversation that may go on over weeks or months or even years.

• Let each other know that it is emotionally safe to express any idea or feeling; that neither of you will be threatened by what is said; and that no matter what confessions are made, you will each accept them in the spirit of love.

Building on the Positives—Another way a couple can use the technique of stocktaking as a tool for growth is to emphasize the positives they once shared, or still share, and use them as a source of future strength. It is human nature to take for granted the good in our relationships and focus on whatever is displeasing, to overlook satisfactions and keep close tabs on dissatisfactions.

Counselors are sadly familiar with women and men who embark on a non-stop litany of complaints about a lover or spouse. They seem unable to find anything good to say. But if a counselor channels the conversation so that a couple are virtually *forced* to think about the qualities they first admired in each other, the pleasures they once enjoyed together, the hopes they once shared —"then," says one therapist, "you can almost see the antagonism begin to dwindle and drain away."

After one such session a man said, "Until I actually made a mental list of the things I like and respect my partner for, I didn't realize how many there were or how important they are to me." Building on the positives in a relationship can be as literal an exercise as writing down everything you and your partner have in common. We are usually all too aware of differences and not aware enough of similarities in attitudes, tastes, and temperaments.

Recapturing old memories is another way of inventorying your "positives." A middle-aged couple have an unusual "flower diary" that makes use of the past to mend present rifts. "We met and fell in love on a hiking trip in the Rockies," the woman says. "Later when I found an Alpine rose I had tucked into my knapsack during that hike, I dried it and kept it as a memento. From then on, whenever we wanted to preserve the memory of a special moment we picked and pressed a flower. Here's dunegrass," she continued, turning the pages of a scrapbook, "from the beach where we were when he proposed. Here's a violet from the bouquet he gave me when our son was born."

Past "positives" can also be called upon to remedy current "negatives," as this case history shows:

> I hate to admit it, but my marriage is awfully boring. I'm not interested in most of the things my husband wants to do, and he's not interested in what I want to do. The saddest part is that things were not always so with us, and I miss the pleasure we used to have from shared interests.

Growing apart is a common problem. It creeps up on older couples whose marriages no longer have the built-in "hookup points" that link their interests. And it sometimes occurs with startling suddenness to younger couples who develop new interests that take them along divergent paths. But no relationship starts out with two people who have nothing in common, or there would never have been a relationship in the first place. So what we suggested to the "bored" wife may seem simplistic, but it does work almost every time:

> ML: Set aside an hour or so when you won't be interrupted. Then each of you, independently, make three lists. In one, write down whatever activities you do now, either alone or with each other, that you would enjoy doing more often. Second, make a list of activities you

have never tried but think you might like if you did try
them. Third, list whatever you can remember that you
liked to do together in the past but no longer engage in.
Sometimes, when couples grow apart, it helps to think
back to courtship and newlywed days, to recall interests
you enjoyed sharing then and might enjoy again.

Be as specific as possible. For example, don't just write
down "tennis" or "music"; indicate whether you mean
playing it, attending a match or concert, or watching the
event on television. Then compare lists. Most couples
who take stock of their interests this way find to their
surprise that there are at least two or three items (usually more) that appear on both persons' lists. And if literal list making isn't for you, at least talk out the three
areas we suggest with your partner. Remember, however,
that list making is just a first step toward breaking out
of your rut. You must both act on the results. Pick an
activity, schedule it, and do it. The ability to spend
more time together contentedly must be practiced.

Looking Forward—In the final analysis, making a relationship
grow depends on how much effort each partner puts into the project . . . how much he or she *wants* it to be better. In the relatively recent past, relationships failed largely because couples did
not have the knowledge to identify their problems or the insight
to resolve them. But we are now in an era when failure lies more
often in a lack of energy and will to put our knowledge to
work.

Thousands of couples, for instance, are working toward growth
by involving themselves in "enrichment" programs sponsored by
various denominational and community service organizations.
Such programs are not designed for troubled couples. Rather,
they are aimed at helping couples to enhance relationships that
are basically sound. In general, enrichment programs focus on
opening up an emotional dialogue between partners. Much can
be learned, too, from sharing feelings and experiences (both good
and bad) with other couples in the enrichment sessions. Essentially, these encounters are a way for a couple to take stock of
where they are now, where they are headed, and where they could
be a few years from now. After all, a relationship itself has no

inherent attributes. It is what the partners bring to it and expect from it that determines what it will be like.

In each person, in each couple, is the potential for growth. But it will not develop automatically with the passage of time. We have called this delusion "the myth of the self-improving relationship." On the contrary, conflicts left unexamined only become more difficult to deal with; hopes left unshared become harder to realize. Admittedly, taking stock—using the past to build the future—and then following through with positive changes is not easy. But in a world where relationships between women and men are changing so quickly and so substantially, the choice is no longer between growing or stagnating but between growing or crumbling. The cost of growing is small considering what you can gain.